Praise for *The Forgotten Church*

Glenn Daman takes us on a journey of understanding on why the rural church matters—how they need us, but also how we need them, perhaps more than ever.

ED STETZER
Executive Director, Billy Graham Center

As one who married a farmer's daughter and came to love the rural community from which she came, I recognize the wisdom of Glenn Daman's book. Rural ministry doesn't get the attention that urban ministry does, but the need is huge and the insights in *The Forgotten Church* point to way to faithful and effective service along countless two-laned roads.

MARSHALL SHELLEY
Director of the Doctor of Ministry at Denver Seminary
Contributing editor of CTpastors.com

I'm deeply grateful that many are moving to our growing cities to plant churches and reach a maximum number of people for Christ, but this good movement often comes at the cost or denigration of important work in rural communities. People who live in smaller towns and rural contexts are in desperate need of the gospel and willing shepherds ready to join God on mission. The church must send laborers to these sadly (and sinfully) forgotten places. This book is an important book that should be included in the syllabi of missions and church planting at schools, seminaries, and sending churches. Glenn Daman offers an important work on a vital mission field in the twenty-first century.

DANIEL DARLING
Vice-President of Communications, Ethics and Religious Liberty Commission; contributing editor, CT Pastors; and author of several books, including the forthcoming *The Dignity Revolution: Reclaiming What It Means to Be Human*

Glenn Daman continues to be an important voice in helping ministry leaders recognize both the strategic significance and distinctive dynamics of small, rural churches. In this latest contribution, he walks the reader through various issues that deserve more attention than they typically receive, ranging from historical background to theological foundations to representative case studies that illustrate how to contextualize challenging topics to a rural church setting.

RANDAL ROBERTS
President and Professor of Christian Spirituality, Western Seminary, Portland, OR

Many thanks to Glenn Daman for authoring this personal and informative review of the too-often-overlooked rural arena of church ministry. While the history of this field is rich with sentiments of life in a simpler time, its current challenges are complex, and our response is critical. Glenn writes convincingly as a farmer and pastor—his message is as timely as the harvest is ready!

JIM CARLSON
Former Executive Director of Rocky Mountain Bible Mission
Former president of Montana Bible College

What does rural America look like? The answer depends upon who you talk to. For those whose view has been shaped by popular media, it is a cross between Swamp People and Mayberry R.F.D. For others, it is a beautiful landscape populated by culturally backward gun lovers and political reactionaries. To those who live there, it is simply home. In this book, Glenn Daman dispels the myths, makes a case for the importance of the rural ministry, and offers practical wisdom for those who want to serve the rural church effectively. Glenn's perspective is shaped by the careful reflection and long experience of someone who is both a practitioner and skilled trainer of those who engage in rural ministry.

JOHN KOESSLER
Professor of Applied Theology & Church Ministry at
Moody Bible Institute

Reflecting careful research and a lifetime commitment to rural ministry, and written with clarity and passion, Glenn Daman's *The Forgotten Church* occupies an important place in the recent literature on small-town and rural ministry. It provides an informative and inspiring call to remember what has been largely forgotten.

STEPHEN WITMER
Lead Pastor, Pepperell Christian Fellowship
Cofounder, Small Town Summits

Glenn Daman sends a passionate call for action from the front lines of rural ministry. Ignoring rural ministry has cost the whole church more than we realize. A fresh focus on rural ministry will breathe new life into rural communities and the urban churches that partner with them.

JOHN ADAMS
Assistant Director for Village Missions

I can't think of anyone who understands life and ministry in rural America better than Glenn Daman. He grew up in rural Idaho and has served as a pastor in rural Washington for more than thirty years. His book shatters myths about rural life as either idyllic or backwards. Then he paints a compelling picture of what rural church ministry can and must be for the glory of God. Glenn's insights are stunning! This book needs to be on the reading list for anyone who prays for or serves in rural ministry.

STEVEN D. MATHEWSON
Senior Pastor of CrossLife Evangelical Free Church in Libertyville, IL
Doctor of Ministry Program Director at Western Seminary in
Portland, Oregon
Author of *The Art of Preaching Old Testament Narrative*

The culture and mindset of small-town/rural America is very different from the culture and mindset of urban/suburban America. Unless understood, this poses a real challenge for pastors and spiritual leaders in rural churches. Another challenge is the mindset that successful churches only grow in thriving urban and suburban settings and rural communities are inconsequential. Glenn Daman truly understands these challenges. Anything he writes is worth reading!

LES LOFQUIST
IFCA International Executive Director

The hometown of my youth boasted 365 people . . . and two mostly forgotten churches. Then, one was remembered. A missionary pastor and his family placed their hearts and hopes in the middle of that village. Fast forward. Today missionaries, pastors, church elders, youth workers and even a seminary president have roots there. It reminds me (the now retired seminary president) that underestimating the potential of rural churches borders on sinful oversight and carries a high spiritual cost. Thankfully, Dr. Daman's book will awaken a rural memory in many readers, and with it, stir hearts to harvest the spiritual potential residing in rural America. Some of us may even return to our roots. Thanks, Glenn.

BERT DOWNS
President (retired), Western Seminary

As one who was raised on dairy farms in southern Indiana and served as the bivocational pastor of a rural church for twenty years, I was deeply touched by this book. I particularly appreciated Glenn's passion for the rural church, a passion not found among every Christian leader today. While pointing out the very real challenges faced by rural America and its churches, this book also offers solutions for addressing those challenges. Rural churches provide an important service both to the people and the communities they serve. It is my prayer that this book will spark a needed dialogue among church and denominational leaders about how to best strengthen the rural church.

DENNIS BICKERS
Author of *The Healthy Small Church* and *The Bivocational Pastor*

The Forgotten Church

WHY RURAL MINISTRY MATTERS FOR EVERY CHURCH IN AMERICA

Glenn Daman

Moody Publishers

CHICAGO

All Scripture quotations are taken from the New American Standard Bible®, Copyright © 1960, 1962, 1963, 1968, 1971, 1972, 1973, 1975, 1977, 1995 by The Lockman Foundation. Used by permission. (www.Lockman.org)

Scripture quotations marked NKJV are taken from the *New King James Version*. Copyright © 1982 by Thomas Nelson, Inc. Used by permission. All rights reserved.

Edited by Kevin P. Emmert
Interior design: Ragont Design
Cover design: Brian Bobel Design
Cover photo of sky and clouds copyright © 2017 by ekapol / iStock (691860584).
Cover photo of city copyright © 2016 by MariuszSzczygiel / iStock (504995266).
Cover photo of rice field copyright © 2015 by tassapon / iStock (498024624).
All rights reserved for all three photos.

Library of Congress Cataloging-in-Publication Data

Names: Daman, Glenn, author.
Title: The forgotten church : why rural ministry matters for every church in
    America / Glenn C. Daman.
Description: Chicago : Moody Publishers, 2018. | Includes bibliographical
    references.
Identifiers: LCCN 2018009699 (print) | LCCN 2018004417 (ebook) | ISBN
    9780802496454 (ebook) | ISBN 9780802418135
Subjects: LCSH: Rural churches. | Rural clergy.
Classification: LCC BV638 (print) | LCC BV638 .D27 2018 (ebook) | DDC
    253.09173/4--dc23
LC record available at https://lccn.loc.gov/2018009699

ISBN: 978-0-8024-1813-5

We hope you enjoy this book from Moody Publishers. Our goal is to provide high-quality, thought-provoking books and products that connect truth to your real needs and challenges. For more information on other books and products written and produced from a biblical perspective, go to www.moodypublishers.com or write to:

Moody Publishers
820 N. LaSalle Boulevard
Chicago, IL 60610

1 3 5 7 9 10 8 6 4 2

Printed in the United States of America

To my wife, Becky, who is my partner
in ministry, companion in life, and best friend.

To my children, Nathan and Emily Daman,
and Andrew and Paige Daman.

Behold, children are a gift of the LORD,
The fruit of the womb is a reward.
Like arrows in the hand of a warrior,
So are the children of one's youth.
How blessed is the man whose quiver is full of them;
They will not be ashamed
When they speak with their enemies in the gate.
(Ps. 127:3–5)

Contents

Foreword

I'VE BEEN IN LOVE with the rural areas of our country ever since this urban kid, who saw his first cow in a petting zoo, started spending summers in Vermont with his grandparents. Something about the scenery, lifestyle, and people filled me with longing to be there. Friends grew nervous without the city noise; I reveled in it. Lack of things to do bored my brother and sister, but I liked nothing better than spending a long, lazy afternoon fly fishing on the Battenkill River. They had many friends, but I developed a few close country friends who didn't have the competitive, sometimes cutthroat, approach to interactions. The first day after school ended, I was on a bus out of New York City headed north, and I didn't return on that bus until the day before school started.

Since those early years, I've been on a journey that's taken me to many different rural locations and involved my wife and me in a rural ministry called Village Missions, a ministry dedicated to keeping country churches alive. My passion is to convince couples considering ministry of the potential of rural ministry—a potential that will only be limited by the extent of your willingness to become involved with the people where you live.

I can't think of a ministry that has as much involvement in people's lives as rural ministry. The local school and fire department will need and appreciate your help. The local café will have a seat for you (no reservations needed), and, quite likely, you'll have your own coffee cup! A rancher or farmer will occasionally need your physical help, which often, with patience, will translate later into spiritual help. In most places it will be a natural thing to stop in for a visit. Many opportunities for conversation will come from a walk around town. You will become the community pastor if you're willing to be the pastor to anyone in the community. You'll have to make yourself available and get out of your study—and if you do, you will have a rich, relational ministry.

Of course, rural ministry, like any ministry, will not be easy. Dr. Daman, in the excellent book you are about to read, will disabuse you of any notions that rural areas are not experiencing the same and even sharper societal and spiritual declines. Did you know that, according to a recent Centers for Disease Control and Prevention study, the suicide rate among agricultural, forestry, and fishing workers is higher than any other occupational group, including veterans? In most instances, you will be the one on the front lines of battle, as infrastructure help will be limited if non-existent. We were located fifty miles away from any social worker or psychologist in the church we served for eleven years.

Despite the challenges, a new generation of committed Christian soldiers needs to discover the hidden treasure of rural ministry. You will have not only virtually limitless opportunities to connect with people in meaningful ways, but also limitless opportunities to show them what it means to live for Christ. Half-hearted disciples need not apply! Paul reminded Timothy that "you have carefully followed my doctrine, manner of life, purpose, faith, longsuffering, love, perseverance" (2 Tim. 3:10 NKJV). They will know your "manner of life" and everything else Paul mentions to Timothy. If that's threatening to you—it should be threatening to a certain extent to anyone—then you might want to look for an anonymous ministry, if there is such a thing. Rural ministry will bring you close to people and, if you are real in your walk with Christ, they will be close to you.

Yet this book is more than just an appeal for a new generation of rural leaders. It is also an appeal for a new partnership between rural, suburban, and urban churches. Having been raised in an urban setting, I recognize that rural and urban communities have much to learn from one another. In an age when our country is politically and culturally divided, we can be strengthened only by finding unity in our cultural diversity, by mutually respecting and interacting with one another. This is equally true of the church. The church at large will be strengthened by the urban church and rural church valuing one another as equals and learning from one another in ministry. Dr. Daman calls for greater cooperation and then maps out how it can be done.

Rural ministry matters not only to this transplanted suburbanite, but also to someone who has deep roots in the rural soil—Dr. Glenn Daman. His rural legacy grows from a committed missionary, a life forged from the farm, and a rural church. The church, though small, was big in its impact on his life and others, like so many other rural churches. He knows that the rural church matters because he has experienced firsthand her impact. You will find his book to be an ideal intersection between able research and personal knowledge.

Here is where Glenn and I intersect. The same mission, Village Missions, that served the rural church my wife and I attended in northern Idaho and that we have been privileged to serve with since 1983 is the same mission that has served Glenn's home church in Tensed, Idaho. Our paths have crossed over the years, and Glenn now serves ably on our board. We both ask God to grant the same thing—that the body of Christ would discover the overlooked potential and the needs of the rural church and develop partnerships between the rural church and its urban counterpart. May God grant you the same insight and passion as you read this book!

BRIAN WECHSLER
Executive Director, Village Missions

Seeing
as Christ Sees

WHAT DO YOU SEE when you drive through the fields and forests of rural America? When you drive by dilapidated and neglected towns, what thoughts enter your mind? When you catch a glimpse of an old broken-down house with the laundry hanging in the breeze, do you think of the people who live there, or is it merely a place you're passing through, hurrying along to your next destination?

For many, rural America is a place to retreat from the noise and confusion of the city. It's a place to relax and enjoy recreational activities. Others see rural America as a decaying and dying landscape where people are stuck in the past and are as rundown as the old homes that dot the landscape. Still others see rural people as close-minded bigots who reject modernity and perpetuate long-standing racial and economic biases.

Christ sees people who are without a shepherd. To Him, these communities represent individuals who have been devastated by the ravaging effects of sin and are in desperate need of the gospel. In Matthew 9:36–38, Jesus opens the eyes of His disciples by challenging them to do more than just look at what's around them. He wants them to truly *see*, for the vision that Christ has of the people is radically different from what the disciples saw. Too often, when driving through the countryside of rural communities, we fail to truly see.

And what do you see when you drive by a boarded-up church? Do you see a church that died because it was stuck in tradition and legalism? Do you become sad, knowing that it represents a light on a hill that has become darkened? When you pass a small church on the side street of a small town, do you see a vital part of the faith community providing a witness of the gospel? Or do you see a church that drains denominational resources and should be closed so that resources could be utilized better elsewhere?

Rural America is rapidly becoming a spiritual wasteland, where churches are being closed because they are overlooked and cast aside by the larger church community as a place deemed too insignificant or unworthy of our attention.

The strategy of many today is to focus on urban ministries.[1] Yet there remains another ministry that is equally important, one that is essential if we are to "make disciples of all the nations" (Matt. 28:19). Recently, rural studies has received renewed interest. But, as Christians, we should move beyond just looking at the rediscovered political clout exhibited by rural America. Christ calls us to look at rural America with His eyes. When we do, we see the spiritual condition of rural communities for what it is. Studies show that rural areas are quickly becoming the new ghetto, with persistent poverty (which exceeds that in urban areas), drug use among young people, and crime—all of which are becoming systemic problems. We also see incredible long-standing and increased racial tension. When we see the true spiritual condition of rural America, we simply cannot ignore it. We need to ask "Why?" and "What would Christ have us do to help?"

To see with the eyes of Christ is to see rural people who are "distressed and dispirited like sheep without a shepherd" (Matt. 9:36). When we drive through the countryside in the fall and find golden fields of wheat ready for harvest, we are reminded of the spiritual harvest where the problem is never the potential for the harvest. Rather, the crisis is the availability of workers, which should drive us to our knees to pray that laborers would attend to rural America (Matt. 9:37–38).

We cannot ignore the need, for to do so is to undermine the very nature of the gospel. The opportunities for ministry are great, but they will require the whole church to become involved. The rural church needs the involvement and assistance of the urban church. The church was never meant to be a collection of independently franchised congregations working in isolation from—and, tragically, often in competition with—one another. It was meant to be both a local and universal community where each congregation recognized the responsibility to assist and strengthen others—where the congregation of Macedonia would contribute to Paul's ministry as he planted churches in other communities, and the church at Philippi would assist the congregation in Jerusalem (1 Cor. 16:1–4; 2 Cor. 8:1–5; Phil. 4:15–20). Christ's prayer for unity within the church goes beyond unity just within the local congregation. It reflects a desire for mutual care and concern of each congregation for one another (John 17).

To see rural churches for what they truly are, we should examine the remarkable strengths found in those small churches—and that includes diving into the history and culture of rural America and the rural church. Rural churches are not the minor leagues or insignificant ministries. They are vitally healthy congregations that have a great deal to teach and contribute to the larger church in America. Paul encourages us to recognize the contributions that every person makes to the health and growth of the church (1 Cor. 12). Paul's image of the church functioning like a body is not limited to describing the necessity of each individual in a local congregation. It also describes how the church at large should function. Just as the rural church needs the contribution of the urban church, so also the urban church needs the input and strength of the rural church. The goal and purpose of this book is that the church at large might understand the importance of and need for rural ministry, as well as identify ways that rural and urban churches can partner together to mutually encourage and strengthen the larger body. In doing so, we will carry out the Great Commission more faithfully.

The Forgotten Ministry

IN THE LATE 1800s, the Northwoods of Minnesota developed into a vibrant logging industry that covered over 200 square miles and employed over 30,000 men who were a "rude, rough, roistering, brawling, and lusty generation."[1] It was a place where men were as savage as the land they sought to tame. As the population grew in the region surrounding Duluth and Bemidji, the call went forth to establish ministry efforts to reach the logging camps. But those who responded found the primitive conditions unbearable due to the lice and maltreatment by the lumberjacks. So, few ministers remained.

Jack Higgins didn't set out to be a pastor to lumberjacks. However, in 1895, after serving urban churches, he was asked by the Presbyterian congregation in Barnum, Minnesota, to serve their congregation. Like most young men, the idea of going to a remote rural community was not appealing. Years later, he would reflect, "I could not understand why I should go to Barnum. Had I been permitted, I should have chosen a farming community rather than a logging village. There seemed no chance to advance; and I had an eye on big churches in those days."[2]

While in Barnum, a lumber baron invited Higgins to visit his lumber camps in the Kettle River area. After being introduced as a pastor, they promptly invited him to preach a message. He accepted and gave an invitation that changed the course of his life as his eyes were opened to the desperate needs of the men in the lumber camps.[3]

In 1899, Higgins moved to Bemidji to serve as a pastor. In that place, he received his second education. His teachers were not trained theologians. No, his teachers were "saloonmen, gamblers, grafters, and the rag-tag and bobtail of humanity"[4] who taught him to understand the rugged logger and speak their language. It was here that he began to develop a passion for the lumberjacks of the Northwoods. Throughout the week, Higgins trekked by snowshoes or skis into the woods to preach to the camps.

After one such week, the elders of the church expressed their frustration and gave Higgins an ultimatum: either discontinue his work with the loggers or be fired. For many, the decision would have been easy: stay in the city and let the loggers come to them. But Frank was cut from a different cloth, and his response was immediate: "I don't need any time, and I have made a decision. This pulpit is vacant right now! A thousand men could take this church. The boys in the woods have only me." Submitting his resignation, with no salary or housing, he began a ministry of traversing into the woods on skis, snowshoes, and dog sled. He often traveled in forty-below weather to proclaim the gospel to men who seemed to be the most unreachable. Eventually, his territory would extend 200 miles west from Duluth, south to Brainerd and north to the Rainy River, encompassing 250 logging camps.[5]

It is one thing to preach to loggers; it is quite another to gain a hearing. To do so, he would first need to prove to the loggers that he was as tough as them, a man among men. They judged a man, not by the clarity of his mind or the eloquence of his sermons, but by the power of his arm and the toughness of his spirit. To survive and thrive in the Northwoods, a man had to be able to stand on his own two feet. He had to be willing to fight the elements, the demands of the job, the tediousness of working months on end, and, when necessary, other men.

Years later, reflecting upon his work, he would tell a reporter, "If I were getting ready for my work again, I would take lessons in boxing. The men that goes [*sic*] into the woods to preach to men has to be a man first and a preacher afterward."[6] The March 2, 1907, edition of *The Bemidji Daily Pioneer* describes the challenges of his ministry: "In nearly every camp there are men who seem to hate the sight of a missionary. They sometimes try to break up the meetings, but 'The Sky Pilot' relies upon the other element to assist him in all such cases."[7] The book *The Last of the Giants* describes one such occasion when "the other element" was needed. "At one camp, the narrator states, Frank was having a Sunday afternoon service, and a man was heckling him. After vainly trying to shut the fellow up by appealing to his better nature, Frank hauled off and struck the disturber a mighty blow"—certainly the recommended practice of seminaries and missions agencies. "The force of the punch lifted the heckler off his feet, turned him over in the air, and left him headfirst in a rain barrel! While his friends pulled him out, Frank calmly proceeded to finish his sermon."[8] As he proved his toughness, they accepted him as a peer and grew to respect him as their "Sky Pilot."[9]

If the brawn of Higgins's fist earned him the respect to be heard, the size of his heart earned the reception of his message. What defined his ministry more than his willingness to engage in a scrape was his willingness to be with them. In a time when the saloons would welcome the loggers with open arms, the churches saw them as dirty and corrupt. While others rejected them, Higgins saw a mission field where few were willing to go.[10] Yet he soon recognized that to reach them he needed to be more than present; he needed to become involved in their lives. This meant going to the camps and bars and other places they lived.[11] It meant traversing the wilderness in blizzards to visit camps. It required carrying a passed-out drunk back to his home and helping to clean and sober him up. It entailed loving and befriending the saloon owners he sought to put out of business.[12] It was said of him, "His religion consisted more of service than of expounding theology; his hand was more eloquent than his voice, and his heart gave greater help than his mind."[13] Throughout his ministry, the loggers, gamblers, and even saloon owners would count Higgins as one of their friends.

By 1904, with his ministry expanding, Higgins recruited others to assist him. These men were cut from the same cloth as Higgins, men who stood among men. Unlike the others, however, Richard (Dick) Ferrell (1855–1956) did not remain in Minnesota, but migrated to the logging camps of Idaho, where he continued holding evangelistic meetings in logging camps and small towns. He was an ex-prizefighter and blacksmith who accepted Christ during a message by Rev. John Stone at the Fourth Presbyterian Church in Chicago, Illinois. After his conversion, Henry P. Crowell, president of Quaker Oats Company, paid his tuition to attend Moody Bible Institute, where he served as a student pastor at First Presbyterian Church, one of the largest churches in Chicago.

One night, John Stone visited Ferrell and introduced him to Frank Higgins, who was looking for rough and tough men to go into logging camps. Several days later, Ferrell walked into the president's office and, to the president's surprise, submitted his resignation, affirming that his calling was not to come to Chicago and preach to "silk plug hats and jewel bedecked women."[14] Instead, he was called to preach to the lumberjacks in Wisconsin. Like Higgins, Ferrell spurned the prevalent attitude of pursuing an urban church and recognition to pursue the obscurity of rural ministry. Consequently, in 1914, the Presbyterian Church (USA) Board of Home Missions commissioned him to go to logging camps in Northern Idaho, Eastern Washington, and Western Montana. The assignment was simple: "Go into the lumber camps, where there are no churches and no preachers, and do what you can to spread the Gospel and help the men."[15]

During the 1930s and '40s, Ferrell traveled throughout Washington and Idaho preaching in the camps and conducting services in the small logging and farming communities. His "congregations" included a roll call of logging empires of the day: Anaconda Copper, Clearwater Timber, Diamond Match, Lincoln Lumber, McGoldrick Lumber, Ohio Match, Weyerhaeuser, Winton Lumber and more. In an average year, he traveled 19,048 miles; delivered 217 sermons; visited 222 camps, hospitals, missions, Sunday schools, and day schools; called on 902 families and 83 sick persons; wrote 380 letters; and handed out 633 Gospels and tracts plus hundreds of pounds of secular books and magazines.[16]

By the 1940s, the nature of lumber work changed. Rough, transient camps gave way to permanent housing and loggers commuting from nearby towns. Consequently, along with preaching the gospel to the logging camps, Ferrell began to establish Sunday Schools in isolated schoolhouses and abandoned camps.[17] In 1933, he helped to organize a Sunday School in a small farming community in Tensed, Idaho. From 1933 until after his retirement, he would frequently visit the struggling congregation, helping them establish a vibrant church. While holding evangelistic services in the community, Wayne Daman, a part-time logger with McGoldrick Lumber and farmer from Tensed, responded to the invitation to accept Christ.

As Ferrell helped establish the church, they enlisted the assistance of Stonecroft Ministry and Village Missions. In response, Stonecroft sent two young women, Lola Theisen and Ruth Goodrick, to aid in the establishment of a Sunday School. Beginning in August 1952, they provided leadership and teaching for the struggling church.

Ms. Goodrick grew up in Appleton, Wisconsin. Later she attended St. Paul Bible Institute and served as the youth director for the South-side Alliance Church in Chicago under the leadership of A. W. Tozer. Although she grew up in the city, she too answered God's call to serve the rural church. Likewise, Lola would marry a local logger named Olle Flolo, while Ruth would marry Wayne Daman. Both families would then become long-time pillars in the church.

On August 3, 1953, the building was completed and the church established. The congregation dedicated the new basement to Rev. Ferrell, calling it "Ferrell Hall" in honor of his contribution to the church. Today, after over 70 years of ministry, the church continues to serve the small community. The founders are no longer present, but the ministry continues under the leadership of their children.

The Forgotten Ministry

Certainly, this story shows the importance of rural ministry. But it does more than that, for the events describe my own story of redemption. Wayne Daman, the part-time logger and farmer who came to Christ in that rustic evangelistic service in an out-of-the-way corner of the panhandle of Idaho, was my father, and the missionary, Ruth Goodrick, sent by Stonecroft Ministries, was my mother. The church they helped to establish became the church that provided my own spiritual foundation. It was in this little church that I not only learned the stories and lessons of the Bible, but also saw firsthand the reality of Christ lived out in the lives of its people. It was there that God began to prepare me for rural ministry.

Is rural ministry insignificant because it does not touch the masses? I pray not, for my very spiritual destiny was influenced by two men's willingness to abandon the masses and instead serve the lost in the Northwoods of Minnesota and rural communities of northern Idaho. Their work may not be important to the writers of church history, but it continues to be desperately important to me. If not for the ministry of Frank Higgins and Dick Ferrell, you would not be reading this book.

But the story goes far deeper than my own personal history; it goes to the heart of the gospel and confronts our assumptions about ministry. For some today, the measure of success is found in *how many* we serve rather than *whom* we serve. We assume that success can be determined by what occurs within the rolls. Consequently, churches growing the fastest and having the most in attendance receive recognition in church and denominational conferences. Yet we must ask, "Is this the biblical definition of success?" When we turn to the pages of the New Testament, we find a different perspective, where "success" is measured by faithfulness and obedience. And we can be faithful and obedient only when we truly see the real need and then act to meet that need.

Yet, just as in Higgins's and Ferrell's day, rural ministry has become neglected. In their day, the church forgot that the call of the gospel is "to the remotest part of the earth" (Acts 1:8), even if it means traveling into the back country of Minnesota and Idaho. Today, rural America has been neglected by a society enamored with cutting-edge urban lifestyles.

In 2015, US Agriculture Secretary Tom Vilsack submitted his resignation. After nearly eight years of seeking to protect and promote the needs of rural people, his frustration of dealing with Washington reached a boiling point. In an age where policies are driven by votes and votes are obtained in urban areas, rural communities are no longer important. The *Washington Post* reported, "Vilsack was frustrated with a culture in Washington that too often ignored rural America's struggles and dismissed its virtues. 'I just sometimes think rural America is a forgotten place,' he often said."[18] So also Thomas Lyson and William Falk, after reflecting upon decades of dismantling of federal programs and policies to combat rural poverty, lament that Washington has neglected the poor of rural America.[19]

Tragically, what is true in Washington D.C. has become true in the church. In an age when the siren's call is for relevance and innovation, the rural church seems irrelevant and outdated. The rural church does not make headlines, and rural pastors are not asked to speak at conferences.

The common perception is that the rural church is bound by legalism and antiquated tradition.

Ask a Bible college or seminary student to pastor a rural church, and they will look at you like you were asking them to pastor a church on the moon, with no people, no potential for growth, surrounded by dust and empty lands. In one survey of students in a Bible college, only thirty-three percent did not consider the size of the community important for prospective ministry opportunities. Further, only twenty-one percent agreed that growth potential was not a critical factor when considering a ministry.[20] When the same question was asked of the Pastoral Ministries students, only seventeen percent agreed that the size of the community and the growth potential was not a factor, and only twenty-eight percent agreed that the size of the church was unimportant.[21] This raises serious concerns as to why so few are willing to serve small churches in rural areas.

Read a book on the history of the American church, and beyond the days of the pioneers, the rural church will be absent. For many, the rural church has nothing to offer in advancing the kingdom. They view rural ministry as the minor leagues, a place to hone their skills before moving on to the major leagues of a larger urban church. It's no wonder that when I decided to pursue a doctoral program in ministry, some within the church I had been pastoring felt that I was merely using the church to advance my career and that as soon as I graduated, I would be moving on. It had happened too often in the past, and so they had good reason to be distrustful.

With a few exceptions, Bible colleges and seminaries exist in large urban centers. Consequently, those who attend receive extensive exposure to the urban church. As they begin their education, their introduction to ministry often begins as first volunteers and then staff members of the larger urban congregations. As a result, when they complete their education, it's natural for them to gravitate toward a larger urban church. Conversely, the student has received very little exposure to the small church, and especially the rural church. It's not that they oppose going to the rural church; it's that small and rural churches aren't on their radar of places they would go. Because of their exposure to the multi-staff church, they are comfortable seeking a position in the urban church but find the prospect of serving as a lone pastor in a rural or small church to be frightfully intimidating.

The lack of visibility of the rural church in the educational process is compounded by the reality that those recruited to serve as instructors often come from or are pastors of large urban churches. This again goes back to the previous misconception that the size of the church measures success. However, this is not necessarily a deliberate bias against the small and rural church, but a result of the lack of representation of the small church. One of the problems is that those who pastor rural churches often lack the educational requirements necessary to be a professor. But the real tragedy is not just that denominational leaders, Bible colleges, and seminaries ignore the rural church. It is that, when confronted with the needs, people respond with a yawn of indifference. Unfortunately, the rural community and the rural church are becoming the forgotten ministry.

What would have happened if Frank Higgins played it safe and stayed in Bemidji where he had financial security? What if Dick Ferrell followed the conventional wisdom and remained in the large church in Chicago? What if Ruth Goodrick remained in Tozer's church, where she would have gained recognition? What if Phillip had stayed in Jerusalem, where the action was, rather than go into the wilderness of Sinai? What if there is no longer anyone willing to go "to the boys in the woods" or "to the ends of the earth"?

That brings us to the heart of this book. The message outlined in the following pages is not a rejection of the need for urban, suburban, and ethnically focused ministry. Without question, these ministries continue to be desperately needed today. Rather, the purpose here is to bring the rural ministry back into focus. Overlooking the rural church and the forgotten places of rural America neglects seventeen percent of our nation's population.[22] The ministry may not be glamorous. It will not bring recognition and invitations to speak at conferences. It may not be trendy and cutting edge. But the people of rural America are just as important to the heart of God as the people in metropolitan areas. For this reason alone, they should be important to the church as well.

Effective ministry in rural communities begins with understanding. We must understand—and truly see—the incredible needs and opportunities if we are going to reach these forgotten communities. This starts by pulling back the curtain of our preconceived ideas and taking a fresh look at rural communities and the contribution that they can make to the health of the broader church in America.

2

The Misunderstood Ministry

IF RURAL AMERICA has been forgotten, it has equally been misunderstood. Often, perceptions distort reality and our understanding of people. As the nation becomes increasingly divided in the conflict of worldviews—which touches upon the division between conservative and liberal politics, traditional versus progressive morality, and urban versus rural cultures—misconceptions become more prevalent. Rather than strive to understand and then engage others in dialogue, we tend to huddle into our own enclaves that promote and reaffirm our biases and misconceptions.

This is true in our understanding of rural life and rural people. Many people tend to view the resistance of rural people to progressivism as being backwards and naïve, stuck in a mentality that existed thirty years ago. As Richard Wood discovered, "Today, more than ever in our history, the 83 percent of Americans who live in metropolitan areas have about as much real-life knowledge of the other 17 percent, and of rural America in general, as they do of central Africa. Worse, much of the little they think they know isn't true."[1] When we fail to understand and value a culture and people, we will eventually devalue and probably ridicule them. This is true of the rural culture. Even more tragically, it is also true within the church. Ask students from urban backgrounds to describe the rural church, and the adjectives will likely be negative: old-fashioned, legalistic, unwilling to change, driven by tradition.

In a success-driven culture, what can the rural church offer? In a culture enamored with achievement and recognition, the rural church offers obscurity. As a result, in recent decades, the rural church has largely been ignored. In an age of hipsters, the rural church is unfashionable. Read books on church planting, and you'll find the focus is often on planting churches in urban and suburban areas. Peruse books on church growth, and you'll read measurements of effectiveness marked by numerical growth. For worship to be effective and the church to be relevant, there must be a dynamic team that leads the congregation in a contemporary music style. If we buy into these models, the rural church is doomed to failure before it even starts. And who wants to go to a church where failure is already guaranteed?

Defining Rural America

Accurately understanding and assessing rural ministry and the opportunities, challenges, and needs of rural America begins with defining what *rural* is. But the complexity and variety of rural communities dotting the landscape make any encompassing definition elusive. In rural America, communities vary greatly, from stable farming communities to transient tourist communities, from poverty stricken mining communities to upscale, technology-driven areas. The meaning of *rural* becomes ambiguous. Consequently, there remains disagreement within the social sciences regarding how we define the term. Instead of defining what constitutes *rural*, often it is defined by that which is not urban, "with no attention given to the intrinsic characteristics that contribute to the place's rurality," as David Brown and Kai Schafft point out.[2]

Defining Rural Demographically

Many researchers focus on the demographic makeup of the community. To delineate what constitutes rural, they begin by defining what constitutes an urban or metropolitan area.[3] The remaining area then is designated as rural. Although this approach provides the basis of the official federal government's definition, inconsistencies exist among different agencies. For example, the US Census Bureau defines *rural* by population density. *Urban* is defined by population clusters with at least 2,500 people. *Rural* refers to the population, housing, and territory that is not urban.[4] Thus, *rural* are those places in open country that have fewer than 2,500 people and are not part of the urban fringe.[5]

Other government agencies define the terms based upon metropolitan and nonmetropolitan counties. *Metropolitan* describes counties that either have a town or city with a minimum population of 50,000 or a county that has a total population of at least 100,000. But the problem is that one can live in a city and still be classified as rural (if it is not over 50,000), and a farmer living in the country can be classified as metropolitan because he lives in a county with a population of over 100,000.[6]

To alleviate some of these problems and confusion, a third category has been introduced. *Micropolitan* has been used to describe those counties with a population of 10,000 to 49,999 that also have an urban core. *Nonmetropolitan*, then, refers to those counties with fewer than 50,000 residents within the county and no urban core.[7]

The United States Department of Agriculture, Economic Research Service identifies nine levels of metro-nonmetro counties based on the total population of the county.[8] They distinguish three different types of metropolitan communities based upon the size of the urban center. They then identify five different types of nonmetro counties based upon both the population of the county and the proximity it has to an urban area. In his book *Small Town America*, Robert Wuthnow defines *small town* as incorporated and unincorporated towns under 25,000 people and not part of an urbanized area.[9]

While the demographic designation of rural provides the basis for government programs, it does not reflect the complexity of rural life and the true character of rural people. The result is that we do not know what rural truly is. We know only what it is not. This leads to a failure to understand rural people. Our perspective of rural people becomes based upon a perception influenced by popular myths. Understanding rural people starts by dispelling the myths and misconceptions, and accepting them for who they are, not for how we perceive them. It is important to move beyond merely looking at demographic statistics and instead move toward understanding and accepting rural people *on their terms*. Rather than define *rural* by what it is *not* (that is, not urban), we need to understand it for what it *is*.

Defining Rural *as a Way of Life*

A far more complex way to understand and define *rural* is not demographically but multidimensionally, by looking at rural life itself. Growing up in rural Idaho, I soon became aware of the vast differences between urban and rural people. They dress differently, they live by different values, they express different political views, they develop a different perspective of work and play, and they worship and view the church differently. Examine a church parking lot in a rural community, and the pickups are not the accessorized 4x4s seen in a city. Rather, they are as beaten and worn as the people who drive them. Recently, one pastor's wife wrote on her Facebook page,

> Loving Life in Rural America: Is it really normal to have a tractor pull into a library parking lot? After I was putting something away in my pickup, I was heading toward the building. I heard a noise and looked back. 'Oh, it is Sarah!' What a nice surprise

it was to see her. As she opens the door and is talking, of course it is a bit difficult to hear with the motor noise, so I hoist myself up the step, pop my head inside the cab and have a nice little chat with my friend. When we got done and we waved good bye to each other I thought . . . I had never pictured myself in a place like this. Where you go to work, and see your friends working too, driving their tractor to their next field, and not only that, but pulling their tractor into the parking lot. All I can say is—Loving Life in Rural America![10]

For rural people, work is not just a job one does merely to earn a living; it is a way of life. There is no line of demarcation between career and leisure. Work is who they are and what defines them. People in rural areas do not merely work on a farm, in a mine, or in the woods. They *are* farmers, miners, and loggers who see their work as their life and their life in their work. "Through most of world history rural people have been dramatically different from urban people, and rural life has diverged strikingly from urban life; that reality continues now in much of the developed world. Until very recently, rural people in Europe and North America had unique experiences. . . . And they pursued an occupation that was at least as much a way of life as it was a way of making a living."[11]

When President Obama first campaigned for the presidency, he revealed his lack of understanding of rural America when he stated, "You go into some of these small towns in Pennsylvania, and like a lot of small towns in the Midwest, the jobs have been gone now for 25 years and nothing's replaced them. And they fell through the Clinton administration, and the Bush administration, and each successive administration has said that somehow these communities are gonna regenerate and they have not. And it's not surprising when they get bitter, they cling to guns or religion or antipathy to people who aren't like them or anti-immigrant sentiment or anti-trade sentiment as a way to explain their frustrations."[12] While he rightly identified the frustration with economic tensions in rural America, he misjudged the way that rural people expressed their frustration, for he was looking at them through the eyes of one who had spent his life in the city.

This is what brings us to the heart of what rurality truly is. Rurality is not just a demographic delineation; it is people and a way of life. Certainly, as is revealed demographically, rurality begins with where people live. The standard definition described above is helpful in our understanding. But population density does not account for the cultural differences. Frank Farmer points out three other important qualities that distinguish rural and urban people.[13]

First, rurality encompasses the isolation of where people live. This involves not just the sparseness of the population, but, more importantly, the distance to, availability of, access to, and cost for necessary services and goods. For many urban people, medical facilities and social services are closer. Rural people often have to travel significant distances, which make these services largely inaccessible to them. When I served a small church in rural Montana, the nearest mental facility for those experiencing emotional issues was over 250 miles away, making it unattainable. Consequently, rural communities place greater emphasis upon the church and the local pastor to provide help and counsel.

Second, rurality encompasses the way people earn their living. Rural communities are more dependent upon farming, ranching, forestry, mining, oil, and gas extraction and natural resource-based industries. The result is that rural people have more limited and less diversified career opportunities than those available to their urban counterparts. Rural people are much more tied to the land and its resources. They measure a person by their willingness to perform physical labor.

Third, rurality encompasses the values people share. To truly understand and serve rural people, we want to understand their individual and corporate values. Socio-cultural dimensions refer to the values and ideals that underpin the community. While rural America is more diverse in values than people realize, there exists certain values that define the community. Specific norms and institutions characterize rural communities of all shapes and sizes. These include the importance of religion, self-control, and social conservativism.[14] For those of us in ministry who live in specific communities, we need to first learn and understand the values and worldview of a community, otherwise we run the risk of superimposing preconceived values upon them.[15] Without this understanding, we cannot effectively work with the people and institutions that shape the community and adapt our ministry to their specific needs.

Because our understanding of *rural* encompasses both demographics and culture, any definition of *rural* is fluid at best. As Farmer points out, "The major point of agreement among those involved in the debate has been that there is no singular or multifaceted definition that will suffice to satisfy the research, programmatic and policy communities that employ the concept."[16] However, for the purpose of this book we define *rural* as: *communities and towns with a population base less than 10,000 people, that are not in close proximity to an urban core, that exhibit characteristics of rural culture, and that are often (but not exclusively) economically and emotionally connected to the land upon which they live.*[17]

Conversely, we define *urban* as: *communities of 50,000 or more in population and a population density of over 1,000 people per square mile.* I recognize that this latter definition is ambiguous. Certainly, not all such communities are "urban" in the same way, and this definition does not identify the scope of cultural diversity existing between large urban centers (over 1,000,000 in population) and smaller urban centers (those under 250,000). It also does not account for the differences between *urban* (how 26 percent of Americans describe the area in which they live) and *suburban* (how 53 percent of Americans describe the area in which they live).[18] However, I will leave it to those writing on urban ministry to develop a detailed examination of the differences existing between various urban communities. Still, the definition of *urban* that I have provided here is accepted by sociologist, government agencies, and most literature on the rural-urban divide.

Rural-Urban Divide

Dispelling the misconceptions of rural America begins with the recognition of the gulf existing between rural and urban worldviews. Recent presidential elections have highlighted not only the radical division in how urban and rural people vote, but also the differences in their perception of the world around them. After the 2012 election, Josh Kron wrote in *The Atlantic*, "The new political divide is a stark division between cities and what remains of the countryside. Not just some cities and some rural areas, either—virtually every major city (100,000-plus population) in the United States of America has a different outlook from the less populous areas that are closest to it."[19] Politically, urban areas vote Democratic and rural areas vote Republican, a trend that has increased since 1984. But the divide between rural and urban perspectives goes far beyond politics and culture, encompassing all aspects of one's viewpoint. From morality to the environment, rural and urban residents look through completely different lenses. As Neil Levesque, director of the New Hampshire Institute of Politics at Saint Anselm College, states, "The difference in this country is not red versus blue. It's urban versus rural."[20] These differences spring from completely different life experiences. While a larger portion of urban dwellers buy smartphones, foreign-made cars, and read fashion magazines, those in the rural area are more likely to attend church, buy American cars, shop in local stores, and spend time in the outdoors.[21]

These differences infiltrate the church as well. While there are significant similarities between rural and urban small churches, the distinctions between small and larger urban congregations (those over 300 in attendance) become apparent. And the distinctions between the rural church and larger urban church leads to the misunderstanding of the rural church.[22] The rural church focuses primarily upon developing and maintaining community and relationships, while the urban church is driven more by casting vision and carrying it out through various forms of mission. This does not mean, however, that the rural church neglects vision and mission, or that the urban church neglects community and relationships. Rather, both the rural and urban church typically order their priorities differently, and their understandings and embodiment of those respective priorities take on different forms. Because urban pastors often fail to recognize this chasm, they tend to struggle in rural churches—and so would rural church pastors struggle in an urban environment. They often seek to implement urban principles of church leadership and practices within the rural church. In the end, the pastor becomes discouraged, the congregation becomes frustrated, and the ministry struggles.

The dividing line is more than political and cultural; it goes to the core of people's moral and ethical beliefs. While many in urban America have plunged into a postmodern worldview, rural Americans have remained more steadfast in their adherence to a Judeo-Christian ethic. For many in rural America, this ethic governs how they understand their own community and how they see the world. While the cities became centers of relativism and pluralism, rural communities are more likely to hold fast to the belief that the Judeo-Christian ethic is grounded in absolute and uncompromising truth. As a result, urban people often see rural people as closed minded and legalistic, while rural communities can view the urbanites as morally corrupt.

However, this adherence to a Judeo-Christian ethic often conceals the spiritual and social crisis confronting rural people. While upholding traditional values, they replace biblical faith with self-reliance. As we shall see, the belief in a Judeo-Christian ethic does not equate to a genuine redemptive relationship with God. Just as the Jews of Jesus' day held to a biblical ethos but failed to embrace the transforming faith to which the Law pointed, so also many in rural areas affirm the ethic of Scripture but rely upon personal merit when it comes to salvation.

Because of differing worldviews, rural and urban people hold different views of the centrality of religion in their personal lives, with rural residents three times more likely to state that religion is important.[22] This religious orientation differs sharply on social and political issues—deficit spending, military defense spending, gay marriage, transgendered restrooms, amnesty, sanctuary cities, affirmative action, gun control, and abortion.[23] However, these rural values are often misunderstood. A common rural worldview is shaped by their conviction about God, the Bible, and the basis by which morality is determined. Even though they might not regularly attend a church, they hold to an ethic grounded in traditional norms passed down from previous generations. The church is seen as the guardian of the values of the community, both in shaping those values and protecting those values. However, while they hold to traditional norms and values, that does not necessarily mean that they are truly biblical. If the urban value is driven by pluralism, the rural value can be governed by deep rooted tradition. If the error of pluralism is cultural and moral accommodation, the error of traditionalism is legalism and self-reliance.

Dispelling the Myths

For many, the reason rural Americans hold to traditional values stems from their bigotry, racism, and lack of education. Tragically, this characterization is based upon misconceptions people superimposed upon rural people. If you are pro-gun, you are violent. If you support traditional marriage, you are bigoted. If you believe in traditional roles within marriage, you are misogynistic. If you promote the enforcement of immigration laws, you are racist. If you lack a college degree, you must be uneducated and ignorant.

This is not just an issue of interest to students of sociology. This also affects the church in several different ways. First, pastors who come from other backgrounds often view the rural church as traditional, old fashioned, legalistic, and unwilling to change. What they fail to recognize is that rural churches are often willing to change, but they are not willing to adopt changes that conflict with the values they believe to be biblically driven. Second, it also leads to greater tensions and conflicts in the church. As urban people move into rural areas, they tend to bring progressive values and viewpoints that conflict with the conservative values of long-time residents. Thus, conflicts arise in the church between the old-timers and newcomers. To be effective, the pastor needs to carefully help people discern between what is truly biblical and what is cultural. He needs to help the "old-timers" see that some of their values are cultural rather than biblical, while at the same time helping the "newcomers" learn to respect and value the rich traditions that undergird a rural church and dispel the myths and misconceptions that popular culture has of rural people.

Myth #1: Rural America Corresponds to Popular Media

For many, popular culture and the media shape their perception of rural America. As David Brown and Louis Swanson point out, "Regardless of the content of their attitudes, most Americans form their opinion about rural people and communities from a distance—through literature, art, and music, but not through direct experiences. The true nature of rurality—the worldviews of rural people and the conditions of their lives—is often at variance with the typical perception of most Americans."[24] People watched the *Beverly Hillbillies* and *Petticoat Junction*, which portrayed rural people as backwoods, bumbling hillbillies, and where the smartest living creature was a pig. Thus, they see rural America as uneducated and ignorant. This perspective was revealed after the 2016 election when one television persona tweeted, "Rural = so stupid."[25]

Others see rural America through rose-colored glasses, where people live romanticized, simple lives. *The Andy Griffith Show* and, more recently, the Canadian show *Corner Gas* present rural communities as a place where life is simple, crime is absent, and everyone lives happily ever after. It is a place where *The Waltons* and *Little House on the Prairie* exists in real life. A place where families live in harmony, both with the land and themselves, and people demonstrate superhuman moral fiber.[26] Thus, country life is seen as a serene, peaceful, and slow-paced lifestyle that is both idealistic and picturesque.[27]

In recent years, the media presented a different view. With the popularity of "reality TV," rural people are often portrayed as country hicks. *Ax Men, Moonshiners, Swamp People,* and others depict rural people as crass, cussing, moonshine-drinking rednecks who love nothing more than to kill ducks, alligators, and trees. Rural America becomes defined by white, gun-loving racists who are homogeneous in ethnicity, culture, and values.

The result is a dichotomous view of rural people. They represent traditional values that are outdated; their life is more relaxed and slower-paced, but harder and more grueling; they are friendlier but intolerant of outsiders; they have a richer community life but are deeply independent and individualistic.[28] But the representation of popular media fails to convey the complexity, challenges, and struggles confronting rural people. The characterization is a far cry from reality.

Myth #2: Rural America Abuses Land

When urban people travel into rural communities, they usually seek relaxation and recreation. For them, the natural resources exist for enjoyment rather than economic sustainability. Forests exist for camping, not for harvesting. Clear-cuts are not acceptable practices of the forestry industry but examples of big corporations raping the forests for profit. Streams and lakes provide fishing, boating, and kayaking opportunities rather than resources for electricity or irrigation. As a result, many urban people promote legislation to preserve the pastoral recreation. As Fern Willits and A. E. Logoff observe, "The greater the contact with rural areas, the less likely these persons were to support economic development either through promoting extractive industries or other businesses/industries."[29] Consequently, "efforts to attract new manufacturing plants, develop tourist sites, or build shopping centers often have been blocked by urban-based protest groups in the face of local support for these activities, regardless of economic costs to the rural residents."[30]

For those who work and live in rural America, the land is more than just for recreation. It is the lifeblood of their existence. Farmers, ranchers, loggers, and miners recognize the importance of preserving our natural resources. They are environmentalists in the truest sense of the word. They are deeply concerned about the health and future sustainability of the land and resources. Nevertheless, there is a fundamental difference between a rural and urban view of what constitutes a healthy environment. The urban environmental view focuses upon the sustainability of the natural habitat, where the intrusion of man is destructive. For them, any management and alteration of nature—such as Genetic Modified Organisms—exploits and destroys the environment. On the other hand, rural people, especially those in the various land-use industries, see the environment as a resource to use and manage.

Myth #3: The Mystique of Rural Life

Among many in America, there is a growing positive view about rural *life* and the quest to get back to nature. When people drive through the countryside, they see rural life as serene and stress-free. However, this perspective, shaped by an idealistic view of country living largely disconnected from reality, remains driven by a rural mystique. Brown and Schafft observe, "The mystique is composed of treasured or almost sacred elements. It is an idealized form of community that stands in contrast to urban life. It is the antithesis of the modern urban world, somehow more moral, virtuous, and simple. In other words, rurality reflects what people feel has been lost in the transformation from rural to urban society."[31] People want to both preserve their view of rural life as well as get back to nature. Consequently, they support public policies for rural areas and environments if they preserve the traditional view of country living, but oppose policies promoting economic development and the change it brings. They desire to preserve the family farm while opposing the "corporate farm" even though the definition of "corporate farms" often encompasses many family-owned and operated farms today.

Recently, I was in a local coffee shop where the barista expressed this perspective. She moved from an urban area into our small community so that she could have a garden and a couple of goats. Her goal was to have a self-sustaining farm on a few acres in her pursuit to get back to nature. She further complained that all the farms were now becoming corporate farms operated by large companies that were destroying our food supply by genetically modified organisms in their pursuit of profits. But the reality is that 96.4 percent of all farms are still family owned.[32] What urban people are seeking to preserve is the mystique. They lament the loss of the Norman Rockwell version farm life where families are pictured working together, children swimming in the watering hole, and the farmer enjoying the benefits of his hard work. Thus, *The Real Truth*, a magazine published by the Restored Church of God, laments the disappearing family farm and the devastation that will bring: "A class of society is being lost, and with it, iconic barns and sprawling rural landscapes are fading at an alarming rate. The concept of a small family farm—one that has been owned and operated by one family for possibly several generations—has been all but destroyed."[33]

Such a life is not only lost; it never existed to begin with. Growing up on a small family farm was an invaluable experience, but it was hardly the idyllic view presented in this article. As a child, our playground was 280 acres of wheat fields and timber ground. It was not uncommon for us to leave the house, come back home for a brief lunch, and then head back outside for an afternoon of exploration. Long before we were old enough to help my dad haul the hay, my brothers and I would rearrange the haymow into our own castle, complete with separate rooms and even a dungeon. We made forts in trees and conducted military raids against the pigs in the pasture.

But life was also filled with work, whether it was helping my dad unfreeze the stock pipes at thirty-below or pulling a Red Flyer wagon hauling buckets of grain to the barn to feed the pigs. By the time we were in our early teens, we worked all summer for either our dad or neighbors. We worked six days a week, twelve hours a day, unless it was spring planting or harvest, then it was fourteen to sixteen hours a day. As a youngster, I did not spend hours tranquilly watching turtles. After school, there were pig pens to clean, livestock to feed, and chores to do. Urbanites decry child labor and pass laws to prevent it, but my dad never got the memo. For a farm to be successful, the entire family has to be involved. Beginning when I was twelve, I spent the summers working first for my father and then for the neighbors driving tractor and combine. While the work was hard, I learned invaluable lessons that prepared me for life in general and ministry in particular. Don't get me wrong. I loved every minute of it. As the saying goes, you can take the boy out of the farm but you can't take the farm out of the boy.

Nevertheless, to live off the land, one must work the land with each crop being harvested with blood, sweat, and even tears. You spend the whole summer tilling the soil to raise a crop, only to watch that crop slowly be consumed by drought. You truck the wheat to the elevator knowing the current price will not cover the expenses. You see a forest fire devastate the timber that you were counting on for your retirement. You see your kids move away because there is no job opportunity. There was no better life than growing up on the farm, but it is not for the faint of heart.

Myth #4: Rural and Agriculture Are Synonymous

When most people think of rural residents, their first thought is that of a farmer in the field tilling the soil in his John Deere tractor. The small villages populating the rural landscape provide the parts, tools, and hardware to support the agricultural community. As a result, when it comes to public policy, there is the natural, albeit inaccurate, conclusion that farm policy is synonymous with rural policy.[34] Today, however, less than a quarter of rural counties depend on farming as the primary source of the economic base of the community.[35] When you immerse yourself in rural America, you find that it is as diverse as any city.[36] Depending on the location and region, there are significant differences as it relates to the farm population. In some areas, such as the Northeastern states, the farm population is relatively small. On the other hand, the Western and Northcentral states have a much larger proportion of farm people. To say that the country is only farmers would be like saying that the city is only office workers. Today, you will find factories, information centers, commercial fishing, forestry, mining, and a host of small businesses prospering in rural areas.

Myth #5: Rural America Is Culturally and Ethnically Homogeneous.

The popular perception of rural America is that it remains white, both ethnically and culturally. While we will look more in depth at the ethnic diversity and racial issue later, it is important to dispel the myth that rural America is ethnically homogeneous. A closer examination reveals that rural areas are more ethnically diverse than people realize. While it is certainly not as ethnically diverse as the urban counterpart (where approximately twenty percent of the population are ethnic minorities), approximately ten percent of the rural population consists of minorities.[37] In the South, there is a larger population of African Americans, while in the West, there are a significant number of Hispanics. Throughout the Midwest and West, there are many Native American reservations. Unlike their Hispanic and African American counterparts, who predominantly gravitate to urban centers, Native Americans live predominantly in rural areas. Growing up on an Indian reservation in Northern Idaho, and now living near fruit orchards where the Hispanic population maintains a strong presence, the rural America that I encountered was certainly not monocultural. Native Americans, African Americans, Hispanics, and kids from India and Iran were enrolled in a small school where my kids attended. While rural America is not as racially and culturally diverse as urban areas, the differences between them are gradually decreasing.[38]

Myth #6: Rural People Are Uneducated and Ignorant

Back in the 1970s, the University of Idaho, in conjunction with the Water and Soil Conservation District, conducted a pilot program on my father's farm to prevent water erosion in the fields. The plan consisted of a series of waterways and earthen dams to slow the water run-off and thus prevent erosion. When they presented the plans to my father, he pointed out that it would fail the first year because the snow would clog the ditches and prevent the water flow, resulting in the failure of the diversion ditches. They were unconvinced, assuring him that research data on weather and soil composition confirmed that their design would withstand whatever the weather threw at it. In the minds of the "experts," my father was ignorant. He never went past the eighth grade. But to say that he was uneducated would be a gross misnomer. He did not obtain his education at the desk of a classroom, but in the school of experience. However, for the PhDs from the University, he simply was an uneducated farmer. Consequently, they brushed aside his suggestions and implemented the plan as designed. A year later, they came back and rebuilt the whole system because it had failed. They subsequently implemented many of the recommendations of my father, though I doubt they admitted that he was right. Ultimately, true education is not determined by how many degrees a person has, but how well a person can understand the situation and develop the right course of action in response. Rural people may not have academic degrees, but that does not mean they are uneducated and ignorant. Their education comes through the experiences of life and common sense.

Many often make three assumptions about the educational background of rural people and thus misrepresent them. The first is that they are uneducated. While it is true that rural people still lag behind their urban counterparts in terms of college education, it would be false to say that rural America is uneducated and ignorant. In comparison, forty-eight percent of metro adults obtained at least some college education, while thirty-five percent of nonmetro residents attended at least some college.[39] While it is true that many of the chronically poor rural counties have substandard education, it is not true for all rural communities. In the three rural churches I have served, within the congregations there was a college professor with a PhD in mathematics, several people with master's degrees, as well as retired executives from Fortune 500 companies and a number of college graduates.

Second, many people mistakenly conclude that the quality of rural education substantially lags behind urban training. As a result, they assume rural schools provide inferior education, so that the students are hamstrung when it comes to obtaining further education and advancing in the national workforce. But the research of achievement scores of eighth and twelfth graders reveal virtually no difference.[40] Consequently, Ruy Teixeira remarks, "To summarize, the message conveyed by these data on educational achievement could not be clearer. Rural students are not receiving inferior quality education, and the general public presumption that they are receiving an inferior education is simply wrong."[41]

Third, many assume that because rural people lack a college education, they are ignorant and thus lack a comprehensive worldview. In our culture, we often judge people based upon their academic degrees. People who are uneducated are often looked down upon as being uninformed and lacking academic abilities to make it in the real world. Yet if you were to look more closely, you would discover that simply is not the case. Many farmers run million-dollar businesses, requiring management and business skills that rival any MBA. Tractors and combines are now computerized so that the farmer can get up-to-date analysis of production. Home computers and cell phones enable a farm to keep track of market trends and international agricultural news to assist them in making decisions related to what to plant and when to sell. While driving the tractor, they may be on the phone negotiating contracts with foreign buyers.

The Perception of the Rural Church

As we have already seen, on a popular level, many urban elites disregard the rural perspective. But, tragically, this disregard also has crept into the church. Denominational leaders sometimes look down upon small rural churches as outdated and insignificant. Newly graduated pastors who start their ministry in a rural church see the rural church as unenlightened and archaic, ignorant of not only the current trends in the church but of the Bible itself. A quick search of the internet reveals many seminaries offering programs in urban ministries, but a complete absence of schools offering even a class in rural ministries.

For those who have never served in a rural church, the rural church usually remains an enigma, a mystery defying understanding. Thus, many have developed misconceptions about what it truly is. Just as the rural residents have a different culture and perspective than their urban counterparts, so also the rural church views itself and the church differently.[42]

Myth #1: The Rural Church Is Bound by Tradition and Unwilling to Change

When people first interact with the rural church, they soon become aware of the importance and significance traditions play in the life of the congregation. At first glance, it appears that tradition seems more important than Scripture. From the place people sit on Sunday to the structure of the church government, unspoken traditions guide the decisions the church makes and the way people interact in worship. In the words of Tevye in *Fiddler on the Roof*, "Tradition, tradition!" Yet people do not blindly follow tradition for tradition's sake. Too often, people look only at the *what* of traditions rather than the *why*. Traditions connect the present generation with the past and serve to keep the memories of former members still present in the congregation. They keep the pulpit in the front, not because they believe a pulpit is the only place a person can preach, but because Uncle Joe, who long served in the church, built it. The furniture becomes the "Ebenezer" celebrating the faith and witness of the saints upon whose shoulders the church was built. Traditions serve to provide a sense of stability in a chaotic world. Rural churches remain open to change, but not at the cost of abandoning the witness of the former generation. They are willing to change traditions if they understand the necessity for it and how it will benefit the ongoing ministry. However, they will also evaluate the change based upon how it will affect their connection with the people in the past. It has been my observation that, in most cases, when a pastor criticizes the rural church for being tradition-bound and unwilling to change, it says more about the pastor and his approach to leadership than it does the congregation. Rural people are open to change, but not unfounded change that is driven by popular culture and the latest fads. They want to know that the change is necessary and how it will affect them both positively and negatively. When they resist a proposed change, more often than not, it is because the leadership has not adequately explained the reasons for the change and given people an opportunity to express their concerns.

Myth #2: The Rural Church Is Dying

When denominational leaders evaluate the life and vibrancy of a congregation, the first criteria they typically examine is the number of people attending the church and the number of baptisms. When the church is not growing numerically, in their estimation, it is either becoming stagnant or dying. With this as the criteria, it is little wonder that the perception persists that rural churches are dying a slow and agonizing death. For many, the answer lies in either starting new churches or consolidating smaller congregations into a large regional church. However, when we look closely at the qualities defining a biblically healthy church (gospel-centered, strong sense of mutual care, both for people in the congregation and those in the community) the rural church often shines. The church I grew up in is a good example. Located in a small farm community (approximately one hundred residents) in Northern Idaho, little has changed in the past fifty years. At its peak, the church averaged seventy people in attendance. At other times, it dipped into the thirties. Even today, its attendance fluctuates between those two numbers. But for the people who attend, it is more than just a place to go on Sunday. It is a community of believers who encourage and support one another and deeply care about outreach into the community. If the church were to close, the nearest large church would be forty to fifty miles away, and an important and necessary witness in the community would be lost.

Myth #3: The Rural Community Is Already Evangelized

Because rural people tend to be more conservative, both politically and morally, many people assume that rural areas no longer need a strong evangelistic focus. However, a vast difference exists between being religious and following a Judeo-Christian ethic, and being a genuine disciple of Christ. As a member of the Board of Directors of Village Missions, an organization devoted to rural ministry, my colleagues and I call people to be missionary-pastors rather than just pastors. We want to ensure that people realize the rural ministry is a mission field where people need to be reached with the gospel of Christ. While rural communities have a strong affinity to a local church, it often does not translate into weekly attendance. Research indicates that only thirty-six percent of the residents in nonmetropolitan communities attend services weekly or nearly every week—only five percent higher than the national average.[43]

Rural areas are becoming a mission field as the city is now coming to the country. As people retire and move back to the country, many rural areas, especially those high in natural resources, are seeing a growth in the population base. These individuals not only bring new opportunities for growth for the rural community, but also new challenges as people transitioning to the rural communities bring greater expectations of the quality and services a small church is to provide. They desire the same services and ministries offered by the larger urban church.

Toward a New Understanding

Again, we will delve more deeply into these issues as we move forward. Gaining a vision and passion for the rural church requires us to stop looking at rural America through either the rose-colored lens of popular culture or the judgmental eyes of political commentators. We need to gain a new appreciation for the value and contribution these congregations make to the global body of Christ. The rural church can teach the global church about the nature and importance of community and the dangers of seeing the church as a business. Instead of preconceived ideas and judgments, we need to listen to what the rural people say, not just asking what they do but why they do it. Only then can we become effective in reaching rural America with the gospel of Christ. We need to get beyond the perception that the rural church is unimportant and unnecessary and bring the rural church back onto the ecclesiastical radar. We need to delve beyond the misconceptions, mystique, and idyllic view of rural life and see the rural church and community for what it is—with all its problems, struggles, and opportunities. To understand the present crisis in rural America, we need to understand the historical context that has influenced and shaped the people who live there.

3

Rural Life:
A Historical Perspective

OUR COUNTRY TODAY is urban. The industrialization of our society has led to the mass migration to urban centers, where the rapidity of change has swept the nation culturally and morally. People who grew up and live in urban centers often see rural people as stuck back in the '50s with their values Victorian and their culture antiquated. For the politician, the rural areas are a wasteland, which they ignore and disregard. The way to Washington is paved through the cities, for it is the cities that provide both the finances and votes. However, this was not always the case. When the nation was first formed, it was an agrarian country that stood in contrast to the urbanized Europe. Political and national leaders saw the rural areas and farming communities as the lifeblood of the nation.

People don't exist in isolation from what happened before them. Rather, the events that happened in the previous century still shape the present. As Miona Uffelman points out, "It is impossible to understand

American history unless you understand agricultural history."[1] But herein lies our greatest challenge: Those who record history often focus upon major events that shape the nation in dramatic ways. But the story of rural America centers upon the story of ordinary people who live ordinary lives and achieve ordinary accomplishments. The events that shape rural America are often the small events of daily life. Rural history is the study of slaves, farm laborers, tenant and migrant workers, and ordinary people whose lives were influenced by production, land, and agricultural markets.[2] However, we are hindered in our understanding because rural history has often been approached by its connection with urban centers and the formation of society. As a result, the focus of rural history has been upon men and women forming families, obtaining land, and building churches and local towns, making it seem as if they did almost everything except work in the fields.[3] We need to understand rural history from a broader meaning of community, where community is understood as a group of people who are socially interdependent, sharing the same story and providing mutual support for one other—people who not only share a place but share "human networks such as family and kinship groups, market systems, church membership, and voluntary associations."[4]

The Formation of a New Nation

When the colonization of America began in the sixteenth century, many saw the opportunities from different perspectives. For some, the idea of moving across the ocean brought the hope of religious freedom. They came to America to escape religious persecution and establish a new society governed by their religious beliefs. They quickly adapted to the New World, learning from the Native population. They quickly achieved economic self-sufficiency by adapting their crops and methods to the new environment. While most of the Puritans who came to America were craftsmen and artisans from urban areas, they quickly recognized the value and richness of the cultivated fields they saw. In most cases, they settled upon land that had previously been farmed by Native Americans.[5] But it was their religious viewpoint that served to be the binding force within the community and would weave the Judeo-Christian ethic into the fabric of rural society. Yet, even as they sought to instill a biblical worldview, it was not without compromise. While some enjoyed the benefits of the newly formed society, others were relegated to servitude. The 1648 Laws and Liberties established two categories of people who did not experience the freedom promised to those who came to America: "Indians captured in 'just wars,' and 'strangers as willingly sell themselves, or are sold to us.' The 'strangers,' in this case, were indentured servants from *outside* the colony as well as imported African slaves."[6] Thus, the stage was set that would ultimately lead to not only the racial tensions we see in our country today, but the chronic poverty of those who were reduced to servitude.

The Need for Land and Labor

From the beginning of the colonization of the British American colonies, nearly all were engaged in farming. This agricultural focus continued to define the early formation of American society so that by the time of the American Revolution, approximately seventy-five to ninety percent of the population still practiced agriculture in some capacity.[7] While the initial focus was on mere subsistence, it was soon replaced with "*commercial mentalité*," producing goods for local, regional, and foreign markets as well.[8] Along with the shift of focus upon trade and commercial production came the need for more land and labor. But these would come at a cost not only to the farmers, but also to others and to society, a cost that is still being realized today.

Throughout history, there has always remained a symbiotic relationship between rural people and the land. The well-being and livelihood of the family intertwines with the productivity of the soil. However, for those dependent upon the land-driven industries, they faced two critical shortages: the shortage of land and the shortage of labor. The need for land pointed west, but it brought them into conflict with the Native Americans. In 1795, under the Treaty of Greenville, Indians in Ohio relinquished most of their territory to the government. This was then repeated as the movement west gained steam.[9] For the colonists, with their agrarian viewpoint, the "Indians did not significantly cultivate and improve the land, and hence had no moral right to it."[10] While the nation was driven by the expansion, it did so at the cost of Native Americans who were left with little choice but to capitulate or die. To the immigrants from Europe, the Natives were savages and barbarians who, because of their nomadic lifestyle, were regarded as part of the wasteland.[11] Eventually, they would be forced to live upon reservations, which led to their marginalization that continues to this day.

Along with the need for land came the need for labor. For production and profits to increase, there had to be people to work the fields. This became even more critical as the three most profitable commodities—rice, tobacco, and cotton—were labor-intensive. As the need for labor continued to grow, the colonies found another source of labor that was not only economically cheaper, but also served as a symbol of social status: slavery. In August 1619, the first slaves arrived when a Dutch ship brought twenty Africans to Virginia. By 1708, slaves outnumbered their white masters; and by 1720, sixty-five percent of the Carolinians were black. As one writer stated, "A 'society with slaves' was rapidly becoming a 'slave society.'"[12] At first, the African slaves proved expensive, costing nearly twice as much as an indentured servant. But soon the advantages became more compelling. Slaves would work harder and longer than English servants and were less demanding. Further, unlike the indentured servant who would eventually compete for land, the slaves remained slaves for life. By the time of the American Revolution, the population of many South Carolina regions was ninety percent black. While slavery as an institution ended with the Civil War

150 years ago, the rippling effects of its evil are still felt today—not only in the racial tension that still exists in our country, but also in the chronic poverty remaining in the rural south, and elsewhere in our country.

This need for cheap labor continues to impact present rural communities as well. In recent years, farmers turned to the migrant Hispanic worker for their labor needs, who now face chronic poverty as rural areas need cheap labor to survive economically. There are too few jobs and career opportunities in rural communities for many workers to move beyond poverty.

The Rise of Agrarianism and Mystique of Rural Life

In 1776, the land gave birth to a new nation "conceived in Liberty, and dedicated to the proposition that all men are created equal" with the unalienable right to "life, liberty, and the pursuit of happiness," as the Gettysburg Address puts it. This new nation was one of farmers, with farming envisioned by the Founding Fathers as the noblest occupation of society. It was the farmer who embodied, as the Declaration of Independence states, the "economic independence and self-determination that was as essential to their own sense of well-being as to the health of a democratic republic."[13] This perspective became the rally cry of Thomas Jefferson and the agrarians.

For the agrarians, farming as a lifestyle was the economic, social, and moral backbone of society, and it was this perspective that became indelibly woven into the fabric of our culture that even today finds expression in the romanticized view of rural life. For the Founding Fathers, agriculture and farming were more than just occupations, but rather the cornerstone of the new civilization. Thomas Jefferson affirmed the standing of agriculture in civilization when he wrote to John Adams, "Cultivators of the earth are the most valuable citizens. They are the most vigorous, the most independent, the most virtuous, & they are tied to their country & wedded to it's [sic] liberty & interests by the most lasting bonds."[14]

The supremacy they gave to farming was not just due to their perception of the economic prosperity of the early colonies, but was derived from their understanding of God's plan for humanity. For the agrarians, "those who labor in the earth are the chosen people of God, if ever he had a chosen people, whose breasts he has made his peculiar deposit for substantial and genuine virtue."[15] While the Industrial Revolution brought about the urbanization of our society, rural life was considered nobler and more moral.

We still hold to the myth that independent subsistence farming is desirable and to be actively promoted in public policy, even though it vanished long before the agrarians promoted its ideology. Douglas Hurt rightly concludes, "Although the belief in the agrarian tradition remains, it is colored with myth. It paints a mental image of a past that never was while denying the reality of contemporary agricultural life. Agrarianism now, as in the past, remains more myth than reality."[16]

The Agricultural Revolution

As the Industrial Revolution brought massive changes to industry, it also brought growth and prosperity to rural communities. But this had a price, with the effects reverberating in rural America today. First, the prosperity of farming resulted in long-term economic consequences. While the markets were expanding and the profits increasing, the rural people were increasingly being governed by the three Ms: markets, middlemen, and money.[17] The markets would fluctuate as production exceeded supply and demand. Middlemen—those who would purchase the produce from farmers and then sell to the regional and international markets—would set the prices not only paid to the farmer, but also received from the market. Further, capital was needed to finance the farmer from the time of planting to harvest, but the money was not always readily available; when it was, interest rates were often exorbitant. This problem at the turn of the century remains today in rural communities, where the farm pays for the transportation of the types of produce they purchased and for the shipping of their products to regional ports. Like the farmer at the start of the twentieth century, the present-day farm continually struggles with cash flow, with most farmers borrowing money at the start of the year to pay for the cost of planting the crop and with little assurance that at harvest there will be enough to cover the expenses. While striving to be independent, they became more and more reliant on the government to serve as their representative at the economic table.

The second consequence, however, ultimately undermined the well-being of rural communities. While they enjoyed the benefits of technology, the urbanization of the country was eroding the favored position the rural community enjoyed under the agrarian movement. While the agrarians of the Founding Fathers elevated the position of farmers to the top of the social structure, the Industrial Revolution turned the tables upside down. Instead of being held up as the ideal, farmers began to be looked down upon as outdated and backwards. Although they welcomed the benefits of the binders and windmills, "they also felt victimized by monopolistic business interests and sensed that their public standing was diminished."[18] David Danbom summarizes the effect it had upon the perception of rural people, a summary that is equally true today:

> Farmers were ambivalent about the future at the turn of the twentieth century. While they enjoyed greater material abundance than their parents or grandparents had, they believed themselves to be at the mercy of an economic system whose rules they could not influence. More and more they felt like strangers in their own country. They no longer controlled the government, if they ever had, and they saw the standards and values of their country defined increasingly by others, often

at their expense. To live in the countryside in 1900 was to have the sense that the nation was passing you by, leaving you behind, ignoring you at best and derogating you at worst.[19]

A century later, little has changed.

Rural to Urban Flight

The prosperity that rural communities enjoyed at the turn of the century was short-lived, as the realities of the new market-driven agricultural economy that once brought prosperity turned against them. This coincided with the greatest ecological disaster to confront rural America, which would devastate the Midwest. The result was a mass migration to urban areas that would subsequently depopulate rural communities.

The decline both of population and economic prosperity of rural areas resulted from the convergence of several different factors. The first was economic. The prosperity enjoyed at the turn of the century collapsed as the prices for farm commodities plummeted in the 1920s. In 1919, wheat sold for $2.14 per bushel. In 1929, the prices had fallen by half as production increased and demand fell for all agricultural products. Three years later, the price dropped to $.38 per bushel. Between 1929 and 1932, the gross farm income declined sixty percent.[20]

A second factor, one that grew from the first, stemmed from government programs and intervention. In the attempt to stabilize the supply and demand to stop overproduction and thus arrest the fall of prices, the government established programs such as the Agricultural Adjustment Act to pay farmers to reduce the number of acres in production. While it provided some stabilization in the crop prices, it had the unintended consequence of driving sharecroppers and tenant farms off the land. As acres decreased, so did the demand for laborers, resulting in people not having work. Hit especially hard were African American sharecroppers and laborers who found themselves without land and income. As a result, a mass migration of people into the cities in search of jobs began—as did the depopulation of rural America.

A third factor came from agriculture itself. As the country went through the industrial and agricultural revolution, mechanized farming quickly replaced human power as the primary source of labor. Farms no longer needed droves of laborers, and the children raised on the farm would no longer be able to make their living on the farm. Further, as farms became more mechanized, those unable to afford the new technology would no longer be able to compete economically, which in turn forced them to sell. At the same time, the demand for agricultural workers decreased while the need for workers in urban industries increased. Thus, the migration came from both a rural push as well as an urban pull.[21]

The fourth factor influencing the migration occurred when the dust bowl swept across the plains. As the drought struck and the dust blew, nature seemed to conspire against the farmers and ranchers of the Midwest. They lost not only their crops to the dust, but also their farms to the bankers. From 1930 to 1935, 28,280 farms were forced into bankruptcy.[22] Between 1930 and 1940, the rural population declined between nine and fourteen percent in the states of Kansas, Nebraska, and Oklahoma, with depopulation particularly severe in Western Oklahoma, the Texas panhandle, and the Rio Grande valley.[23] This started a trend of migration from rural to urban centers that has continued to the present. At the turn of the twentieth century, 40 percent of the total workforce in the United States worked on a farm, and by the year 2000, that number would drop to 1.9 percent.[24]

What the demographic data does not show is the effect this outward migration had upon rural communities. Many schools either closed or consolidated. Small towns once thriving became ghost towns, plagued by poverty, and were forgotten by the rest of America. And churches faced not only the challenge of declining and aging membership, but also the frustration of seeing their young people continually drawn away by the luring bright lights and prosperity of the cities. The land that once promised economic prosperity and freedom became the breeding grounds of poverty and despair.

The Farm Crisis

By the late '70s and early '80s, farmers increasingly faced the frustration of an agricultural economy where they had no control over the profits they needed to sustain their livelihood. Unlike any other realm of business, where the company sets the price of its product based upon the manufacturing cost, farmers have always been at the mercy of forces beyond their control. As costs have increased, commodity prices decreased. Farmers faced markets controlled by corporations who not only influenced their costs for production, but also the markets and the price they would receive. In some cases, the same company that sold products to the farmers also purchased their commodities. For example, ConAgra is a leading distributor of pesticides and one of the top producers of flour. While the cost of chemicals rose dramatically, commodity prices steadily decreased. In 1932, wheat sold for a national average of $0.38 a bushel (which would equal $6.67 in 2016) compared to $3.45 in 2016.[25]

The inability of farmers to control their own price came to a crisis point in the late '70s and early '80s when the agricultural economy again turned against farmers, leading to an agricultural depression paralleling that of the '20s and '30s. Due to the economic depression in the global economy, grain exports fell by half. In 1980 alone, farm income fell by forty-six percent, which exceeded any such decline during the Great Depression.[26] Adding to the crisis, high interest rates and land devaluation made it difficult to get operating money. Consequently, many farms faced severe financial pressure, leading to a farm strike sponsored by the newly formed American Agriculture Movement. The goal of the movement was to address the economic problems of the farmers who had no control of either expenses or price indexes. Seeking to rally the farmers, they proposed a national farm strike in 1979 with the demand that they would receive one hundred percent parity—that is, the fair equivalent value between the cost of farm production and the amount they receive in payment.[27] While it achieved little in terms of structural change in the agrarian business, it did raise awareness about the struggles confronting farmers.

But the effects of the crisis went far deeper than merely the economic health of the farms. For rural people, their self-worth and personal identity is intimately bound together with the sustainability of the farm. When confronted with economic stress because of the crisis, farmers blamed themselves. They felt they failed both their family and the previous generations that entrusted them to maintain the family farm for the future. The result was an increase in depression, suicide, family breakdown, alcoholism, and family violence.[28] During this period, the suicide rate among farmers was three times that of the general population.[29]

Although the crisis was over by the end of the decade, it brought a dramatic shift in rural communities. Before the 1980s, there was already a decline in young people remaining on the farm, but it was the crisis of the '80s that served to put the final nail in the coffin. Since that decade, the number of young farmers remaining has steadly declined, meaning that the median age of farmers has steadily risen.[30] Consequently, rural America experienced an out-migration of young people, which has had devastating effects on the future of rural America, as many of the achievers left to flee to the cities.[31]

At the same time as the farm crisis, the logging industry also faced serious challenges. At its peak in the 1940s, 90,000 workers engaged in the logging industry in the state of Oregon. While there was a slow decline, even as late as 1990, there were still 70,000 employed in the state. After 1990, however, the logging industry likewise took a sharp downturn, so that today only approximately 25,000 are still working in the industry.[32] A big factor in the downturn of logging was the closing down of federal forests to large scale harvesting. Hit especially hard was the West, where 70 percent of all forest land is publicly owned. Until 1990, the National Forest Service harvested approximately 10,000,000 board feet of timber a year. Under the pressure from environmental groups and recreational users, it rapidly declined until there was only 2,500,000 board feet being harvested.[33] As a result, not only did many rural communities lose mills and employment, but schools and counties lost critical revenue from the timber sales.

Rural Rebound

While much of the history and trends in the last hundred years have been depressing for rural residents, a population and economic rebound revitalized many rural communities in the 1970s. Brown and Schafft list four factors that have slowed, and in some cases reversed, the rural to urban migration: (1) "deconcentration" of employment, (2) modernization of rural life, (3) population aging, and (4) preferences for rural living.[34] While the migration reversal has not been sustained, there are several encouraging trends drawing people back to rural communities. First, older people are choosing to relocate to rural retirement communities centered around outdoor amenities. Second, manufacturing companies are seeing greater opportunities for relocation in rural communities where worker wages are lower and there are fewer regulations. Third, people who enjoy the outdoors can work from offsite locations. All these bring new hope for rural communities. But these changes bring both opportunities and struggles for rural people. As new people come into the community, they bring new ideas and serve to revitalize the economic and social structures in the areas. On the other hand, as new people arrive, they serve to challenge and disrupt established social networks and structures, which can create tension between long-term residents and the newcomers.[35]

Implications for Rural Ministry

Effective ministry begins with an understanding of the people and communities we serve. The issues confronting rural America are not a recent development, but stem from the long-standing struggles existing throughout its history. Issues of poverty, race, and economic development in the past continue to impact the way people understand their community and shape their world. If you were to move into the area where I was raised, in northern Idaho, without an understanding of the historical background of Native Americans and how it shapes the relationships on the reservation, you would be ineffective in reaching the Native Americans with the gospel. So also in my current community, which was economically devastated by the closing of the national forests to logging, an understanding of the tension that exists between older residents who are strongly opposed to the environmental movement and the newly transplanted urban residents who want to see more environmental regulations is central to understanding the relationships within the community. This creates a tension not only within the community, but even within the church.

This also has broader implications for the universal church. The issues facing rural America are issues that the church cannot overlook. Just as the suburban church cannot remain indifferent to the plight of the inner city, so the urban church cannot ignore the plight of rural America. The rural church needs financial assistance if it is going to continue to exist in impoverished communities. They need instruction on dealing with long-standing racial tensions. As the inner-city church has developed strategies to deal with these issues, they can come alongside rural congregations that are struggling to understand the historic struggles of minorities, especially Native Americans. The urban flight that led to the depopulation of rural communities should not have led to the disappearance of the church. Just because the numbers are fewer does not mean that those who remain are any less important to the kingdom of God.

But our understanding of rural communities does not end with this brief overview. Rather, as we move into or partner with a community, we seek to understand the past that has shaped the present. For those of us who are pastors, we also need to be historians, in a sense, if we are to be effective in ministry. We need to understand the history of the community, the church, and the individual lives of the people we serve. Only then will we be effective in addressing the struggles that rural communities face.

4

The Rural Church: A Historical Perspective

THE HISTORY OF THE rural church is not a history of the re-nowned and influential, but of the obscure and forgotten. While church historians examine large-scale movements of society and religion, the history of the rural church exists on a minuscule level. In the rural church, there are no great national leaders who gain national promi-nence, simply because the rural church dwells in the shadowy fringes of American ecclesiology. If rural America has become the realm of the "Forgotten Places,"[1] the rural church has become the forgotten church.

But the fault does not lie with church historians, as if they have de-liberately overlooked and devalued the rural church. The first hindrance to a comprehensive history lies within the nature of rural ministry itself. The history of the rural church is not found in the overarching trends governing and influencing the national religious scene, but is discov-ered by looking at individual churches and the history they have experi-enced. While there certainly have been historic trends that governed the rural ministry, the full depth of understanding comes only by studying each congregation. Here we also find our second hindrance. Roger Finke and Rodney Stark rightly point out that "nostalgia is the enemy of history," for it corrupts our perception of both the past and the present.[2] Our perception of the spiritual landscape of the rural church has been largely colored by our nostalgic interpretation. We see the rural church though the lens of the popular hymn "The Church in the Wildwood" as a little brown church in the vale, where there is no lovelier place, where the whole community attends for fellowship and spiritual growth. As a result, the perception is perpetrated that rural communities are largely Christian and in little need of new strategies of outreach. Yet when we look more closely, we discover a different story.

The Wild West

Being educated in a small country school, I remember the stories and pictures of the first Thanksgiving, with Pilgrims sitting peacefully at a large table loaded with succulent dishes in celebration of God's bountiful blessings. We heard the stories of their pursuit of religious freedom that drove them to the new country in search of a spiritual utopia. The popular perception is that the early settlers were a God-fearing people, who established a Christian nation governed by biblical principles and morality. While it was true that the Pilgrims came for religious freedom, most of the early colonies were cut from a different cloth. Many of the colonists came from the poor and criminal classes. As a result, many thieves, rebels, prostitutes, and convicts were banished to the colonies because of their previous crimes.[3] In many colonies, life resembled more the Wild West with its drifters, gamblers, prostitution, and saloon keepers than the moral order of the Puritans.[4] Historians generally agree that in the colonial period, only ten to twenty percent of the population belonged to any church.[5]

This trend continued as the migration pushed westward. As the country grew and people continued to expand the frontier, those drawn to the outskirts of society were those who fled punishment or disgrace and lacked any social or relational attachments.[6] It's no wonder that the frontiers were often characterized as morally impoverished and irreligious. Throughout the history of America, the frontiers have been a place where the law was marginally enforced and people had little interest in the church.[7] For some, the frontier, with its moral and civil bankruptcy, existed beyond the reaches of the law and redemption. Timothy Dwight (1752–1817), the eighth president of Yale, wrote that the pioneers "cannot live in regular society. They are too idle, too talkative, too passionate, too prodigal, and too shiftless to acquire either property or character."[8] Another missionary wrote that the nations of the world had cast their "scum" into his Kansas congregation.[9] This challenge was compounded by the nature of the people who traveled to the frontiers. The diversity of the people's cultural and ethnic backgrounds served only to make any social organization more difficult. Lacking any social stability, the people who came to the frontiers were transitory by nature. It was not uncommon for a settler on the frontiers to move several different times. One settler, for example, had twelve children, each born in a different location.[10] This made it difficult to establish a church based on social stability rather than chaos.

Because of these challenges, the frontier—first in the colonies themselves and then later in the westward fringes of society—struggled with a continual shortage of clergy. Those answering the call often lacked moral character and spiritual fervor. In 1724, Giles Rainsford, an Anglican clergyman in Maryland, complained to his superiors about three of his colleagues: "Mr. Williamson is grown notorious and consummate in villainy. He really is an original for drinking and swearing. Mr. Donaldson is so vile that the other day, being sent for to a dying person, came drunk, and the poor expiring soul, seeing his hopeful parson in that condition, refused the Sacrament at his hands and died without it. Mr. Maconchie is a mere nuisance, and makes ye church stink. He fights, and drinks on all occasions, and I am told *alienas permolet uxores* [forces his attentions on the wives of others]."[11]

Life was difficult not only for the people, but also for the pastors and missionaries who sought to minister to them. Food was meager, and people were isolated. To serve on the frontier required a willingness to forsake the comforts of civilization and live in one-room cabins, eat an unvaried diet of wild game, and wear homemade clothing. With a continual shortage of pastors in urban areas, the pastors were selective in their placement, most choosing to serve well-established congregations rather than plant churches on the wild frontier.[12]

The Rise of the Itinerant Preacher

While some churches, seeking to maintain their ties to the old-world affiliations, sought to protect their ecclesiastical territory by focusing upon urban areas, George Whitefield challenged and questioned their religious zeal. Instead of following the normal pattern of pastoring an established church, he traveled as an itinerant preacher, going throughout the colonies and preaching wherever he gained an audience. For the Congregationalists, he served to undermine the church with his noisy, uneducated, and critical intrusions into communities that angered the local pastors and caused division among the people.[13] Consequently, the Congregational clergy of Boston and Bristol County met on January 22, 1744, to discuss how they could stop this new brand of preacher. For them, this itinerant preacher constituted a threat not only to the established churches, but to the social order of the entire community.

But George Whitefield and his fellow preacher Jonathan Edwards did more than usher in the first Great Awakening. They established a new method, which would ultimately bring about the taming of the wild frontier. They brought attention to the need for a new approach that eventually would effectively appeal to the masses of the uncivilized west.

The people of the frontier were people of the land who, like the loggers in the Northwoods, measured the value and worth of a man not by his education and economic status, but by his toughness and physical prowess. As a result, they rejected the "educational rationality of the Enlightenment."[14] This brought them into conflict with the established denominations of the colonies who not only upheld the necessity of education for all preachers, but also looked down upon the uneducated, rugged frontiersmen. Because of this tension, the frontiersmen saw the church as an institution established by women for women.[15] It was into this arena that the itinerant preacher stepped.

While Whitefield introduced the frontier to the itinerant preacher, it was Lyman Beecher who brought attention to the need. In 1835, Beecher wrote his tract "A Plea for the West," in which he argued,

> It is equally plain that the religious and political destiny of our nation is to be decided in the West. There is the territory, and there soon will be the population, wealth, and political power. . . . It is equally clear, that the conflict which is to decide the destiny of the West, will be a conflict of institutions for the education of her sons, for purposes of superstition, or evangelical light; of despotism, or liberty.[16]

In response to the call, the Baptists and Methodists commissioned itinerant preachers and circuit riders to travel not only from community to community but from house to house, sharing the gospel with any who would listen. Many did not receive any formal education and were often persecuted and sanctioned from preaching from the mainline churches.[17] Regardless of the response from the East, those in the West flocked to them, for they came preaching the gospel in words they understood. "Many frontier ministers were bombastic, conceited, arrogant, crude, and illiterate; they were products of their times. Despite their odd traits of character, they had a humanizing effect on the pioneers."[18] As a result, small churches began to spring up across the frontier, bringing not only social and moral structure, but spiritual transformation as well. The evangelicalism that would become an influential force in America's culture and morality was in part built upon the backs of these nameless men and women who gave up the comforts of the East to labor tirelessly in reaching the Wild West. As the churches took hold, they provided not only the moral standards for newly formed communities but a gathering place for the community to support one another in both their faith as well as trials of life.[19]

But here again, history takes a personal turn. For one of these forgotten men was my great-great grandfather. Born March 17, 1835, George W. Daman was hardly a candidate to become an itinerant preacher. Possessing a natural talent for music as a young man, he became popular for providing music for the local dances. This would change when D. S. Davis, a circuit rider and evangelist of the Methodist Episcopal Church, provided both music and evangelistic services in a nearby town. Being drawn to the service by his love for music, George responded to the invitation to embrace Christ, and his life was radically changed. After leading a Bible class, he found a new calling, and it was not long until he entered the ministry. At age thirty-three, he began the work of an itinerant pastor traveling throughout the Sandhill's of northcentral Nebraska. His office was not in the corner of a local church with a view, but on the back of a horse as he traveled about the small towns and villages, preaching the gospel and assisting in the establishment of churches. While the pages of history have long forgotten Rev. Daman, for those he served, his ministry was important. While I never had the privilege of meeting him, I have no doubt that his spiritual DNA contributed not only to my own spiritual growth, but also to my work of serving rural churches.

The Industrial Revolution and the Rural Church

As the Industrial Revolution reshaped America and the social structures within American society, it also reshaped the rural church. As mass amounts of people migrated from rural communities to industrialized cities, churches in rural settings suffered the loss of membership in general and the loss of young people in particular. From 1920 to 1970, rural America declined substantially as more and more people left. While a number of reasons have been posed for the cause of the depopulation,[20] it is certain that the rural church suffered continual decline because young people chose to pursue opportunities in urban America. The first to feel the pressure were the small town and country churches that saw their membership slowly decline.[21] More and more, denominations consolidated country churches, while others disappeared in the shifting sands of time.

The second effect was the shortage of clergy willing to serve rural communities. With the opportunities of church growth and recognition of urban ministry, the rural church became less and less appealing. Why go to a forgotten cornfield in the Midwest where you will be overlooked for any career advancement? It was natural for ministries to focus on reaching the new masses of growing, regional cities. In 1924, the Institute of Social and Religious Research published research revealing that 54.5 percent of churches located in urban areas had full-time pastors while only 4.7 percent of country churches had full-time ones. For the country church, the majority (71 percent) were served by non-resident pastors.[22] With the focus on urban ministries, rural churches were only able to attract those who lacked theological training, and the few who did come to rural churches often lacked an understanding of rural society.[23] Consequently, the rural church served as a place to either start one's ministry or roost as one coasted into retirement.

But the greatest effect was upon our understanding of church itself. From the beginning, the diversity of religious beliefs, the lack of a state-sanctioned church, and the freedom of religious practices led to an ecclesiastical economy where churches competed for membership. While this was a natural outgrowth of the freedom of church attendance, it was the Industrial Revolution that brought its full acceptance by the church itself.

Concerning the nature of religious economies, Finke and Stark write,

> Religious economies are like commercial economies in that
> they consist of a market made up of a set of current and poten-
> tial customers and a set of firms seeking to serve that market.
> The fate of these firms will depend upon (1) aspects of their
> organizational structures, (2) their sales representatives,
> (3) their product, and (4) their marketing techniques. Trans-
> lated into more churchly language, the relative success of reli-
> gious bodies (especially when confronted with an unregulated
> economy) will depend upon their polity and local congrega-
> tions, their clergy, their religious doctrines, and their evange-
> lization techniques.[24]

In such a world, the market strategist has had as much to do with the
success of churches as the theologian.

In the Industrial Revolution, the definition of success shifted as
well. In an agrarian culture, success is not measured by growth, but
sustainability. But in an industrial society, success would be measured
by the increase of assets, sales, and production. For the church, success
then became measured by the bottom line of attendance, programs, and
facilities, where growth indicated success and decline equated to spiritual stagnation. Consequently, the rural church not only faced decline;
it became overlooked, and at times, even maligned. With the absence
of the church providing a moral foundation in rural communities, it
was not long before rural areas were not only declining but also facing
significant social problems that needed serious attention.

Rural Church Movement

As a result of the neglect of rural communities,[25] several national leaders
became concerned with the loss of the values and virtues of rural life.

In response, President Theodore Roosevelt, in 1908, appointed a Commission on Country Life. After conducting thirty hearings throughout the country and circulating over half a million questionnaires to farmers and leaders, the Commission published a report recommending, "We urge the holding of local, state and even national conferences on rural progress, designed to unite the interests of education, organization and religion into one forward movement for the rebuilding of rural life."[26] For the Commission, the needs went beyond the spiritual condition of the country and affected the very social structure of a forming nation where "the rural church was the greatest factor in the molding of an enduring democracy through the union of these new population groups which built up the great States of the Middle West."[27]

In response to the rising need of rural churches, Warren Wilson formed the Town and Country Church with the purpose of providing training for rural pastors and serving as a clearing house for common action on problems related to the rural church.[28] This preparation not only included training for pastoral care in rural churches, but also gave trainees an understanding of rural life, for "a major handicap of many rural ministers is their lack of knowledge of agriculture and country life, a knowledge which is essential for them to understand the problems and attitudes of their parishioners. As yet very few theological seminaries give any special training for the rural ministry."[29] Tragically, this is still the case today.

Gifford Pinchot, the first Chief of the United States Forest Service, likewise saw the need for rural church renewal. He coauthored two books on the country church, and in his opening address to the Conference on Church and Country Life in December 1915, stated, "The country church is one of the greatest roots from which spring national integrity, vitality, and intelligence. Its life and power are of nation wide [sic] concern."[30] As society became more urbanized, some recognized that something inherently valuable was being lost, and that the rural church and rural community needed to be valued and reached.

With the increased awareness of the distinctive needs of the rural church and rural America, awareness of the need for specialized ministries for rural churches increased. As a result, ministries were established to address the needs of rural communities. The American Sunday School Union (later to be named American Missionary Fellowship, and subsequently InFaith), Rural Home Missionary Association, Village Missions, Rocky Mountain Bible Mission, and the United Indian Mission are just a few of the organizations that arose in response to the need to reach rural America.[31]

Hogs, Calves, Chickens, and Even a Dog

The real history of the rural church is not just found in the movement of ministries and programs, but also in the work of farmers and ranchers who had a vision to establish a church and reach a community with the gospel. The story of the church in which I grew up illustrates this point. After the allotment of land was given to the tribal members on the Coeur d'Alene Indian Reservation, the remaining land was opened to homesteaders in 1909, with land set aside for the town of Tensed. As homesteaders arrived, Robert Thomas organized a Sunday school and conducted preaching services. When the ministry floundered, they approached Dick Ferrell to help them reorganize the church in 1933. With his assistance, the local congregation began the task of organizing the congregation and building a church. A building committee was formed from the small group of people whose names were never mentioned in the history books, but etched in my mind as the pillars of the church upon whose shoulders my spiritual heritage was built—people like Frank Daman, Harold Wilson, Lynn Mumau, Pearl and William Weaver, and Art and Sallie Johnson.

Like so many communities of that day, however, their plans were interrupted when World War II began. With the war came a scarcity of money and building materials as the nation turned its resources toward the war effort. The small amount of funds available were used to purchase war bonds. On February 13, 1944, as the nation was starting to see an end in sight for the war, people met once again and "decided to try and build a church."[32]

The building went slowly, as the project was "stopped thru the summer as the men had to return to farm work."[33] On April 3, 1948, the auction committee organized the first auction sale at the Grange Hall. "This consisted of old machinery of every kind brought in by the men, hogs, calves, chickens, and even a dog. The ladies contributed fancy work, old household furnishings, and lots of food was brought and a very good dinner served."[34] By the end of the day, $611.23 was raised. But even as the floor was laid and sheetrock put on the walls in the spring of 1948, work again was "postponed until the spring of 1949 because of field work and an extremely cold winter in which many had the flu—and as we did not have a flue in the building yet."[35] Finally, on Sunday, October 2, 1949, the church was able to hold its first Sunday School service in their new building. Through the years, the church has experienced the ups and downs and trials that beset any congregation. There were the years when eighty to ninety people would pack the small building, and years when the congregation would dwindle to a few dozen. But through it all, the church has remained faithful to the gospel. In visiting the church today, one would hear the same gospel preached as it first rang through the halls sixty years ago. Some of the names of the families are no longer present; others remain, with the torch of faith being passed on to the third and fourth generations. But to read the history of the church is not just to step back in time; it is to step back to the names and faces of people who have since gone to glory. Their legacy remains in my own life and in the lives of my children, for many of the lessons I sought to teach my children were those taught to me in a small Sunday School room by the very people who nailed the siding, filled the gaps and sanded the floor. If you visited the church today, you would see not only the same floor—although now covered in carpet—

and the same sheetrock, but also the true history of the rural church. History that is not discovered in a book, but in the lives of people that they touched. And this history is a picture of true success.

But here again the rural church stands at the crossroads. At the 1928 Jerusalem meeting of the International Missionary Council, Kenyon L. Butterfield summarized the need for a renewed focus on rural ministries:

> The rural people have been neglected in movements for economic and social reform. . . . The huge numbers involved in rural life, the segregated groupings, the less obvious exigencies, have made the rural problem difficult and have caused a relative neglect of the rural population. Even in missionary areas not yet industrialized, where reform movements are not so obviously at the front, the political, economic and educational interests of the cities are given first and major attention, the urban and industrial problems press for solution, and there is this same tendency to neglect rural interests.[36]

This is equally true today. Once again, rural America needs people who have a new vision for the forgotten ministry. To help us, we now turn our attention to the present, not only to understand the culture of rural America, but also to move beyond the mystique so we can see the full reality that is rural America. This begins by identifying the problems and challenges confronting rural communities so we can then see the new opportunities to reach people with the gospel of Christ.

5

Understanding
Rural Culture

GROWING UP ON the farm and spending my life living and serving rural areas, it did not take long to realize that there is a marked difference between urban and rural cultures. Some of the differences are easily identified, such as the style of clothing and type of music. Other differences are more subtle. Visit a local coffee shop and you start to see these differences. In the local coffee shop in a small town, conversations between patrons are ongoing. By the time you have finished your coffee, you have not only talked with the person you entered with, but with almost everyone else as well. If a visitor from outside the area walks in, soon they will be invited to join a table, and people will be asking them where they are from, how long they will be in town, and who they are visiting. Whether or not the visitor asks, they will be given all kinds of input regarding places to visit, the best food in town, and the current activities happening in the area. I have long since learned that if I want to schedule a meeting with someone to talk about anything remotely private, the local coffee shop will not do. In a small town, the coffee shop is not a place just to get coffee; it is a place where people socialize, share community information, and discuss local politics. It is a place where there are no private conversations, for even those not directly part of the conversation will chime in with their opinions and insights.

Contrast this to the urban coffee shop. When you walk into the coffee shop, the conversations are much more subdued and private. People often isolate themselves behind a screen. If you were to say hello and attempt to sit at a table that someone else occupies, your intrusion will be unwelcomed and rebuffed. In the urban area, the coffee shop is usually a place to get coffee, catch up on the news via the internet, write a report for tomorrow's meeting, or have a private conversation with someone.

Defining *Culture*

Paul understood the importance of understanding and adapting to culture. He wrote,

> For though I am free from all men, I have made myself a slave to all, so that I may win more. To the Jews I became as a Jew, so that I might win Jews; to those who are under the Law, as under the Law though not being myself under the Law, so that I might win those who are under the Law; to those who are without law, as without law, though not being without the law of God but under the law of Christ, so that I might win those who are without law. To the weak I became weak, that I might win the weak; I have become all things to all men, so that I may by all means save some." (1 Cor. 9:19–22).

While the gospel is transcultural in that it embraces all cultures as well as stands apart from the confines of culture, it needs to be shared within a culture if it is to be communicated effectively. This is true not only of missionaries, but of pastors as well. All ministry to some degree is cross-cultural, where we step outside our own personal cultural norms and understand and relate to people who think and act differently from us. Effective ministry involves appreciating and accepting others within the context of their individual cultural setting. Shannon Jung and Mary Agria rightly point out, "Understanding the interconnectedness between economics, social issues, and theological underpinnings is essential for any pastor serving rural families as they respond to the realities of their lives—not only from a congregational studies perspective, but from the point of view of faith formation and spirituality."[1]

When we speak of culture, we are not just referring to the tangible things we often associate with a specific group of people—that is, food, shelter, art, music, clothing styles, and even language. Culture also includes the intangibles such as the values, relationships, hopes, dreams, and rules that serve to govern a community and which people are expected to follow. Understanding rural culture begins with understanding the practices, objects, beliefs, and values influencing the way people live and see the world. Pastors from urban backgrounds, educated in an urban context, taught by professors from urban churches, often do not understand that rural people and the rural church have a different worldview.

Sociologists have long recognized that the church is not only the channel by which a congregation shapes its theology and a biblical worldview, but also one of the primary agents by which culture is shared and transmitted within the community.[2] Within the rural community, the local church is the place where the values and morals of the community are sustained. It is not uncommon within a rural community to have many people send their children to the church for instruction, even though the parents do not attend any of the services. They see the church as a place not just to learn religious truth, but also to teach their children the values shaping the world in which they live. While a pastor needs to confront and change cultural values that conflict with Scripture, if the pastor fails to understand the differences in viewpoints in a rural community, he will no longer be the guardian of the values of the community. Instead, he will be an outsider who undermines these values. In the end, the pastor will be ostracized and dismissed.

Rural People and the Land

If you were to walk into my office, you would see an array of commentaries and religious books, which you would find in any other pastor's office. What is not as common is the display of approximately one hundred toy farm tractors that I have collected over the years. Most are 1/64 scale, but I have a few that are detailed 1/16 scale models of the tractors and combines my dad owned and I drove as a youth. They remind me of my roots—that no matter where I am and where life takes me, there is a part of me that is forever linked to the land upon which I was raised.

As we saw in previous chapters, the land is more than just a location for rural people; it is intimately connected to their identity. In urban areas, people live in one place, work in another, and recreate in a third. For rural people, the place they live is also where they work, socialize, and recreate. Their identity is tied to the land itself. The contrast between urban and rural attitudes toward the land can be summarized this way:

> Whereas land is simply the foundation for the construction of towns and cities, whose urban culture and economy thrive on human ingenuity and industry that may have little direct attachment to the physical ground over which it occurs, historical discourses of rurality place the land at the heart of the rural economy and society. Rural people, such discourses hold, live on the land, work the land, tend the land and know the land.

The land formed not only the base of the rural economy, but also shaped rural culture and the rural calendar, and contributed to the constitution of the rural character. As such, the land is central to rural sense of place.[3]

When my father went on vacations, which was rare, to other parts of the country, people would ask what he thought of the scenery. His response was always the same: "It is nice, but it is not Idaho." Everything he saw, from the Grand Canyon to the ocean, was always second place to the farm in Idaho. The reason went far beyond the natural beauty of the pastoral scene of farm land and fir-covered mountains. Idaho, and the farm on which he lived, was his home and identity. The land was where all the connecting points of his life converged together. As Jung and Agria summarize, "The land is a powerful factor in people's lives and identities. At heart, as one southwestern Iowa pastor put it, all rural residents are farmers. Even if they themselves are no longer actively farming, their lives are intrinsically bound up with the land."[4]

Those who live and make their living on the land see themselves as stewards of the earth. Grounded in a theology of Genesis 2, they see their role as being the gardeners of the land ultimately belonging to God. Thus, while they may have legal ownership of the land, they never fully see the land as belonging to them. They have been given stewardship for a time to work the soil until they pass it on to the next generation. When surveyed, a consistent theme emerges for multigenerational farmers: they will "'do whatever it takes' to pass a viable farm operation on to the next generation."[5] Their goal was never to become independently wealthy or to retire and travel the country in a motorhome. Rather, it is to "pass down wealth in the form of knowledge, equipment, land, capital, and credit to the next generation" while at the same time instilling traditions and values to the next generation to carry on the family and farm legacy.[6] The loss of the farm can be almost impossible to accept, for it brings not only a sense of failure but guilt as well as they fail to keep in the family the land that has been a part of their history for generations.[7] As mentioned before, when the farm falls upon hard times, there is a dramatic increase in depression, suicide, family breakdown, alcoholism, and family violence.[8] However, this connection between personal identity and land is not just ingrained in farmers; it is ingrained in all those whose livelihood is bound together with the land on which they live. It is true for loggers and miners as well, who see their work as part of their personal identity.

Rural People and the Family

Working the land is a family event. Unlike many urban families, in which the father and mother leave the house to go to separate jobs in different locations that may or may not even be in the same town, members of the rural family not only eat and live together but also work together. During the busy times of the year—spring planting, harvest, calving season, etc.—the whole family becomes involved, each doing their part. Long before I could legally drive a car on the highway, I was driving tractors in the field. The first time I was pulled over by a policeman after I obtained my driver's license was not because I was driving too fast, but too slow. I was taking a tractor down the road and was stopped because I did not have a slow-moving vehicle sign on the back. By the time I was twelve, I was working for neighbors, bucking bales in the summer. And when I was fourteen, I was driving the combine for my dad since my two older brothers—who were fifteen and seventeen—were employed full-time by neighbors. A typical harvest day on any farm would find the teenage children—both boys and girls—driving the combines, the wife driving trucks to and from the grain storage, the father emptying the trucks and filling the storage, and the youngest, who was barely old enough to reach the clutch and brake, jockeying the trucks around in the field. This mutual involvement in all aspects of life brings a type of closeness within the family that urban families sometimes do not experience.[9]

For the rural family, life is centered upon the family unit. They work together, they play together, eat their meals together, and attend church together. The importance and centrality of family can also be seen Sunday morning. In larger urban churches, families arrive together but often go to different age-appropriate services. In rural churches, the children worship with their parents. The idea of separating the children—except for the small preschool children who might go to children's church—from the parents is not only foreign, but also sacrilegious to many rural Christians. We work together, play together, and worship together. While most teens' social activities revolved around their friends, my brothers' and my social activities involved doing things together, as brothers. And my experience was not unique, as rural siblings are more likely to spend time together than their urban counterparts.[10]

This family interconnectedness extends across generations as well. In rural areas, often several generations will live on the same farm, work the same mine, or log the same forest. I grew up with my grandfather living in a house thirty feet from the house I lived in. While I left the farm to pursue ministry, on the farm, within less than a quarter of a mile, still lived both my brothers and their families and my sister. As a result of this tight-knit family culture, rural children are taught values that are reinforced by generations of influence. They learn the values of "hard work or industry self-reliance and a sense of responsibility, a commitment to family life, social trust and a value system that is not devoted to money and consumerism."[11]

While many of these same traits exist today within the rural family, there are changes and struggles confronting them. First, children in rural areas today are faced with greater challenges than children in past generations. As schools consolidate, children are spending more time commuting to school, with some having to ride the bus for an hour or more. They also face a lack of career opportunities that would keep them in the area. As extractive industries have become more mechanized, fewer opportunities for employment are available. Consequently, even though young adults in rural areas want to remain, they are forced to leave the rural areas and move to the metropolitan areas in pursuit of jobs. The result is the loss of young families.

Second, as more and more young adults are leaving, many of the elderly in rural areas find themselves living without any immediate family in the area. Consequently, more elderly in rural areas are at risk of not having their caregiving needs met. This is further compounded by the fact that older people in rural areas have lower income and higher poverty rates than their metropolitan counterparts.[12] As a result, older people in rural areas rely upon friends and the church for assistance, an issue the church needs to address.

Third, single moms have greater difficulties providing for their family. Because rural life centers on the traditional family, single moms can be overlooked and even ostracized. This, coupled with the lack of available jobs, results in a higher rate of poverty. Further, they lack access to public assistance programs—such as childcare and welfare—making it more difficult to provide for their families. This again provides the rural church an opportunity to minister to the needs of people and introduce them to Christ.

Rural People and the Community

Beginning with Ferdinand Tonnies in the late 1800s, there has been a debate regarding the nature and differences between urban and rural people's understanding of community. Tonnies distinguished between rural communities, which were characterized by face-to-face interaction in small groups such as family kinship groups and small villages (*Gemeinschaft*), and urban communities, which were based upon means-end orientations where relationships were impersonal and indirect and not carried out face to face (*Gesellschaft*).[13] Since his introduction of these differences, many would agree that his characterization of urban culture largely missed the sense of community often existing within urban settings. However, he did provide us with a framework by which we can understand rural community. Rural people maintain a strong sense of community through their involvement and volunteerism.[14] Relationships are built within and between the different associations and activities as the same people interact within the church, school, local government, businesses, and county services. Because of this interconnectedness, people develop a sense of mutual responsibility where supporting one another is both honored and expected.[15]

Community means more than geographic and relational proximity. It refers to a specific place and location where a group of people interact. It includes the existing social systems such as the schools, churches, government, and businesses. Lastly, it describes the sense of identity held by a group of people.[16] In the past, all these elements of community existed in one place, as rural people lived, worked, worshiped, shopped, sent their children to school, and socialized in the same place in which they shared the same values and identity.[17] As society became more mobile, the community was broadened as people shopped and conducted business outside their immediate area. Even in rural communities, people no longer shared the same sense of identity as their needs were no longer met within a specific location. However, even as the realm of community was broadened, there remained a strong sense of local community as people shared the same social capital—natural, cultural, human, social, and other resources that can be utilized to meet local needs—providing the basis for a healthy and vibrant community.

Within many rural societies, sharp disagreements over local and national politics sometimes take place, but the people still share a sense of personal responsibility for the well-being of the community and members within it. If a family is unable to harvest their grain because of a sudden illness or accident, the surrounding neighbors will leave their fields unharvested and first harvest their neighbor's field. When a house catches on fire, even before the firemen put the fire out, people will already be mobilizing to meet the immediate needs of the family. If a medical emergency happens, the community will have a change jar in the local store and a fundraising dinner to help with the medical costs.

Community in the rural areas stems not only from the sense of personal responsibility for others, but from the relationships that interconnect people. For many in rural communities, the family network, neighbors, work, and church all overlap. You see the same people at church or at a neighborhood barbeque that you see when you go to a basketball game or a fundraiser for the local museum, which creates a "high density of acquaintanceship" where "daily life is carried out among a cast of familiars rather than among strangers in an anonymous city."[18] As a result, there is a mutual expectation that in a time of crisis, people will be there to offer aid. Consequently, in rural areas, people more often look inward to the community to meet the needs of the community. The church and pastor are expected to do more than just provide spiritual instruction and support. They are an integral part of the social capital (we will expand upon this in later chapters). If they fail to be a part of the community, they will be ignored by the community.

The downside of this strong sense of community identity is that often newcomers are viewed suspiciously, making it difficult for them to become part of the community relationship. Even within the church, a new member must pay his or her "dues" before they will be fully accepted and given leadership positions. Likewise, community decisions are heavily influenced by power structures governed by longtime or lifelong residents.[19] Decisions are often informally discussed and made at the local café rather than at government meetings where "the hidden agenda of such interactions constitutes the working out of subtle consensus building about town issues."[20] This can be equally true in the church, where longtime members become powerbrokers and decisions are made over a dining room table and only confirmed at a congregational meeting. If a pastor tries to usurp or dismantle the structures, he will soon find himself looking for another church. Thus, the challenge for pastors and denominational leaders is to work within the power structure of the local church, recognizing their place within the church, yet also confronting those structures that become exclusive and controlling. For the pastor and denominational leaders to effectively work with local leadership, they need to develop leaders who understand that leadership is not about control and authority, but service.[21]

Rural People and Rural Values

Many of the values shaping my life and those I sought to instill within my children stemmed from my own childhood, imparted to me by my parents and reinforced by the community. Unlike many urban areas where pluralistic values result in conflicting value systems, rural communities often maintain a uniform value structure passed on from one generation to another. The smaller, more stable nature of rural communities exerts pressure on people to conform to the local culture and moral ethos. As Aaron Morrow points out,

> For a variety of reasons, people in small towns are not typically open to change in comparison to people who live in larger cities. . . . The lack of change in small towns often leads to a high degree of conformity. For better or worse, there is a relatively narrow range of acceptable behaviors, choices, and ideas that people are generally expected to adhere to in a small town. And the smaller a town is, the narrower the range![22]

The values that my parents sought to instill within me were also the same values shared by the rest of the community. In rural areas, you can be different, but only if you conform to the rest of the community! We were taught the value of self-reliance. Whether you were out in the field fixing a broken piece of equipment or providing for your family, it was expected that you would take care of it yourself. You performed your work without complaint because it had to be done, no matter how unpleasant the task. There was no point in complaining about the heat while putting hay in the peak of the barn on a hot summer day. No matter how hot it was, the barn had to be filled for the winter. We were taught the importance of hard work and were judged by our willingness to "get our hands dirty." A person with manicured fingernails and hands without calluses was considered soft and "citified." The Pledge of Allegiance was recited at the start of school, followed by the reading of a chapter from the Bible. While the Bible is no longer read, the conservativism and respect for religion remains. Recent surveys reveal what rural people knew all along: rural people are more conservative and hold to traditional moral values in stark contrast to the secularization and moral liberalism of those in more populated areas.[23] Soon after the election of Donald Trump as president, Matthew Spandler-Davison identified the frustration felt by rural people towards elite Americans who they perceived to have abandoned small town views of faith and individual freedoms. Spandler-Davison summarizes, "Their pro-guns position is presented as sinister. Pro-life values are portrayed as being anti-women, the desire to run a business in line with their religious convictions is reported as bigotry. [The overall message, they perceived,] was like, 'We're progressive, you're regressive, we're moving forward and leaving you behind.' Small town America said 'no.'"[24]

Those who dwell in rural America are expected to conform to these values. As Jung and Agria point out,

> All these factors—geography, economics, demographics, values, and lifestyle issues—suggest an inherent tension in rural life, a tension that influences the capacity or resistance of the rural community or church to respond to the enormous problems facing it. Economic and other factors in many rural communities are urging change. At the same time, the people who advocate such change are often considered suspect. If the

impetus for change is internal, it can be perceived as disloyalty; if external, as an outright threat.[25]

When a person, or even a pastor, does not uphold these traditional values, they typically are branded an outsider and will find it difficult to gain acceptance. This conformity is grounded in the close interpersonal relationships existing within the community, where people know not only you but also everyone else. This connects people to the community and pressures them to conform to community standards.[26] When coming into the community, the pastor should recognize that he serves not just the church but the whole community. Gaining respect of those in the church and community at large begins with the pastor valuing both the relationships of people and the culture of the community. This is equally true of denominations and urban churches that desire to get involved in assisting rural communities. Effective ministry in rural areas is built upon trust, and trust comes when we accept and value people within the context of their culture rather than seek to impose our own cultural views upon them.

Rural People and the Church

The farm that I was raised on was five miles from the nearest small village. The town itself had a population of ninety people, with two gas stations, two bars, two sawmills, a small mom-and-pop grocery store, and one church. The bars and gas stations have since closed, the sawmills have been swallowed up by large mills, and the grocery store struggles to exist as a small mini-mart. But the church remains. Within the surrounding community and farmland, there were two other churches, a Free Methodist church connected to a local church camp and the Catholic Church started by Father Pieree-Jean De Smet. The next closest church was twenty miles away in another valley. The church was more than a church for the forty to sixty people who met each week. It was regarded by many to be "their church" even though they never attended. As is often the case in rural communities, people are religious and will identify with a church in the community even though they may never attend. For them, the presence of the church is a part of the community identity. As Aaron Morrow writes, "Small towns tend to be loaded with religious non-Christians. They may not go to church very often, but they generally believe that God exists and the Bible probably has something to say about him."[27] In many rural communities, there will be a specific denomination or "faith family" that dominates the area.

Within the rural church on any given Sunday, there may be two or three different generations present. Those who do not have grandparents near may often be "adopted" by older couples whose children have moved away. It is through this intergenerational worship that values and faith are passed down from one generation to another. As a result, rural parents are involved in the church community, and that involvement is matched by their children. There is a natural progression from generation to generation. Every Sunday morning and evening, my parents would pack all four of us children into the car and head to church. The only time we did not attend was when we were ill—and you better have a doctor's note confirming it! It was so engrained within us that even when we were teenagers and our parents were away on a trip, we still went, never even thinking that attendance was optional. Our parents never forced us to go to church. We just never realized it was an option. But it was there that we learned about the Bible and saw it lived out in the lives of the people who attended, people who cared about us and were as much a part of my life as any blood relative. When I go back, I do not see a white building located between a small town and a wheat field. I see people, each of whom left their imprint on my life. Understanding the rural church requires us to look beyond the building and see the people.

In rural communities, the church plays a more important role than just offering a meeting place for the local congregation. It brings stability and supports the whole community. In many small communities, especially those isolated from large urban areas, the church plays an important role in providing help and assistance for people. In rural communities, the church functions not only as a religious center, but also as a social center. In times when a tragedy strikes the community, people will look to the church and the local pastor to provide support and a sense of community, even though they may never attend the church. Because of the lack of social services, many times people will look to the church to fill the gap in food and clothing. Thus, in rural communities, the civil and social well-being of the community is interwoven with the vitality of the local church.[28]

So far, we have seen rural America in its best light and, in many ways, it corresponds to the idealistic stereotypes we have of rural people. But we cannot be fooled into thinking that all is perfect in the heartland of America. A dark and sinister underbelly exists, hidden from many casual observers. The decaying storefronts dotting the small, rural landscape betray a moral, spiritual, and economic decay creeping through rural America. It is to this that we now turn our attention.

6

The Rural Ghetto: Poverty in Rural America

IN RECENT HISTORY, the church at large has focused on cities and the plight of the urban poor and the inner city. In response, seminaries rightfully have developed programs to equip the next generation to meet the crisis. Following the lead of the evangelical social justice movement, young pastors with a strong sense of social responsibility turned to the inner city to plant churches and ministries designed to bring social, economic, and spiritual renewal to the inner city. However, the unintended result was that rural communities became "faceless places we road-trip through on our way somewhere else."[1] What the evangelical church failed to recognize was that, even as they turned their attention to the inner cities, rural America was rapidly becoming the new ghetto, with high poverty, drug use among young people, and crime all becoming systemic problems. Evangelicals have viewed rural America through idealist eyes as over-churched, over-evangelized, and overly-prosperous. As Harland Padfield summarized, "It is a fundamental illusion of American culture: the persistent celebration of rural life in the midst of its destruction."[2] After evaluating the plight of rural communities, Osha Gray Davidson concludes,

> Conditions in America's rural communities are far worse than is generally recognized. Contrary to national assumptions of rural tranquility, many small towns—even those white-picket-fenced hamlets in our fabled Heartland—today warrant the label "ghetto." No other word so vividly, and yet so accurately, conveys the air of ruin and desolation that now hangs over our rural communities. The word "ghetto" speaks of the rising poverty rates, the chronic unemployment, and the recent spread of low-wage, dead-end jobs. It speaks of the relentless deterioration of health-care systems, schools, roads, buildings, and of the emergence of homelessness, hunger, and poverty. It speaks, too, of the inevitable outmigration of the best and the brightest youths. Above all, the word "ghetto" speaks of the bitter stew of resentment, anger, and despair that simmers silently in those left behind. The hard and ugly truth is not only that we have failed to solve the problems of our urban ghettos, but that we have replicated them in miniature a thousand times across the American countryside.[3]

We tend to view rural America through the rose-colored glasses perpetuated by the false caricatures of modern television, all the while failing to see that rural people are facing a crisis. While the church rightfully has focused on the crisis of the inner city, it has mistakenly neglected the plight of rural people.

Growing up Poor

Both my father and mother knew the reality of poverty. While my mother grew up with the stigma of poverty in urban Appleton, Wisconsin, my father spent his early life in South Dakota, where he experienced the trauma and economic disaster inflicted during the Dust Bowl. Even after my father resettled in northern Idaho, if he had "two nickels to rub together," he would have thought he was rich. With my mother working as a school teacher in the local grade school and my father diversifying the farm—he farmed about four hundred acres and maintained a stock of twenty-five cows and thirty sows—they made ends meet. While not rich, we never considered ourselves poor. Living without luxuries was just a normal part of life for not only my family but many of those around us. The house we grew up in was less than a thousand square feet with three small bedrooms and a small living room, which sometimes served as a nursery for baby pigs or a calf when the weather was too cold for them to survive in the barn. My two brothers and I always thought that life was not fair because we had to share one small bedroom while my sister enjoyed one to herself. We grew up using plastic bread bags as extra socks to keep our feet dry when our boots got holes in them.

Yet even as my parents struggled to pay the bills, we were aware that others in the community were poorer than we were. We never looked down on them. Rather, we recognized that they were "less fortunate." Like others in the community, we tried to help them by purchasing their eggs or giving their kids rides to school events. In rural areas, the poorest family may be neighbors with the richest family in the community. While a person may face financial hardships, they would still be elected to positions of leadership within the church and valued for their down-to-earth wisdom. I remember one rural church I pastored in which some of the most respected members of the church were a couple that lived in a small travel trailer with an old boxcar attached to it as bedrooms for their two children. Poverty was just a part of life, not an indication of personal worth.

While rural people accepted people regardless of their economic status, there was one group of people that were looked down upon. These were the "welfare" people who accepted government assistance. Tragically, for many who needed this assistance, they were judged and mischaracterized as being lazy and unproductive. Regardless of how poor a person was, they were pressured to "carry their own weight," and if they did not have a job, it was because of their own choices rather than any external circumstance beyond their control. Unfortunately, this judgmental attitude still prevails today. We failed to understand that many people faced severe poverty because of circumstances beyond their control rather than because of some character flaw. We did not realize that this attitude not only was misguided, but perpetuated poverty in rural communities.

Poverty in Rural America

When discussing systemic poverty, many people naturally shift their focus to urban areas. This is not surprising since poverty in the inner city is concentrated and visible. Because rural poverty is not as visible, many assume that poverty is not a rural problem except perhaps in African American communities in the southern states. Because people typically associate poverty with the urban setting, rural poverty as a social problem is frequently under-recognized.[4] Consequently, the church has focused its attention almost strictly on the plight of the inner city.

Yet surprisingly, studies spanning across several different decades consistently tell a different story, revealing that rural areas not only experience equal or higher poverty rates than inner-city areas, but that they are more likely to remain persistently poor.[5] In 2007, the poverty rate of rural areas was 16.59 percent compared to 17.23 percent in center-city areas and a 12.95 percent national poverty rate.[6] Over 9 million people in rural areas live below the poverty line, with some counties experiencing a poverty rate near 30 percent.[7] Especially plagued by poverty are rural children. In rural areas, there are more than twice the number (3 million) of low income white children living in poverty than in the central cities. Hit especially hard is the most-overlooked people group, Native Americans, and in their communities, over 50 percent of the children live in poverty.[8] Unlike the urban city where poverty is linked to residential or neighborhood segregation by race, rural poverty is more likely to be associated with the isolation of rural communities where assistance is unavailable.[9]

While rural America suffers under the weight of poverty, the real tragedy is that the church and general society have largely ignored it. While many religious and governmental programs funnel resources to urban centers, little effort is made to assist those living in outlying areas of the country. They have become the forgotten poor. As the church and society turned their attention to the problems of the inner city, they failed to recognize that almost ninety percent of all the "persistent-poverty" counties—those that have experienced poverty rates above twenty percent for the past thirty years—exist in rural areas.[10] As a result, the most significant distinction between the rural poor and the urban poor is not the amount of poverty but the absence of options and programs to assist them in transitioning out of poverty. Of those in poverty—both in nonmetropolitan and metropolitan areas—people in rural communities are least likely to improve their lives because of factors and circumstances beyond their control. It leads Thomas Lyson and William Falk to conclude, "The forgotten places . . . are being by-passed in the newly forming global economy."[11] As manufacturing jobs are outsourced to other nations, rural areas are hit especially hard because over one-third of rural employment is dependent upon goods-producing industries.[12] To understand rural poverty, it is important to realize that the problems go far beyond the farm crisis of the '80s and '90s. Not only is poverty greater in rural areas, but rural unemployment has exceeded urban areas since 1980. This, coupled with the fact that the rural workers are more likely to be underpaid with a decrease in real earnings per job, provides few opportunities for rural people to move beyond poverty. The issue is not the lack of willingness to work, but rather the lack of opportunities to work. As a result, the income inequality has increased more rapidly in rural areas than in urban areas, with the rural poor falling further and further behind. In 2005, for each dollar earned in urban places, rural workers earned only seventy-two cents.[13] Even for those working, they are still falling further behind.

Contributors to Rural Poverty

It's easy to depersonalize statistics and draw conclusions regarding why people exist in poverty based upon misconceptions fed by attitudes of moral superiority. We jump to the conclusion that poverty, especially in the United States, stems from personal choices and attitudes. We believe people live in chronic poverty because of moral and social deficiencies. We assume they are not willing to work or are lazy workers, that they take advantage of welfare to avoid working, that they are plagued by alcohol and drug addictions, that they are sexually immoral so that they have children out of wedlock, and that they are guilty of a host of other self-destructive behaviors. Cynthia Duncan comments on the attitude of people in the Appalachians: "Because this minister's parishioners are the well-to-do county-seat residents who have no contact with the poor, they will have difficulty finding people who they can be sure 'need' help. The social isolation that keeps the haves out of contact with the have-nots means that all long-term poor are stigmatized and lumped together as an undeserving group."[14] But this observation fails to understand the complexity of circumstances contributing to people becoming impoverished, trapping them in a cycle of chronic poverty. As sociologists attempt to identify the causes, it soon becomes apparent that there is no single factor. While some trends can be identified, the full complexity of persistent rural poverty points us to a diverse problem. In addressing the causes of poverty, it is as important to take each community individually and recognize that there are unique factors contributing to the problem within each group. Along with identifying some of the common causes, it is equally valuable to identify the unique causes that plague a specific area. Concerning the universal causes, they may be categorized into two broad factors: structural/economic factors and individual factors.

Structural and Economic Factors

Contrary to popular perception, the greatest cause of poverty stems not from the person's choices but from the economic and structural instability that makes it difficult for people to obtain jobs with sustainable incomes. Those who live in areas of chronic poverty have few options available. For instance, rural communities remain more dependent upon a few industries for their economic livelihood. So when a downturn occurs, it has a wide-ranging impact on the whole community.

The persistent poverty found in the so-called Black Belt—counties in southern states where thirty-three percent or more of the population is black—is well documented. Rural communities in these areas experience forty-one percent greater poverty than rural white counties, with a poverty rate of forty-two percent for blacks and thirteen percent for whites.[15] As with many cases in rural areas, a major contributing factor was the loss of manufacturing jobs. When we think of rural economy, we tend to focus on the ebb and flow of agribusiness. But for many rural communities, especially in the Southeast and Northeast rural areas, manufacturing also plays an important role in providing jobs, where one in five rural workers find employment.[16] In recent years, as companies have relocated plants overseas, there has been both a loss of manufacturing jobs as well as a shift to service industries. Between 1980 and 2006, the rural workforce in manufacturing declined by twenty percent, while the service industries only increased by eighteen percent.[17] This is especially true in the Southeast region where the manufacturing industry is the biggest employer. However, the service industries replacing them pay lower wages and provide fewer opportunities for career and economic advancement. As a result, the area is doubly disadvantaged. The region is losing jobs and has fewer better-paying, high-skilled jobs, thus leaving the poor few options to better themselves.

The second economic factor is the collapse of mining, affecting those counties, especially in the Appalachians, dependent upon the extractive industries. Until the 1980s, Kellogg, Idaho, a mining town near our farm, was a thriving silver mining community. But a series of events brought an end to the century-old livelihood for the people in the area. In 1971, one of the mines experienced one of the largest mining accidents in the country when ninety-one men died from an accident, which led to the closure of the mine from 1971 to 2001. In 1980, labor disputes and the economic downturn of mining led to the closure of other mines, causing thousands of workers to lose their jobs in the surrounding area and forcing many to migrate out of the community. As a result, the population of the area decreased by half between 1970 and 1990. This devastated the local economy and businesses with a loss of patronage. Not only that, schools suffered decline in enrollment, and, as a result, received decreased federal funds. This experience was not unique to Idaho, but was repeated in other mining-dependent areas, especially in the Appalachian and other coal mining communities that were dependent upon the coal industry. In West Virginia and Kentucky, the number of mining jobs declined by twenty-three percent and twenty-eight percent, respectively, from 2015 to 2017.[18]

For the Northwest, the decline of the timber industry undermined the economy of many rural communities. The recession in the early 1980s caused a sharp decline in timber prices, devastating the timber industry. This was further fueled by the new environmental restrictions on logging in federal forests in 1990, which caused a sharp decline in timber prices and jobs. In Oregon, for example, from 1983 to 2011, the number of jobs related to the Oregon wood products industry declined from approximately 64,000 to 27,000.[19] In the community in which I currently live, over 90 percent of the county is federal- and state-owned forest. Since 1990, the amount of annual timber sales from federal forestland in our county declined from 400 million board feet to 82 million board feet. The local employee-owned plywood plant was forced into bankruptcy, which not only caused a loss of jobs for many in the community, but also a loss of their retirement as they had invested in the stock of the company. Today, almost 70 percent of the county's earned income comes from jobs outside the county.[20] As a result, the Pacific Northwest became known as the new Appalachia because of the economic and structural instability experienced in many of the logging-dependent communities.[21]

If these issues were not enough, the farm crisis of the 1980s brought about an economic crisis in the Midwest and other farm-dependent communities. In the 1970s, the future of farming seemed bright. Commodity prices were increasing as the overseas markets pursued American grain. In the face of an optimistic future, farmers sought to expand their operations. But the prosperity only served to set the stage for the crisis of the '80s. As farmers expanded, available land—always a limited resource—became scarce, and land prices increased substantially, resulting in further debt as they purchased the increasingly high-priced land. However, farm incomes began to dramatically decrease so that the cash-flow—always a problem—became even more critical. The '80s brought about a three-pronged assault upon the economic stability of farmers. The first was a sharp decline in commodity prices as other nations began to flood the market with their products. The second was the high rise of petroleum, which increased the price of both fuel and fertilizer. The third was the rapid decline of farm land values, which made it difficult for farmers to obtain operational loans and necessary refinancing of outstanding debt. With the economic downturn, many lost their farms and were forced to seek off-farm employment in a time when the job market in agricultural communities was already in recession. This brought about not only the foreclosure on farms and the displacement of families but also the "psychological effects of the loss of land on farmers—land that had often been in families for generations."[22] Consequently, the poorest counties are no longer in Appalachia or the Deep South, but in the Great Plains, where ranchers struggle to make ends meet and farms struggle to survive.[23]

Personal Factors

Poverty is not just an economic structural problem. There are also personal factors that contribute to individual economic status. Poverty often breeds poverty, as people develop lifestyles further contributing to their inability to make necessary changes. People make choices resulting in a culture of poverty. While some want to attribute poverty only to class and societal structures, we also recognize that people are moral beings who make choices that affect their ability to find and maintain a job. Brown and Swanson describe the contributing culture of perpetual poverty that spans generations as including the "lack of integration with formal institutions and society in general, early initiation into sex and consensual unions, feelings of dependence and inferiority, and a present-time orientation and sense of fatalism that hinders people from seeing and seizing opportunities and planning for the future."[24] We are never solely a product of our environment, just as we are never fully a product of our individual choices. While poverty contributes to self-destructive behavior, so also individual self-destructive choices contribute to poverty. Teen pregnancy and single parenthood often put a person in a position where she or he becomes more dependent upon the state for assistance.

Likewise, the individual's human capital contributes to personal poverty. Human capital refers to the assets each person possesses that contribute to their ability to be successful members of society. This includes health, formal education, skills, knowledge, leadership potential, etc.[25] A significant part of a person's human capital enabling the individual to transition out of poverty involves their level of formal education. Here, again, we find the rural poor at a distinct disadvantage. The most poorly performing schools are found in impoverished areas, including poor school districts.[26] Further, because rural communities are small and isolated, they do not have access to adult education programs. As Jensen and Jensen point out, "The comparatively low education of rural residents has been linked to (1) poorer quality schools, (2) a rural 'brain drain' where the best students migrate to opportunities found in more urban locales, and (3) the possibility that rural residents, sensing a local economy that yields a low payoff to education, rationally underinvests in their own human capital."[27] While it is true that a person does not need a college degree to be successful in rural communities, when confronted with job loss and forced migration to an urban center in search of a job, the lack of education becomes a major hindrance to obtaining a sustainable income.

Personalizing Poverty

In examining the causes of poverty, however, it is important to realize that there is no single factor driving it. The causes of poverty are complex indeed, and the danger is that we too readily jump to focusing on the cause of poverty rather than listen to individuals voice their struggles. It is easy in examining statistics to depersonalize people. We become detached and indifferent. Instead of understanding the person, we try to fit them into our preconceived box. Understanding the poor requires us to see them as individuals who struggle to overcome the obstacles confronting them.

We need to see the single mother struggling to provide for her children after she has been abandoned by her husband, for she faces seemingly overwhelming obstacles. The rural mother often finds employment in jobs with lower pay, so that even though she is working full time, she is more likely to be on food stamps (compare 29 percent of rural single mothers to 19 percent of urban single mothers), but less likely to rely on welfare benefits (15 percent versus 29 percent).[28] They further struggle to find jobs that pay a good wage and affordable childcare, so that they have "the triple disadvantage of higher poverty, more barriers to the work, and lower economic incentives to return to work."[29]

We must see the children gripped by poverty. I remember the first time I realized the tragedy of children in poverty. It was in Manila when we were driving along the cardboard boxes stacked up to form a shelter under the freeway, and a young girl was washing her hair in the water flowing in the street gutter. But you don't have to go to Manila to see children living in poverty. You can find the same children on the Indian reservations where Native Americans face 65 percent unemployment.[30] You see it in the homes of single mothers, where the poverty rate of children parented by a single mom is over 60 percent.[31] And 27 percent of rural children live in poverty.[32] It's not hard to find children in despair, children who face "deep poverty"—where the annual household income is less than half of the poverty threshold—which is slightly more prevalent in rural areas (12.2 percent) than urban areas (9.2 percent). The highest levels of children experiencing deep poverty are found in the Southwest, Pacific Northwest, Michigan, and the historically poor regions of the rural Southeast.[33]

We must understand that those who have become trapped in a lifestyle of substance abuse often deal with inner struggles pushing them to try to find some level of peace and joy through the wrong method. People trapped in persistent poverty often lose hope, and so they are more prone to substance abuse. This is especially true on reservations, where the "lack of economic opportunity, limited access to quality health care, persistent poverty, and unemployment rates near 80 percent on some reservations have led to increased violence and drug and alcohol abuse among reservation residents."[34] It is far easier to condemn than to help, but help we must.

We must see the farmer who struggles with depression and suicidal thoughts because he believes he failed not only his family, but also previous generations who worked hard to establish and maintain the farm. The loss of a farm is more than the loss of an income and a career; it is the loss of a person's identity. In a culture that values self-reliance and equates masculinity and self-worth with the ability to sustain and strengthen the family farm, a man would rather die than admit he failed. And die they have. In Oklahoma, during the farm crisis, the suicide rate among farmers was a shocking three times that of the national average.[35]

We must identify with the elderly poor of rural America. In our search for the poor, we often overlook the rural elderly who are at higher risk of poverty, more likely to slide into poverty from one year to the next, and less likely to escape poverty than their urban counterparts.[36] Their plight is exacerbated by lower lifelong earnings—thus, lower Social Security payments—and less access to pensions. Their struggle is compounded when they do not have any family nearby to care for them.

Walk onto the campus of a Bible college or seminary or peruse the books on poverty, and the talk will be focused on the plight of the inner city. The plight of the rural poor has become forgotten. For all the talk about social justice in the church today, we have been grossly unjust in our treatment and response to the poor of rural America.

The Response of the Church

The church in rural communities has long struggled with responding to the problem of poverty. Limited resources often make it difficult for the church to develop strategic programs to assist the poor in the local community. Along with the lack of resources, the rural church's perception of the poor can become clouded, thus hindering any compassionate ministry. We can attach a stigma to poverty that places blame upon the poor themselves and causes us to remain indifferent. To minister to the poor, we need to change our thinking.

Recognize Our Responsibility

Changing our perception begins with a recognition of our biblical responsibility. When the social gospel abandoned orthodox faith and adopted theological liberalism and the ecumenical movement in the turn of the twentieth century, evangelicals reacted by refocusing on the redemptive truth of the gospel. Rightfully, people recognized the bankruptcy of a social gospel that neglected to address the greatest need of humanity—the need for redemption from sin. But in the process of defending the integrity of the redemptive work of Christ in the face of ecumenicalism and theological liberalism, we lost sight of the responsibility that God gave His people to care for the poor.

But here again, the answer is far more complex than the question. Helping the poor begins by recognizing the means by which God provides for them. In Scripture, we discover a fivefold safety net established for the poor, who are the most vulnerable members of society.

The first safety net is the individual himself or herself. Paul writes in 2 Thessalonians 3:10, "For even when we were with you, we used to give you this order: if anyone is not willing to work, then he is not to eat, either." Paul was not directing this injunction toward those who were unable to work or could not find work, but to those who refused to work and were solely relying upon the wealthy to provide for their support.[37] People who have the ability and opportunity to work but refuse to do so cannot expect any assistance from the church. The first step is not to cast money but to help address the issues in their lives and develop skills to help them find a job.[38]

The second safety net is the family of the poor. In 1 Timothy 5:3–8, Paul reminds believers of the responsibility to provide for the financial and physical needs of their immediate family: "But if any widow has children or grandchildren, they must first learn to practice piety in regard to their own family . . . but if anyone does not provide for his own, and especially for those of his household, he has denied the faith and is worse than an unbeliever." Children and grandchildren who have the ability to do so are responsible in the sight of God to care for their elderly parents and grandparents.

The third safety net is the church community. There are numerous Bible verses challenging us to care for those unable to provide for the necessities of life. This begins within the church, so that the congregation takes responsibility for those within the church who are destitute and in need of assistance (e.g., Prov. 29:7; Gal. 2:10; Rom. 12:13).

The fourth safety net is the community at large, including the government. The reality is that the church cannot help everyone. Rural churches continually struggle with insufficient resources to operate the church and face limitations in their ability to help others. While the Bible does not specifically lay out the responsibility of government to provide for the poor, there are verses pointing to the role of government in upholding justice and the well-being of those most at risk for poverty (Prov. 29:14). In Ezekiel 16:49–50, God condemns Sodom for their failure to help the poor and needy. Further, all of society bears a responsibility to care for the poor, as evidenced by the command to allow for the poor to reap the corners of the fields (Lev. 19:9–10; 23:22).

The last and ultimate safety net is God Himself. When people fail to provide for the poor and needy, God takes responsibility in providing for them (see 1 Sam. 2:8). Because God ultimately cares for the poor, He holds us responsible to care for them. In His provision for the needy, He seeks to use people as the means to meet their needs. Consequently, giving to the poor serves as an act of worship in which we are giving to God (Prov. 19:17).

Focus on the Solution Rather Than the Cause

Often, when we evaluate poverty, we focus on the cause of poverty rather than the solution. We judge people in terms of why they are poor rather than help them develop strategic plans through cooperative efforts to alleviate their poverty. The heart of the gospel is not condemnation, but forgiveness and grace. When we confess our sins, God restores and forgives our sins regardless of the manifestation of our depravity. In rural communities where self-sufficiency and self-reliance are central values, we can easily turn a blind eye to the poor because we assume it is their own fault and "as you make your bed, so you must lie on it," as the saying goes. Instead, our responsibility is to seek to help people find avenues to escape poverty. This does not mean we do so without some level of accountability. The apostle Paul already pointed out that if a person is unwilling to work, then that person is to be held responsible. Nevertheless, many poor in rural areas face obstacles restricting their ability to overcome their struggle. A single mother faces low wages and so struggles to pay for child care. Even though she may have made poor decisions that placed her in that position, merely telling her of her faults does not provide the help she needs. We need to take steps to help her find solutions as well.

Identify Opportunities and Cooperation

The last step is to identify possible opportunities for the church and avenues that will help us work in conjunction with other community groups and agencies to assist people. The church can work with government programs to expand regional cooperation, innovation, and entrepreneurship. In our own local church, we recognize that we do not have the ability to run a food bank; so instead, we take a food collection every other month to support the local food bank. As a church, we cannot do everything. Nor can we solve rural poverty. But that does not mean we cannot do something to minister to the rural poor.

Social Action and the Gospel

As Christians, we must realize that helping to provide for the poor is not enough, for we need to proclaim the gospel to them in both words and actions. When the disciples of John the Baptist came to inquire whether Jesus was the Messiah, Christ pointed not only to His miracles but also to "the poor hav[ing] the gospel preached to them" as evidence that He was so (Matt. 11:5).

We recognize that both the causes and solutions to chronic poverty are complex. There are no easy answers and no magic bullets to solve the problem. Christ Himself stated that we will always have the poor with us (Matt. 26:11). But the complexity of the problem should not cause us to abandon the search for a solution. The church needs to take the initiative and the lead in rural communities to help people who are facing the personal crisis of poverty. The greatest error is not in the misguided attempts to help, but in not doing anything at all.

Racial Tension in Rural America

LIVING ON THE reservation brought both an awareness of the conditions and struggles that Native Americans face as well as the reality of racial tension in rural areas. Through grade school, little difference seemed to exist between Native Americans and Anglo students. As children, we went to school together and played together, not thinking we were all that different from each other. But as we transitioned into high school, the differences began to surface. While we were still good friends, we began to realize that we were from two radically different worlds existing side by side. The academic performance of some of my Native American classmates started to decline as the social problems they faced on the reservation and in their families took its toll upon their understanding of the world in which they lived. Drugs and alcohol began to play a major destructive part in their lives.

As we went through high school, the social and cultural differences between the tribal members and the non-tribal members became more apparent. While we lived near one another and attended the same classes, we lived segregated lives outside the classroom. It was not overt racism, but the reality of two different cultures coexisting side by side. This distinction increased as tensions developed between tribal members and non-tribal residents. The Native Americans resented the presence of the whites living on the land they felt belonged to them, and the whites resented the intrusion the tribe had in local policies and regulations on the reservation. While we cordially greeted one another in the local mom-and-pop grocery store, we remained relationally unconnected, even as we lived in such close proximity.

Tragically, this separation existed in the church. While the small church I attended has existed on the reservation for over fifty years, it remains predominantly white. The only Native Americans who attended were those adopted by a white family in the church. The reasons for the essential absence of Native Americans in that church are indeed complex. And while attempts were made by the church to bridge the gap between them and the American Indian residents, their attempts failed.

All this serves to illustrate that, contrary to popular perception, racial diversity and isolation is not just an inner-city problem; it is a rural problem as well. In recent elections, many pundits portrayed rural Americans as Christian fundamentalist, racist, white Americans. For them, rural America exists in a homogenous bubble, inhabited by people who refuse to listen to anyone who is different from them. When people speak of rural America, they often speak of white rural people. But perception clouds reality.

Yet as urban people fail to see the racial diversity in rural areas, rural people often overlook the reality of racial tensions in their communities. Rural people see racism only from the standpoint of the overt prejudice manifested by white supremacist groups. By and large, rural people vehemently reject the ideology of these groups. Yet what they fail to see is the structural racism existing within the country that remains invisible to whites, but is plain to people of color. If the rural church is to effectively reach people of color, it needs to reexamine the reality of racial diversity and tensions existing within the rural community.

The Changing Demographic

While metropolitan areas remain more ethnically diverse, the popular perception that rural America is "white" fails to appreciate the existing ethnic diversity in rural areas. Historically, the rural African American population in the South along with the Native American and Hispanic populations results in a diverse population in rural communities. In recent years, much of the population growth in rural communities is due to the influx of minorities. Rural America is rapidly becoming multicultural and multiracial.

According to recent census information, 74 percent of the US population is white. However, in rural communities, the percentage jumps to approximately 80 percent. Yet these figures fail to recognize the significant regional variations in ethnic and racial concentrations. For example, 90 percent of rural African Americans live in the Southern areas, with 70 percent living in only five states: South Carolina, Georgia, Alabama, Mississippi, and Louisiana.[1] In the Southwest, a significant portion of the population is Latino, where 70 percent of Latinos live in eight states: Texas, New Mexico, California, Arizona, Colorado, Washington, Florida, and Kansas.[2] The other significant source of diversity comes from the Native American tribes that are scattered throughout the West and Southwest.

What these figures fail to indicate is the growth of ethnic diversity that is coming to rural communities. In the past twenty years, there has been an increasing trend of immigrants moving into rural areas rather than urban communities. This has been especially evident in the Latino population. From 2000 to 2010, the rural Hispanic population increased by 44.6 percent.[3] By 2010, Hispanics exceeded African Americans as the largest minority group in rural and small towns.[4] With the increasing dependency of agriculture and agricultural-related businesses upon migrant and Hispanic workers, this trend will continue to grow. With the predominant population growth coming from minorities, rural America will continue to become more ethnically diverse. As the young people flee rural areas to the city, they are being replaced by minorities.

But this growth also brings further pressure upon rural communities, as minorities continue to lag significantly behind in their economic and social well-being. Rural minorities continue to suffer greater poverty, often employed in low income jobs. They suffer further from substandard housing. Geographically and socially segregated from mainstream America, rural ethnic minorities are often ignored and forgotten.[5]

Racial Diversity in Rural Areas

To understand the diversity and struggles of rural minorities we need to recognize not only the history but also the present struggles and realities they face. We view people through the lens of our own life and experience, and conclude that others have the same opportunities and obstacles we faced. If we overcome those barriers, we assume that everyone should be able to do the same.

However, if we look more closely, we discover that minorities often face challenges in both the community and society at large that we never experienced. This begins with an understanding of the history of the rural minorities. For many people, the migration to rural areas occurred because of voluntary immigration or resettlement. Simply put, our forefathers settled in the rural community because they desired to live there. Historically, however, such was not the case for many of the rural minorities. Instead, their history was grounded in the legacy of slavery, conquest, and racial subjugation. The result was often that rural minorities were isolated and segregated.

African Americans

African Americans make up close to eight percent of residents in rural areas. When we think of ethnic isolation and segregation, our first thoughts shift to the racism experienced by African Americans in the Deep South, rooted in a long history of slavery, segregation, and the belief that blacks were inferior. While the Civil War achieved political freedom for African Americans, it did little to bring about economic prosperity for African Americans living in the Deep South. Rural blacks working in agriculture largely depended upon sharecropping and tenant farming—a form of "debt bondage" in which they were tied to the land owned by white landowners—which did little to give them any economic freedom.[6] Even after the civil rights movement, there remained structural discrimination, making it difficult for African Americans to advance economically.[7]

For example, as recent as 1982, African American farmers received just 1 percent of farm-ownership loans. The USDA did little to help the African American farmer, with only 398 farm-ownership loans being given to black farmers in 1980. It was not until 1997 that a class-action lawsuit by 400 black farmers brought to light the existing discrimination.[8] As a result, rural African American areas suffer chronic and extreme poverty and are still some of the poorest regions in the country. Thirty-five percent of the nation's poor and 90 percent of the poor rural African Americans live in the rural areas of the Southeast.[9] Yet subtle racism still prevents many African Americans from obtaining the necessary tools to move beyond poverty. Rural African Americans continue to be plagued by low levels of education, lower incomes, and poorer health care.

Hispanics/Latinos

Latinos continue to be the fastest growing ethnic group in the country. While many are migrating to the urban areas, the majority are moving to rural communities, where the Latino population increased in the 1990s by 67 percent.[10] While most of the rural Latinos are concen-

115

trated in the South and Southwest, other areas of the country are also experiencing significant growth in Latino residents. Meat-processing industries, looking for cheaper labor, have turned to Mexican and Asian workers.[11] The fruit industries became dependent upon Latino migrant workers to provide the needed supply of cheap labor.

With the growth of the Latino population came many challenges. As with the other minorities in rural areas, one of the biggest challenges facing Latinos is education, where they encounter high levels of school segregation, dropout rates, and pervasive inequities in school funding.[12] This is especially problematic for the children of migrant workers who frequently move with their family as they follow the agricultural seasons in search of employment, resulting in a lack of stability and educational consistency. Further, many communities fail to understand the culture and needs of Latino children, as was the case with Native Americans during the turn of the twentieth century.

Most distressing is the condition of the colonia residents, who are regarded as the poorest of the poor. In 1990, the Cranston-Gonzalez National Affordable Housing Act established the federal definition for colonias as "an 'identifiable community' established before November 28, 1989 in Arizona, California, New Mexico, or Texas within 150 miles of the US-Mexico border that lacks potable water and sewage systems and decent housing."[13] The Department of Housing and Urban Development has designated 86 colonias in Arizona, 15 in California, 142 in New Mexico, and more than 1,800 in Texas.[14] The rural colonias are home to 1.6 million people and are characterized by extreme poverty (20.7 percent), substandard housing that often does not meet housing codes, poor education, and crowded conditions. Especially at risk are the elderly, who often lack even the basic services necessary to meet their needs. The challenges confronting those who live in the colonias is further impacted by the 'contract for deed system' in which the buyer makes direct payments to the developer, who keeps the title until the amount is paid in full. Often, these contracts involve high interest rates where the buyer faces foreclosure if they miss one payment.[15] As a result, residents often encounter major challenges in improving their communities as they have neither a land base nor a secure political status enabling them to obtain vital services.[16]

Native Americans

Perhaps the most overlooked people group in our country—not only by society at large, but by the church itself—is the Native American. And "everything most people know about Indians is wrong," Paul Chaat Smith states.[17] For many, Native Americans share a common culture of fried bread and teepees, a common spirituality involving the worship of the "Great Spirit," and speak the same language (in old Western films, all the Indians spoke Navajo regardless of their tribe). In reality, the tribes populating North America before the arrival of Europeans were as diverse in culture, language, and beliefs as the individual people groups populating Europe. Just as the culture, language, and history of the Germans is vastly different from those of Spain or Sweden, so the Cherokee differed vastly from the Issaquah. However, instead of seeing them as individual tribes, we see them only as "Indian." As Chaat Smith points out,

We only became Indians once the armed struggle was over in 1890. Before then we were Shoshone or Mohawk or Crow. For centuries North America was a complicated, dangerous place full of shifting alliances between the United States and Indian nations, among the Indian nations themselves, and between the Indians and Canada, Mexico, and half of Europe. This happy and confusing time ended forever that December morning a century ago at Wounded Knee. Once we no longer posed a military threat, we became Indians, all of us more or less identical in practical terms, even though until that moment, and for thousands of years before, we were as different from one another as Greeks are from Swedes. The Comanches, for example, were herded onto a reservation with the Kiowa and the Apache, who not only spoke different languages but were usually enemies.[18]

In an age when Caucasians identify themselves by their historical roots as German, English, or Norwegian, Indians remain Indian. The myth of popular perception is difficult to erase.

Despite the rich diversity and culture of the Native Americans, their story is one of genocide and isolation. Most scholars estimate that before the arrival of Columbus, there were fifty million Indians living in both North and South America, with approximately five million living throughout the United States and Canada.[19] When the colonists arrived, strained and sometimes violent relationships developed between them and the Natives. As the United States pushed westward, it increasingly confronted resistance from the various tribes as traditional tribal territories were absorbed into the ever-increasing population growth of the country. By the end of the nineteenth century, many national leaders concluded that the American Indian was destined for extinction. As a result, there was a push to "civilize" the American Indian by absorbing them into the Anglo-American culture. The prevalent motto was, "Kill the Indian and save the man." In other words, the only way we can make them productive members of society was to eradicate their cultural identity. As a result, boarding schools designed to detribalize and indoctrinate the Indian children into the rest of the American culture were established.[20] Children were given European hairstyles and clothing, and their names were changed to sound English. At the schools, they were punished for speaking their native language, even as they struggled to speak English.[21] In the end, however, the result was not the absorption of the Native American, but their isolation as they were assigned to reservations.

Today there are just under 2.5 million Native Americans (about half living on rural reservations), with over 500 recognized tribes living on 326 reservations, mostly located in the western half of the United States.[22] But the policy of absorption and isolation resulted in the American Indians becoming the poorest people group in the US. Brown and Swanson observe, "According to nearly every social indicator—such as income, employment, educational attainment, quality of health care, and life expectancy—American Indians are well below the national averages."[23]

Race and Racism

Race and racism remains a volatile issue in our country. From 2001 to 2010, the percent of people who expressed a great concern about race relations steadily declined to only 13 percent. In the last four years, however, it has skyrocketed to 42 percent.[24] Years after the civil rights movement, race relations have once again become one of the top concerns confronting our country, and it is unlikely that it will go away anytime soon. But racism and race relationships are not just an urban problem. With the increase of racial diversity in rural areas, racism and race relationships are issues in rural communities as well.

Individual Racism vs. Structural Racism

Ask most white people about race and racism, and they would deny that they are racist. Yet ask a minority if racism exists, and you will get a completely different answer. While white Americans may be comfortable with neighbors who are minority and do not feel any animosity toward people of different races, there remains a gap between white Americans' perception of racial issues and those who are minorities. How, then, do we explain this discrepancy? To begin, we consider the difference between individual attitudes towards race and structural patterns resulting in racial inequities.

In their provocative book *Divided by Faith: Evangelical Religion and the Problem of Race in America*, Michael Emerson and Christian

Smith argue that while individuals are less racist than they were fifty years ago, we still live in a "racialized society," a society "wherein race matters profoundly for differences in life experiences, life opportunities, and social relationships."[25] The extent of progress the country has made on an individual level is highlighted with the election of President Obama, something that seemed unlikely as recently as 1965, when the Voting Rights Act became necessary to fully open the door for African Americans to vote. Yet the recent protest by NFL players reveal that we still struggle with racial issues on a societal level. In a racialized society, social structures provide different economic, political, social, and even psychological rewards based upon race.[26] Because we individually may not be racist, we fail to recognize and understand the underlying structural issues contributing to racial division. Our life experience is radically different, and so it blinds us to the existing inequities. Too often, we neglect the reality of racial discrimination. Because many of us have not experienced the constraints of the racialized society, we dismiss the concerns and frustrations of others. The first step toward racial unity begins by listening and understanding the experiences of others and how they differ from ours.

Race and Culture

To understand the attitudes people have towards race, we must look beyond the color of a person's skin or the ethnic background of the individual. Race is ultimately interwoven with culture. Often what we attribute to race and racism has more to do with culture than ethnicity. For example, a person of Hispanic descent who speaks English, watches the NFL, and celebrates the Fourth of July will be more accepted by whites than a Hispanic whose first language is Spanish, watches soccer, and celebrates Cinco de Mayo. Whites will view an African American who wears a suit and drives a BMW differently from one who wears baggy pants and drives a souped-up Cadillac.

With culture often comes cultural arrogance in which we judge people based upon our cultural bias. Edward Stewart and Bennett Milton identify this danger:

> Faced with these cross-cultural uncertainties, people tend to impose their own perspectives in an effort to dispel the ambiguity created by the unusual behavior of host country nationals. They are unlikely to suspend judgment about differences in behavior because they assume unconsciously that their own ways are normal, natural, and right. Those of the other culture, therefore, must be abnormal, unnatural, and wrong.[27]

As a result, we often ascribe moral force to our personal cultural patterns so that those who differ must be flawed, rebellious, or immoral.[28] This is what brings tension into rural communities. With the influx of ethnic diversity there also comes different cultural patterns and expectations of people. When these clash with our patterns and expectations, tensions arise.

Moving beyond Paternalism

The issue of race and racial diversity is not just a theoretical problem that sociologists and theologians debate. It is a real issue affecting real people. For Nathan (not his real name), the issue became real at a very young age. In the 1950s, Nathan was born to a poor family in a log Hogan in a southern reservation where no record was kept of his birth date. Even today, it is difficult for him to obtain medical help outside the VA Hospital—where he is a registered war veteran—because he does not have a birth certificate, although he points to his belly button as his certificate.

When he was six years old, the Bureau of Indian Affairs dictated that native children be sent to boarding schools because of the lack of local schools on the reservation. While white children throughout rural America were being bused to the nearest school district, Native American children were being separated from their families for the whole year. As a result, Nathan grew up hating the thunderstorms of August because it reminded him that he would soon leave his family, only to return for a short visit during Christmas break.

The boarding school was not a place of comfort. Children were arbitrarily divided into four groups: One would be Catholic, one Protestant, one Mormon and one Traditional Spiritualism. They were then forced to attend an assigned church regardless of their preference, and so they grew to see Christianity as the "white man's religion" forced upon them. Because society viewed them as uncivilized savages who needed to be culturally integrated into the "American mainstream," they were not allowed to wear any traditional clothing and were punished if they spoke their native language, even though they did not know English. After high school, being denied any educational scholarships because of his grades, Nathan enrolled in the military. Despite his negative impressions with Christianity, while in the military, he accepted Christ through the influence of a chaplain.

Even though he embraced Christ, his spiritual journey to maturity was fraught with struggles unique to his Native experience. At the beginning of his faith journey, he sought to integrate his new-found faith with traditional spirituality and peyote. But the more he attempted to do so, the more he realized that Christ required his full allegiance and that his native spiritualism was incompatible to the teachings of Scripture. But the transition was not easy, for it involved setting aside not only his beliefs but also many aspects of his native culture. Because our European-Anglo culture was built upon a Judeo-Christian worldview, there is much that remains compatible with our faith. However, for many Native Americans, their culture is interwoven with their native spiritualism so that if one accepts Christ, that faith comes into conflict with many of their cultural norms. Such was the case for Nathan.

While many Anglo missionaries have worked as co-laborers with Native Christians, many others have developed paternalistic attitudes toward them. Instead of understanding the culture of Native Americans and how they relate and function, paternalistically-minded Christians often treat them as inferior. They view the Native Americans as ignorant, lazy, and uneducated—even though they have the same amount of theological training as the Anglos. If an Anglo and Native American are being considered for a church leadership position, the Anglo would be chosen. If Anglo and Native American pastors would fellowship, the gathering would be driven by Anglo culture—with the meeting starting and ending at specific times so that the agenda could be accomplished—rather than be adaptive to Native culture, which sees eating together and building relationships without time constraints as an essential part of their fellowship. In talking with several different Native Americans from several different tribes, I have heard them express their frustration that almost all ministries to Native Americans are led by Anglos. Instead of the relationship being a mutual brotherhood and fellowship of equals, there was a sense of paternalism on the part of the Anglo leaders and Anglo church.

All this brings us back to the structural racialization that exists even when we reject personal racism. Our cultural pride blinds us to it. We agree theologically that we are united in Christ, but we demand conformity to our specific cultural views. The result is that we can develop a paternalistic view that prevents us from seeing others who are culturally or economically different from us as equals in Christ. Consequently, the majority church in rural America often fails to fully accept and value the cultural diversity of fellow believers in Christ.

Toward a Theology of Race and Culture

Ultimately, racism is not a social problem but a theological one. Understanding race and culture begins with our understanding of God and His creative work. From the very beginning of time, when God created the heavens and the earth, He blessed humanity with the unsurpassed gift of being made in His image. One of the most profound statements in all Scripture is when God said, "Let Us make man in Our image" (Gen. 1:26). This not only distinguished humanity from all other creation by bestowing on them a gift that God did not share with any other being in heaven or earth, but also established the dignity of humanity. When God created humanity in His image, He set the value and worth of all humanity. This teaches us that an individual's worth is found not in economic status, race, gender, or social standing, but in being made in the likeness of God. We were given the unique privilege of participating in His nature and character.

Adam and Eve did not have a racial distinction as we think of it. Rather, through them all people would come. They were non-ethnic and non-national.[29] To see one particular race as superior to another ultimately denies the biblical doctrine of the *imago Dei*.[30] Racism, then, is "an explicit or implicit belief or practice that qualitatively distinguishes or values one race over other races."[31] This is why Paul states, "And [we] have put on the new self who is being renewed to a true knowledge according to the image of the One who created him—a *renewal* in which there is no *distinction between* Greek and Jew, circumcised and uncircumcised, barbarian, Scythian, slave and freeman, but Christ is all, and in all" (Col. 3:10–11; see also Gal. 3:28). In Christ, worth is not determined by race, for we are all possess equal value. Moreover, in the church, we all are equally part of the body of Christ in which every member is as equally important as the rest (1 Cor. 12).

However, while recognizing that in Christ we are no longer to judge people by race, we also acknowledge the legitimacy of cultural diversity. Paul affirmed this: "to the Jews I became as a Jew, so that I might win Jews; to those who are under the Law, as under the Law though not being myself under the Law, so that I might win those who are under the Law. . . . that I may by all means save some. I do all things for the sake of the gospel, so that I may become a fellow partaker of it" (1 Cor. 9:20, 22–23). Paul was not driven by the need for cultural accommodation and assimilation. Instead, he recognized the value of culture as a tool to effectively reach others for Christ. Rather than wait for them to share in his cultural background, he entered their world and culture to more effectively present the gospel to them. Too often, in both rural and urban communities, we demand either explicitly or implicitly that people become culturally homogeneous with us, and as a result, we hinder the message of the gospel.

As Christians, our goal should be to proclaim the gospel and live considering the implications of the gospel. For this to occur, we need to strive to promote racial and cultural reconciliation where we accept one another's cultural differences while promoting racial unity and understanding. As Jarvis Williams writes,

> Racial reconciliation means that different races are now members of the same spiritual family by their faith in Christ because of his death for sin, and they have equal access to God by the same Spirit since Jesus recreated all who believe into one new man. This new man is the new race in Christ. This new race transcends our old ethnic identities and our old man in Adam (see Rom. 6:6).[32]

With that as our goal, we should reach out to build relationships with those ethnically diverse in our community, accepting them for who they are, so that we might become one with them in Christ. This is a challenge for both the urban and rural church, yet it is not one that cannot be met without the church working within and as a part of the community.

The Church and the Rural Community

IT IS ONE THING TO identify the problems and quite another to do something about them. We can easily identify the social and economic struggles of rural America, but the challenge for the church is to develop an appropriate response that brings us not only into the sociological function of the church but also into the heart of our theology.

When I first entered ministry, I did not fully appreciate and realize the extent to which the rural pastor becomes involved in the whole community. But one instance brought home to me the reality that a pastor is more than just a leader in the church, that a pastor is a spiritual leader in the whole community. In our community, there was a tragic death of a small child whose parents were also involved in the emergency services, so it was traumatic for all those involved, including the responding emergency personnel. When the tragedy occurred, the sheriff's office called and asked if I would go to the scene to provide counseling. When I arrived, one of the EMTs looked up and with a look of despair cried out, "I am so glad you are here!" This lady never attended our church, but at that moment in time, I served as her pastor. To pastor a rural church is to serve as a pastor to the whole community.

During my ministry, I have served on the volunteer fire department, driven a tractor during spring planting for a local farmer who suffered a broken leg, helped with the harvest, served on a strategic planning committee for the local school, and served as a chaplain for the local police department. I learned early on that to be effective in the rural community, one has to be part of the community. In many rural areas, resources are limited. Professional counselors—especially those who have a Christian worldview—are often not accessible for rural people. Social services, while improving, are still lacking. As a result, they turn to the pastor to fill the gaps.

The same is true for the church. The church is not just a theological institution existing in an ecclesiastical world. The church exists in the real world, in a local community. It is surrounded by real people who face real struggles and issues in their lives, whether it be poverty, racism, or the daily struggles of life. How we engage the community and the people who live in it will reveal our theology far more than words in a church constitution ever could. The previous chapters about race and poverty are not just statistics and sociological mumbo jumbo, but are real issues affecting people on a daily level, both in our community and in the church. To minister to people, we have to become involved in the community by engaging people and structures to address people's physical, emotional, social, and economic struggles as a means of gaining a hearing to address their most important need: the redemptive work of Christ.

The Church, Mission, Community

A quick perusal of books on the church reveals an agreement about the ultimate mission of the church set forth by the Great Commission: to go into all the world and make disciples (Matt. 28:19–20). While the overarching mission remains clear, the process we use to engage our world with the gospel quickly becomes muddled. For some, the strategy is to create a fortress so we can protect ourselves from the corrupting effects of the world, and so people will see the difference and come join us. For others, it is about abandoning the church altogether and just "being real." Still, others see the gospel only from the standpoint of personal and societal freedom. Some see only a God of love who embraces us without any real demands for complete transformation.

Christ, however, provides clarity when He defines what a true disciple is. In John 14, He repeatedly states that a genuine disciple is one who is in a personal relationship with Him, which is manifested by uncompromising obedience to His word (vv. 21, 23–24). True disciples refuse to conform to the morality and worldview of society and culture and instead seek to be transformed so that they are conforming their moral ethos and worldview to the will of God as revealed in Scripture (see Rom. 12:1–2). Anything short of making such disciples fails to embrace the mission assigned to us.[1]

The Church and the Gospel

The gospel is inherently relational. At the center of the gospel is both a doctrinal creed as well as a message of redemption that impacts our relationship with God and relationships with others. The heart and center of the gospel includes the deliverance of humanity from the clutches of hell, sin, and death, and God's restoration of fallen and alienated people back into relational fellowship with Him. It is about the devastation of sin, the divine abhorrence of all that is evil, the isolation of humanity from God, and the remedy that brings us back into a personal relationship with Him through the substitutionary atonement of Christ. It is about a personal transformation where we become more and more identified with and conformed to the person and character of Christ.

Because the gospel is inherently relational, it is not surprising that it is also about the restoration of people to one another. To accept the gospel message is to be placed into a community of believers marked by mutual identification, responsibility, and care. As a Trinitarian God, the three persons of the Trinity exist in eternal fellowship with one another. This internal mutual relationship finds its visible expression in the church as the body of Christ. The unity and mutual interdependency of the church provides the earthly expression of the triune God.

The gospel provides the foundation for racial reconciliation. The church is not just a model of community, it is to be a model of racial reconciliation as we recognize the image of God within all people. God's redemptive plan includes all races and is the same for all people. As Piper points out, "God's concern to include all the ethnic peoples of the world in his saving purposes—in his final, eternal family—is unbreakably linked with the two greatest realities in the universe: God's very being as one God and the way God has ordained to put sinners in the right with himself through justification in Christ."[2] God created all people, imprinted His divine image on all humanity, and established one plan for all races to be reconciled back to Him and one another.

The Church and the Community

If we divorce the gospel from relationships, whether it be with God or others, we remove the heart of the gospel and thus empty its meaning and redemptive power. Through relationships, we connect the gospel to the community. As Rockwell Smith rightly summarizes,

> First of all, the local community is the world which the church faces, with which it is hopefully engaged in a redemptive work. The world is more—much more—than the local community, but it is in the local community that contact with the world begins. Unless we are making a real and significant contact with men and women—all kinds of men and women—in the local community, we shall have precious little chance of

making an impact of any kind upon the larger world of which our community is part.[3]

The church can make an impact in the community only when it engages people through the daily activities of life. This involves being both active and visible as well as serving the needs of others. A healthy congregation is one where people actively serve one another and the church looks for opportunities to serve the community. In 1911, G. Walter Fiske, Junior Dean of Oberlin Theological Seminary, rightly pointed out, "The country church has become decadent where it has ceased to serve its community; and it may find its largest life again in the broadest kind of sacrificial service."[4] Over a hundred years later, this statement still rings true. The importance of community involvement cannot be overstated for rural ministries. It builds the relational connections that become the basis for evangelism. It establishes a visible testimony to the validity of the gospel and the reality of God's love for the world.

Community involvement is essential not only to the health of the church, but also to the work of the pastor. In rural ministry, the pastor is seen as the shepherd not solely of the local congregation, but of the whole community as well. People will introduce me as "their pastor" even though they may never visit my church. In times of crisis, rural people looking for spiritual, emotional, and moral guidance will often turn to the pastor. A pastor who has a heart for the community will strive to become integrated into the whole community, to serve the spiritual needs of people regardless of whether they attend the church.[5]

The Church and the Needs of People

As He prays for His disciples, Christ states to the Father, "I do not ask You to take them out of the world, but keep them from the evil one. . . . As you sent Me into the world, I also have sent them into the world" (John 17:15, 18). According to Jesus, the mission of the church is not accomplished in isolation from the world or *in absentia*. Rather, the mission He assigned us can be accomplished only as we interact with people. This begins by ministering to the physical, emotional, and spiritual needs of others (Gal. 6:10). Rather than responding to persecution with evil, we are to demonstrate love in tangible ways (1 Peter 3:9–18). This involves helping the poor, promoting justice for the immigrant, and providing for those most vulnerable to economic and emotional distress (the widows and orphans; see James 1:27).[6] The church is responsible for upholding their rights and caring for them. But this is not social action merely for the sake of social justice. Rather, it is how the people of God reach others with the redemptive gospel of Christ. When we minister to the needs of people, we give tangible evidence of Christ's love for the world.

The Danger of Isolation

As society becomes increasingly secular, the church is increasingly tempted to remain inside the walls of its building. Freedom of religion has been redefined from the freedom to worship and live one's religious values in all aspects of life to the freedom to worship only in the confines of the church walls. One's faith may be expressed privately but needs to stay outside the public sphere. This pressure is being exerted not only on the individual Christian, but on the larger church as well. In response, we face the temptation of retreating from the public arena.

The danger of isolation has been a struggle for the evangelical church, which has tended to emphasize personal redemption at the cost of undermining community involvement. Robert Wuthnow contrasts the civic involvement of mainline churches and evangelical churches: "Whereas the mainline churches participated in progressive social betterment programs during the first half of the twentieth century, evangelical churches focused more on individual piety."[7] While evangelicals became involved in the Right to Life movement, in other areas they focused more upon involvement in the local church rather than community issues. As a result, the church is becoming less involved in addressing social issues. Rather than being part of the community, the evangelical church withdrew.[8] The church became introverted, more concerned about theological correctness and internal ministries than serving the community. Wuthnow also states, "They do not cooperate with other churches nor with community welfare agencies. Usually they are unconcerned with effective means of community outreach. They are in effect 'little islands of holiness in a great sea of worldliness,' and they have very little impact on this 'sea of worldliness.'"[9]

By withdrawing, the church not only fails to be the salt of the earth by restraining the corrupting effects of sin, but loses the ability to be the light as well. When Christ calls us to be a light to the world, He teaches that our radiance consists of "good works" that bring glory to the Father (Matt. 5:14–16). If we are to reach our community with the gospel, we must first have a "concern for all the people in the community. Not only the people at the center, but those at the periphery need to be served. The rich, the poor, the newcomer, the old-timer, the business man, the factory worker, the young, the old, the hardened reprobate, and the saint; those all are the concern of the church."[10] This cannot happen if we stay within the walls of the church and minister only to ourselves, where we become professional navel gazers. When we disengage, we lose our passion and compassion for the lost. When a church abandons its involvement in the community, it loses the ability to connect with the problems of others. The struggles of poverty, race, and the collapse of the family become cold and detached statistics rather than real problems confronting real people. A church isolated from the community will have little influence in the community. This is especially true in rural areas, where rural people value and judge both individuals and institutions by their contribution to the well-being of the whole community. Being a part of the community involves more than just developing social programs; it requires spending time getting to know people, shopping locally rather than regionally, eating at the local restaurants, and being visible at the local sporting events.[11]

The Church and Social Capital

Being part of the community involves providing social capital. Every community possesses assets contributing to the health, well-being, success, and sustainability of the community. These include *natural capital* (the natural resources), *cultural capital* (the values and symbols defining the culture), *human capital* (the education, skills, knowledge, and abilities of the people), *political capital* (organizations, connections, and powerbrokers within the community to enforce shared values), and *economic capital* (the wealth and income available for the community).[12] Along with each of these assets, there is *social capital* enabling people and groups to work and cooperate for the betterment of the community. Robert Putnam describes social capital as "connections among individuals—social networks and the norms of reciprocity and trustworthiness that arise from them."[13] In other words, when we speak of the social capital, we refer to the social relationships between people within the community that enable them to develop a sense of mutual trust so that both people and organizations can cooperate with one another toward mutually beneficial goals.[14] For example, social capital enables different groups—such as the PTA, the Lions, and the local churches—to work together to build a safer playground in the local park. This trust is based on the existing relationships between people within the organizations enabling them to work together.

Building mutual trust and cooperation involves a willingness to participate on two separate levels of social capital. The first is *bonding capital*, which involves working together with others of similar backgrounds and values to achieve a common purpose.[15] This would include churches working together to address moral issues within the community.

By banding together, they can have a greater voice in addressing community concerns.

The second is *bridging capital*, which involves diverse groups working together within the community as well as connecting with groups and organizations outside the community to address specific issues. Bridging social capital fosters diversity of ideas and brings together diverse people.[16] Putnam describes the difference between bonding and bridging capital this way: "bonding social capital constitutes a kind of sociological superglue, whereas bridging social capital provides a sociological WD-40."[17] That is, bonding capital fosters and strengthens bonds between churches within the community, while bridging capital enables churches to work with other organizations that may not share the same values but have a common interest in the specific issues. Thus, the church may not share the same values with the PTA, but it does share the same desire to see safer playground equipment. While bonding capital focuses more upon shared norms and values, bridging capital centers on specific issues and tasks. Without these social capitals existing within the community, the community lacks the structures necessary to bring about effective and substantive change for the betterment of people.[18]

Rural communities often lack the resources to deal with the issues confronting people, especially those most at risk. They lack the governmental resources to address poverty and the lack of educational opportunities for children. Those who face emotional struggles and/ or domestic violence often find themselves unable to obtain assistance. Thus, by banding together various organizations and people, the community can address the issues that would otherwise remain untouched.

All this brings us back to the church. One of the most important sources for building effective social capital in the community is the church. Putnam argues that "faith communities in which people worship together are arguably the single most important repository of social capital in America."[19] The church is the fertile soil that encourages community involvement and the building of trust. People who attend the church are more likely than others to visit with people and be involved in the various organizations and groups within the community. Further, their participation within the church provides important practical experience enabling them to become leaders in the community as well.[20] The church has historically provided the groundwork for social service and action. For many rural communities, the health and well-being of the community is intimately connected to the health and well-being of the local church, so that when the church declines, rural communities often struggle to survive as well.[21] When disaster strikes a community, the community often looks to the church, as well as to police and emergency services, to be the first line of assistance in helping meet the immediate needs of people. But the social service of the church extends beyond that as well. Rural people often look to the church to provide help for those who are confronting "personal and family crisis, illness, disability, chronic pain, serious accidents, disaster, caregiving, loss of loved ones, and substance abuse."[22]

While some may argue that such social action is a distraction from the mission of the church, it stands at the center, in fact. As we have already pointed out, the gospel is grounded in relationships and gaining a hearing to share the gospel. And we can gain a hearing only if we develop trust. In an age of religious hucksters and secularization, people are suspicious of the church. In the minds of many, the church is either a gathering of bigots or charlatans peddling religion to pad their personal pocketbook. While we might decry such mischaracterizations, we can overcome the obstacles facing us only by building relationships that develop trust and respect. This comes by being a part of the community and utilizing the social capital we possess to demonstrate the love of Christ in a tangible way, so that we can build the necessary trust we need to effectively share the gospel.

Again, what was said over a hundred years ago is relevant today: "the time has arrived when some church body, or some conference made up of representatives of church bodies, ought to make a careful study of the needs and conditions of our average rural communities in America, for the purpose of outlining in a general way, a practical plan of cooperation among country churches."[23] But this cooperation extends beyond just the local churches. To address the struggles of real people in ways that open avenues by which the gospel can be both demonstrated and communicated, it will involve the cooperation of rural and urban churches. The crisis confronting rural communities cannot be solved by one church, or even by a few churches. Just as the crisis of the inner city required the involvement and assistance of the suburban (and rural) church, so also the rural church needs the help of the urban church. The crisis of depression and drug abuse requires trained counselors to address the underlying problems, yet rural churches and communities do not have as much access to professional counselors. By making their staff counselors available to rural communities, the urban church can partner with the rural church to bring both emotional and spiritual healing to people in rural communities. To address these issues, denominations and church leaders can develop strategic plans of cooperation where the resources and involvement of the urban church can assist rural churches in addressing the social crises found in the forgotten places of America.

The Dark Side of Social Capital

Entering the arena of social capital is not without its risks and challenges. Community involvement can become messy. To be part of a community involves working with people and organizations with whom we have fundamental disagreements. The challenge is to work with diverse groups while still upholding biblical truth. Further, there is pressure to "check your faith at the door." For many, social capital is synonymous with inclusion, where we not only respect our differences but also accept those differences. To stand against moral decline is to be labeled a bigot. In other words, people want the church to address the social ills of poverty and race, but remain silent on the moral issues confronting us today. For example, Putnam writes, "So I challenge America's clergy, lay leaders, theologians, and ordinary worshipers: *Let us spur a new, pluralistic, socially responsible 'great awakening,' so that by 2010 Americans will be more deeply engaged than we are today in one or another spiritual community of meaning, while at the same time becoming more tolerant of the faiths and practices of other Americans.*"[24] In other words, promote social responsibility with us but do not try to convert us or challenge our morality.

This misses the most important contribution of the church to the community's social well-being. We are to be salt, standing against the moral decline threatening America and destroying the lives of people. Many today want the church to be part of the social capital without exerting any moral influence, but this is the one responsibility that stands at the heart of the church's involvement in the community. We are to work to help the poor and dismantle both individual and structural racism in our country. But we are also to stand against the sexual revolution that has sought to redefine marriage and ultimately undermine the very foundation of society itself. We also can provide help for those suffering from depression, drug addiction, and family breakdowns.

But this raises the question regarding how we should engage our communities. The key is to be involved where we can set aside differences with others while still promoting community good and disassociate from those activities that promote morality and norms that contradict Scripture. For example, we may work with the local welfare department to promote feeding the poor—a shared value that corresponds to biblical values—but decline to participate in their child development program that includes teaching kids a worldview contrary to Scripture.

Developing a Strategic
Plan for Community Involvement

Ministry in the community begins by developing strategic partnerships with other organizations and churches to meet existing needs within the community. While the goal always remains the preaching of the gospel and building of God's kingdom, an important part of the process involves ministering to the needs of people. Our involvement reveals our genuine love for people and the community. A church isolating itself within its own walls will soon develop a reputation as a closed and uncaring church and will do little to attract new people. It should not escape our notice that in ministering to the spiritual needs of people, Christ often ministered to their physical needs first.

Perhaps one of the most perplexing miracles was when Jesus healed the ten lepers (Luke 17:11–19). The event is often used by preachers to point out the importance of gratitude and the dangers of using God as a tool to obtain what we want. While this is indeed central to the passage, we often miss another important message in the story. The question we often fail to ask is, "Why did Jesus heal the other nine?" Even though Jesus knew that only one would respond with genuine faith to His healing work, He still willingly healed the other nine. Throughout His ministry, Christ healed people not based upon the worthiness of their response, but solely upon their need and His love for them. During my ministry as a part of the local ministerial association, we have helped hundreds of people by providing lodging, food, a tank of gas, or a payment of their utility bill. While they all say that they will repay us, I have never had a single person come to the church in gratitude for our help. Rather, the opposite has at times been the case. Instead of showing gratitude, I have had people become angry that we have not done more for them. But our service to the community should never be based upon their response. Rather, it should be based upon their need, for in doing so, we follow the model set forth by Christ.

When we serve the needs of others, both within the church and within the community, we demonstrate the unconditional love of Christ in tangible ways that open doors for a discussion of a greater need—the need for the gospel of Christ.

This is also true of the pastor. When the pastor becomes involved in community activities and social action, it yields two important benefits.[25] First, being involved in the community raises the visibility of the church. When they see the pastor involved, they become more aware of the church's presence in the community. Second, by helping to address the needs of the community, the pastor gains a better understanding of the people in the community. A pastor has to learn and understand the history, culture, and struggles of the people within the community. The greater his understanding, the more effective his ministry will be.

Essentials of Community Involvement

Presence. The first step in addressing the challenges and opportunities of rural communities is being present. The incarnation of Christ reveals the importance of presence. When Christ came to earth, He didn't come just to die on the cross, but to dwell in the world of humanity and reveal the Father to all (John 1:14). When Christ ascended, He left the church to be His visible presence in the world. This begins with the pastor and the local church as visible members of the community. The pastor is seen at local events, frequents the coffee shop where he can visit with people, and is involved in community activities such as the local fair or founders' day. The church is present by its people being involved in various organizations within the community, such as coaching local baseball and soccer teams, serving as board members for the local museum, and becoming involved in social services. But the pastor is only the "boots on the ground." The pastor and the congregants are only the connecting link to the broader church community, and it is the larger church community that can more fully address the issues confronting people in the community.

Prioritize. The rural church has limited resources—both time and money. We cannot solve all the problems challenging rural people, but we can help in some areas. Therefore, it is important to intentionally identify and work on the areas having the greatest impact in the lives of people and for the gospel. While we may not be able to solve all the economic problems in an impoverished area, we can, for example, help provide school supplies and clothing for the children of poor families.[26] But here again, the urban church can provide crucial assistance. Once the local congregation identifies specific issues confronting the members of the community, it can network with denominational leaders or other larger ministries to identify additional organizations and resources to meet those needs. By involving other churches outside the community, the church can increase both its resources and volunteer base. By doing so, the local church is able to meet needs that it could not meet individually.

Plan. Identify how to become involved. Mark Rich identifies three levels of involvement in community activities: "The church may invite agencies to share in church programs and services; the church and agencies may cooperate in joint projects; the church may lend a hand to agencies in carrying out their programs."[27] Other levels of involvement would include working with other churches to address needs or to recruit and work with outside agencies to address issues. The rural church can work with other churches, both within the community and in urban centers, to then help in the planning and implementation of programs designed to address the needs of people. Because the local church knows not only the needs of people but also the culture and resources, they can work with the broader church community to develop and implement effective strategic plans.

Protect. As the pastor and church become involved in social action, we need to also protect the mission and theology of the church. At no point should our involvement within the community result in a compromise of our beliefs and values. As we work with others, we need to be careful that our actions and involvement do not bring disrepute to the cause of Christ. This involves honesty and openness about our convictions, while at the same time respecting those who do not share our values. This does not mean that every group we cooperate with needs to share our values, but that in the process of meeting the needs of people, we should not undermine biblical truth. When the urban church seeks to become involved in rural social problems, it should work with the local churches so that the testimony of the local congregations, as well as the testimony of the gospel in the community, is safeguarded. Another reason they need to work with the local church is that the local church has a better understanding of the local nuances and how actions will be interpreted by the local people. Consequently, the local church needs to serve as the liaison between the groups seeking to help and the community itself so that what we do, why we are doing it, and how we are doing it properly convey our theology and the character of Christ within that specific culture.

This brings us back to the heart of the gospel. While the gospel is ultimately centered upon personal redemption, we gain a hearing by how we respond to the personal needs of people. Just as Jack Higgins earned the respect of the loggers of the Northwoods by demonstrating personal care for them, so we gain a hearing for the gospel through our love and compassion toward people. While social action should never replace the gospel as the goal of the church, the gospel cannot be divorced from it.

Developing a Theology of Rural Ministry

AS A RURAL PASTOR, I often wonder what it would be like to pastor a large church with multiple staff members and dynamic programs. I've always dreamed of the day when we would have enough people to have vibrant programs for everyone; enough young families with small children so that we could easily draw new families; a full worship team so if one family moves away, we are not left scrambling to find someone else to lead worship. But best of all would be having an associate who would buttress my administrative weakness. I would have a sense of validation for my ministry, that in the end, I have made a difference. To pastor a rural church is always to struggle with having enough people, resources, and programs. To pastor in rural communities is to live in the realm of obscurity and frustration, to always live with a sense of futility in ministry.

But each Sunday, as I stand before the small congregation, I am reminded that for these people, the task I do is just as important to them as it would be to the thousands in a mass auditorium. The call to ministry is not a call to generic masses. It is a call to serve, disciple, and pastor individuals, whether eighty or eight thousand gathered in one place at one time. The gospel was not given to masses and societies to corporately become a "Christian nation." The gospel is for individuals. It presents them with the decision to accept the redemptive work of Christ, a decision that each person must make freely and unconstrained.

After serving in rural congregations for over thirty years, I have learned the importance of having a strong biblical theology of rural ministry. To serve faithfully in a rural church without merely viewing it as a stepping stone for a larger urban church, you have to be grounded in your understanding of the biblical theology of the church. But this is not easily kept in perspective.

Overcoming the Urban Bias

Many classes on church leadership assume that the student will be serving in a multi-staff church. Because few professors in seminaries or Bible colleges have extensive experience in rural ministry, the courses are taught from an urban perspective. Rural ministry is often not even on the radar. Even when it is, it is typically viewed as a dead end for any up-and-coming pastor. Seminaries and Bible colleges, by their very nature, desire to be on the cutting edge of ministry, and the rural church is anything but that. Consequently, there arises an urban bias that looks down upon rural ministry. Don't get me wrong. I'm not suggesting this is deliberate. It's just that most Bible colleges and seminaries exist in urban areas, so there is a natural tendency to see Scripture and ministry through an urban lens, for that is the world in which they live. But that world is not my world or the world of rural ministry.

As our culture moved from an agrarian society to an urban society, the focus naturally shifted to the need for urban ministries. As a result, training institutions, denominations, and literature focused more and more on urban ministry. Even in the early twentieth century, some saw that the rural church was being neglected, and so they helped to establish the Rural Church Movement. Edwin Earp highlighted this trend in 1918 when he wrote, "As a result the whole missionary movement, for a generation or two, was directed to the cities rather than to the rural populations of the world's mission field."[1] The trend continued throughout the twentieth century, so that in the early 1960s, an article published by the National Association of Evangelicals stated,

It is not an entirely undesirable condition that thousands of our open country and village churches have been closed. There are declining populations in most rural communities. Improved transportation makes it possible for rural people to travel fifteen or more miles to church in less time than it takes many city people to go by bus or automobile to their churches. A general centralization of rural institutions in the larger villages and towns appears to be taking place today. It is only sensible to use the material things God has entrusted to us in the most efficient way. Instead of continuing to support small rural churches with missionary funds and part-time pastors who can provide only the most meager services for their people, we will do well whenever it is possible to merge these small churches into larger units which can carry on the work of Christ in a most effective and less costly way.[2]

Little has changed in the subsequent years. Read books on church planting and church missions, and you'll find the focus is on urban areas. Using Acts as the model, missiologists argue that the pattern of Paul—and thus the pattern that we should follow today—was to focus on urban areas. Thus, David Hesselgrave writes, "Paul gave priority to establishing churches in strategically located cities. . . . In church-extension evangelism there is much to be said for giving a certain priority to cities."[3] Even when he mentions rural areas, he makes it clear that cities should be given the clear priority: "Though the need of peoples in rural areas is not to be overlooked, it does seem that the increased attention being given to urban centers—and especially to large cities—is warranted if for no other reason than their sociological significance."[4] In other words, while we should not forget rural areas, if you really want to have a significant ministry, do not go west, young man; go to the cities. So also, Aubrey Malphurs precludes any rural church planting when he suggests that to start a church, a church planter should have at least fifty to a hundred adults before the church goes public.[5] Well, that wouldn't work in rural America.

Stephen Um and Justin Buzzard, in *Why Cities Matter*, a book recommended by prominent Christian leaders, take it a step further. They argue that the redemptive plan of God is urban focused. From their perspective, the plan of God for humanity from the outset was "ultimately an urban mandate, a call to create settlements where people could live and work together to be fruitful, to multiply, to develop, to cultivate, and to flourish."[6] For them, this focus upon urbanization has Trinitarian implications, where cities fully express the community enjoyed between the three members of the Godhead.[7] They find support in Timothy Keller who likewise writes, "The New Jerusalem . . . is the Garden of Eden, remade. The City is the fulfillment of the purposes of the Eden of God. We began in a garden but will end in a city; God's purpose for humanity is urban!"[8] In this line of thinking, the Garden of Eden becomes a city rather than an agrarian setting.[9] For those of us who love and live in rural areas, the Garden of Eden loses its appeal. There's a reason that I never pastored an urban church. I would have gladly done so if it were in a rural setting!

Pete Nicholas likewise sees Genesis 4:20–22 as a mandate for the priority for cities in that they are of central importance to God's plan to "be fruitful and multiply," and of proclivity and cultural development. Even though we should not exclude rural areas, "the church as a whole should have a focus on urban areas."[10]

Um and Buzzard also see the city as the focal point of Christ's ministry. They conclude that even though Jesus began His ministry in a rural setting, the city was His ultimate goal: "To recognize the centrality of the city of Jerusalem for Jesus's ministry is not to deny or undervalue his ministry in rural and presuburban settings, it is simply to acknowledge the shape of his ministry as it is presented in Scripture. As we will see, in Jesus, God's commitment to the city is at its peak."[11]

If all this is what the evangelical community is focusing on, it's no wonder that young pastors are avoiding the rural church like the plague. Why go to the rural church when God's plan is ultimately for the city? If God's plan for humanity is urbanization, we should send pastors and missionaries into the cities. Again, let me affirm that I believe wholeheartedly that we desperately need healthy churches and ministries in urban areas. And I appreciate the passion that Um and Buzzard have. They write an important book outlining the need for ministry in urban areas. But we need to move beyond the urban bias and see that God's plan is *both* urban and rural, and that He desperately desires to build His kingdom in both the city and country, to the ends of the earth.

While much of the book of Acts focuses on events in urban centers, it's a mistake to think that Paul focused only on cities. In 14:6–7, we find that Paul also went into the surrounding region to proclaim the gospel. The Greek term translated "surrounding country" means "'the region around' or 'the people living around them.' When Paul and Barnabas left Iconium, they preached not only in the cities of Lystra and Derbe but evidently also in the towns and villages controlled by these two cities."[12] Likewise, when Paul describes his ministry to King Agrippa in Acts 26:19–20, he mentions that he spent time in the "region of Judea," which no doubt includes the countryside. After his conversion, he preached not only in Jerusalem, but also in the smaller towns and villages of Judea.[13] Does God desire urban people to come to Him? Absolutely! Does God place a higher priority on cities? Absolutely not! Both cities and rural areas play an important part in God's redemptive history and plan.

Developing a Rural Church Theology

All throughout Scripture, we find the story of rural people. The Bible is a story of farmers and ranchers, of shepherds and vineyard owners. It should not surprise us that God even refers to the Messiah in rural terminology, speaking of Him as the Shepherd of His people. When Christ came as the Messiah, His coming was couched in rural terms, and His ministry was conducted in the rural plains of Galilee.

Rural People and the Ministry of Christ

It's not by accident that Christ was born in a small rural village and that the first visitors to pay homage were rural shepherds. But shepherds were not the romanticized people we often make them out to be. They were despised by their own people, regarded as untrustworthy. They were generally considered to be thieves who took advantage of others.[14] They stood in stark contrast to the wealth and nobility of the wise men. In choosing to announce the birth of Christ to the shepherds and wise men, God provides representatives from the full scope of humanity. These two groups represented the poor and the rich, the elite of society and the dregs of society, the near and those distant, Gentiles and Jews, urban and rural. It was in the shepherds that we discover God's heart for the rural people.

Not only was Christ born in the rural area of Bethlehem, but His family eventually made their home in the rural hillside of Nazareth, where an estimated four hundred people lived. It was a small, nondescript rural community where people made their living by tending vineyards, agriculture, and livestock. Although it was overshadowed by the Greek city of Sepphoris, which was the capital of Herod Antipas, it remained traditional and fully Jewish. It was a tiny, poor, country village that was ignored by the rest of Israel. Nathaniel, an urbanite, considered Nazareth to be unsophisticated and the unlikely place from which anyone of significance would arise.[15]

With deep roots in a rural community, it's no wonder that Jesus spent the bulk of His time and ministry with rural people. In Matthew 9:35, we find that Jesus went throughout the area teaching in the cities and villages. According to Johannes Louw and Eugene Nida, a city served as an important population center walled with gates and provided economic significance and political authority over the surrounding area, whereas the village was an insignificant population center lacking any walled protection.[16] In contrast to Paul's strategy in Acts, Christ spent the bulk of His time and ministry in the rural areas and small villages of Galilee. In the ministry of Christ, there was not a preference to urban or rural; both received His attention.[17] When Christ told the disciples to look up and see the fields white unto harvest, He was looking at both the rural and urban people that were gathered around Him. Christ did not see a world where city is more strategically important than country. No, He saw individuals who needed a shepherd. Consequently, it should not be a surprise to the reader that when Christ sent His disciples out to minister, He sent them to both urban and rural places (Matt. 10:11).

Rural People and the Teaching of Christ

The teaching of Christ clearly reflected the rural background of the people. Rather than speaking in metropolitan terms, He spoke parables tied to the land and the farmers and shepherds who cultivated it. The parables of the sower, the vineyard, the tares, the dragnet, and others were all directed toward and understood by rural people who lived on and worked the land and sea.

Growing up in a rural area, Christ understood and spoke in a language they understood. Yet even in a modern world, the parables in which Christ communicated need little explanation for those who live in rural communities and work the land and care for livestock. While a person from the city may be confused regarding the difference between the wheat and the tares, a farmer fully understands the story. Tares not only are worthless and unproductive, but also are virtually indistinguishable from the wheat until the seed is formed. The warning of the landowner to leave the tares lest they destroy the grain as well makes perfect sense to farmers.

But the parables not only spoke in the language of rural people, they also served to remind the people of their value to God. The parable of the lost sheep reminds us that all people are equally important to God. The point of the parable is that the person who is lost is more significant than just the masses, that God does not look at numbers, but sees individuals. The argument often given in support of urban ministries is that cities are where most people live and thus that there we will see greater results. But the parable of the lost sheep reminds us that everyone is treasured and that the focus of missions should never be about the crowds but about the person. The work of the missionary who labors for decades for one convert is just as important as the work of the missionary who sees thousands come to Christ. In God's economy, the one is just as important as the many. Although 83 percent of Americans live in urban areas, it is not a waste to seek to reach the 17 percent of the nation's population who live in the countryside. It has never been about numbers, but always about individuals in need of God's redemptive grace.

The importance of each individual is likewise illustrated for us in the book of Acts. Even as Philip was enjoying profound success in proclaiming the gospel to the people of Samaria, God directed him to leave the city and head into the wilderness. One can imagine the confusion Philip might have felt. The sage fisherman never leaves fish to find fish, so why leave a productive ministry in the city to head into the isolated desert where there were no people? This was something Philip would not have done himself, but God supernaturally intervened because one person, an Ethiopian, was searching the Scriptures and needed someone to guide him. So God sent Philip to teach him. After the work was complete, the Holy Spirit guided him to another area, Azotus. The one is just as important as the many. The priority is not where people live, but where there is a person in need of the gospel. Thus, the priority is on both urban and rural ministry.

Rural Ministry and the Theology and History of the Church

In an age of the supermarket, Wal-Mart Supercenter, and superchurch, the rural church seems archaic and second-rate. What William Willimon and Robert Wilson state regarding small churches can easily be said of rural churches as well: "People also have a gnawing feeling that the small church is somehow second-rate and does not quite measure up to what it ought to be in today's world. Other persons, particularly the clergy and denominational leaders, view the small church as an anachronism, kept alive by stubborn people who are holding onto an institution that should be allowed or even encouraged to die."[18] The answer for some, then, is to bring the city to the country by establishing regional large churches. Leith Anderson argues, "We need Wal-Mart churches: churches that will serve regional rural markets; churches that are friendly, carry lots of programs, are customer-driven rather than institution-driven; churches that transcend the deep traditions of small communities and give permission to worship without alienating family histories and relationships."[19] If we cannot get the boy off the farm, then let's try to get the farm out of the boy. If we cannot get rural people into the city, let's at least get them to adopt the corporate model of urban churches. But this undermines the very nature of the church. As Ruth Tucker warns, "Church represents many things, but every church ought to be a community of believers seeking God and sometimes finding

God in *the least of these* among the poor and needy—people who may be in the congregation or out in the neighborhood."[20] The fact that small churches are present in small rural communities is precisely what makes them effective. We need to remember that in God's program there exists a paradox: the great become the least, and the least becomes the great. Not only do we find that rural people are important to the plan of God; when we examine the biblical theology of the church, we discover that it encompasses the nature and ministry of the rural church as well.

God Calls the Rural Church to Accomplish the Great

The rural church has value because God is the one who uses the rural church to accomplish His purpose. Often, we regard the rural church as insignificant because it is small. Because it has few people and is little known, we dismiss it as being irrelevant. God, on the other hand, is one who takes what the world regards as insignificant and uses it to accomplish His eternal purpose. He used a handful of believers who fearfully gathered in Jerusalem to turn the world upside down for the cause of Christ. Even when this was occurring, what caused people to marvel at the growth of the early church was not the eloquence and charisma of its leaders, but the fact that the individuals leading this groundswell of growth were "unschooled, ordinary men" (Acts 4:13 NIV).

Christ used a small boy with a small lunch to feed a crowd of five thousand. He used an army of three hundred men armed with clay pots, trumpets, and torches to defeat a vast army of Midianites that outnumbered them 450 to 1. God's view of the small is revealed in Deuteronomy 7:7–8, where we discover it was not the greatness of Israel that led to God's selection of them to be His people, but their smallness and insignificance. David Ray rightly points out, "The small church can easily develop an inferiority complex when it measures itself by contemporary standards of success. If it chooses to measure itself by biblical criteria, however, it may find itself being affirmed, worthy, legitimate. Its small size does not guarantee legitimacy, but it cannot be the criteria for damnation or ridicule. Size has nothing to do with the biblical marks of the church."[21] This is equally true of the rural church. Neither size nor location has anything to do with God's redemptive program. Greatness is not defined by growth and numbers but by personal transformation leading to a faith visible to the world in which we live. What better place to have our faith most clearly demonstrated than the rural community where everyone knows who we are and what we believe.

God Used the Rural Church throughout History

As we look at the establishment of the church in the first century, many churches became large even by the modern measure. What we do not see is the growth of the church in the rural communities. Along with the large church in Jerusalem, we find small congregations meeting in house churches (see 2 John 10, for example). If urbanization is a recent phenomenon, then the church has been maintained and perpetuated by rural churches down through history. While we should not overlook the contribution that larger churches have made, we can also recognize the important role of the rural church for the next generation. The rural church has sent a significant number of missionaries and pastors from their midst who have extended the ministry of the rural church far beyond the walls of the church. In many ways, the present health of the church in the world is built upon the shoulders of the small rural congregations who escape the notice of church historians.

God Calls Church Leadership to a Shepherding Ministry

While the church has learned much from the secular community regarding leadership and organizational structuring, and vice versa, we must recognize the fundamental difference between church leadership and secular leadership. Secular leadership focuses upon *organizational* health and growth. Within the biblical model, however, the pastor is not called just to be a leader in an organizational sense. Rather, the pastor is called to be a shepherd who cares for, nurtures, and encourages the people within the congregation (1 Peter 5:2). Pastors are responsible for providing spiritual oversight to the congregation, teaching and instructing them in biblical truth, correcting sinful behavior, and moving the people individually and corporately toward spiritual maturity. We must do more than just run the church; we must place the needs of the congregation above our own agenda and search for those who wander from the truth (Ezek. 34:1–10). The strength of the rural church is found in rural pastors who provide personalized and specialized care. Because they know each person, they can effectively minister individually to them. What large urban churches struggle to do, the rural church does instinctively. It develops a community where people nurture and care for one another in their spiritual growth.[22] For example, when someone has been absent from our church for several Sundays, it's not uncommon for people within the congregation to call them to find out where they have been.

God Calls Us to Service, Not Success

Crucial to our theology of ministry is realizing that we are not called to success, but to a life of service, the foundation of which is faithfulness. The parable of the unfaithful steward (Matt. 25:14–30) reminds us that we will be judged, not by our outward results or accomplishments, but according to whether we faithfully fulfilled our duties and remained obedient to the leading of Christ. It should not escape our notice that the faithful individuals in the parable were rewarded equally, even though their results varied. Further, the service of a pastor is not defined by the secular model of business, but by the pursuit and fulfillment of God's purpose for our life and ministry. This purpose often differs greatly from our expectations. God often calls us to minister in situations where we may not see outward results (Ezek. 2–4). Often, we evaluate our ministry by our outward accomplishments, so when we do not see such results, we move on toward "greener pastures." However,

God's purpose may involve faithfully staying, so that in the end, the people, whether they respond or not, will know that a "prophet has been among them" (Ezek. 2:5). The joy of our ministry is not found in our achievements from an outward perspective. Nor is our joy found in the acceptance of people. Rather, our joy is found in the fulfillment of God's purpose for our life and ministry. This is what sustains us emotionally and spiritually (see John 3:27–30). As Kent and Barbara Hughes point out, "We found no place where it says that God's servants are called to be *successful*. Rather, we discovered our call is to be *faithful*."[23] The urban church is appealing for many reasons and offers the things we desire most: success and recognition. Yet the rural church only offers obscurity and "failure"—from the world's perspective. As Tucker points out, the only way to become a winner is by becoming a loser, by embracing a theology of failure where we give up our dreams to allow God to accomplish His dreams for us.[24]

God's Presence Determines the Success of the Church

In Ezra 3:11–13, we find the remnant who returned to the land facing an emotionally and spiritually charged crisis. As they began laying the foundation of the temple, those who had seen the glory of the previous temple were deeply lamenting its present appearance. The size and splendor of the new temple paled in comparison to the majestic temple that Solomon had built. Their words and response echoed the attitude often prevalent in the rural church, in which the glory of former years has become a millstone of defeat for the present. Often, the rural church, like the people of Israel, live in the past, talking about "how great it was back when," never fully appreciating or perceiving the work of God in their midst. Because of this lack of perception, Israel, like many small churches today, became discouraged, wondering whether God had abandoned them. Consequently, they stopped building, and the temple work remained dormant until the arrival of the prophet Haggai. It was Haggai who brought God's perspective to the minds of people by reminding them that the vitality and significance of the temple is found not in the size and activity of the temple but in the presence and activity of God (Hag. 2:1–9). What makes a church successful and effective is not how great it becomes or how many programs it operates, but the reality of God's presence in the life of the congregation, enabling it to pursue the will and purpose of God. When God is present and working, there is cause for joy, even in the rural church (see Zech. 4:10).

God Calls the Church to Build Relationships

Often, the ministry of the church becomes focused upon outward growth and the fulfillment of programs and visions. We measure the success of the church by external standards of growth, economic viability, and program development. When these do not occur, we become frustrated and discouraged. We become critical, casting blame on others for the failure to fulfill our expectations. Consequently, the church becomes mired in the muck of broken relationships as people point the finger at one another. Instead of working together to accomplish God's purpose, we become deeply divided over which program should be implemented and what specific forms should be put into operation within the church.

However, Scripture continually reminds us that the unity and health of the people of the church are more important than the strength and development of programs (see John 13:34–35). A church sacrificing unity for the sake of program development will become ineffective. This is not to say that programs and strategic planning are unimportant. They are. The danger for a church that has strong interpersonal relationships is that it can become a self-serving clique. While love begins within the congregation as people love each other, it also includes loving those outside the church.

Often, the strength of the rural church is the depth of relationships that people have with one another. Sadly, that same love is often not expressed toward those outside the church. Because people do not manifest their cultural expectations, they avoid or disassociate from them. However, we are called to love them as well, extending the love of Christ even to the most depraved of individuals. Here again we find the importance of mutual interaction between the urban and rural church. While the rural church can provide a helpful challenge to the urban church regarding the importance of people and not just programs, the urban church can provide a healthy balance to the rural church concerning the value of strategic evangelism and outreach.

God Does Not Follow a Specific Format

As certain church structures begin to dominate the ecclesiastical landscape, we often mistakenly think that a specific form is necessary for the church to be effective. However, as we examine Scripture and the establishment of the church, we discover that although the Bible has much to say about what the church is to be (a body of believers in fellowship with God and one another) and what the church is to do (be a witness for Christ in a spiritually dead world), very little is given regarding the format of the church. While we see hints of organizational structure, programs and forms, the only prescription given to the church is that it must have elders and deacons who are responsible for providing spiritual oversight for the congregation. Consequently, in the formation of our understanding of the church, we should caution against ascribing any specific format as necessary for the church if it is to be effective. Instead, we should strive to develop a culturally sensitive ministry that is responsive to the ministry opportunities confronting each congregation.

God Is Most Glorified When Our Weakness Is Most Evident

Today, the focus is often upon multitalented individuals who manifest an ability to efficiently organize the church and communicate effectively from the pulpit. For the average pastor, this focus becomes intimidating, as we hold ourselves up to the standard of the megachurch pastors who dominate the airwaves and religious landscape. We should recognize that the true effectiveness of the ministry is dependent not upon us or our abilities, but upon the sovereign and gracious work of God (1 Cor. 2:1–5). Rather than our weaknesses and inabilities being a hindrance, they become a springboard for ministry because they draw attention to God's activity rather than our skills. While this is never to be an excuse for laziness or a failure to sharpen our ministry skills, it should cause us to relax, knowing that the basis for effectiveness is found in God rather than ourselves.

The Rural Church Is Part of the Universal Body of Christ

The rural church is part of the universal body of Christ in which Christ is the head of the church. In ministry, it's easy to become microscopic in our focus by directing all our attention on what's happening within the walls of our individual church. We need to continually recognize the importance of being part of the universal body of Christ. This is not only the basis for missions and for thinking beyond our local ministry, but also the foundation for maintaining positive morale within the church. As part of the universal body of Christ, there are no unimportant members (1 Cor. 12). Every church, no matter the size or location, is important to the overall health of the body. As we have already seen, the broader church community can learn much from the rural church regarding the importance of a solid theological foundation, the value and nature of genuine community, and the importance of avoiding the entrapment of turning the church into a business.

God Desires All People to Come to Him

We should focus on rural ministry for no other reason than the command of Christ to go into all the world. Approximately sixty million people live in rural areas. If rural America was gathered together and formed into a separate nation, it would constitute the twenty-third largest country in the world. Harold Longenecker points out why we often overlook rural ministry:

> This, it appears would be a sufficiently loud call for an aggressive evangelistic program in rural America. However, the scattered nature of the population, which almost precludes the building of truly large churches, and the small size of the existing rural churches, has served to dampen the enthusiasm of many. Since our approaches to church ministry are geared to the larger church, the small ones continue with little assistance. Relatively few men will give themselves to a lifetime of service in a rural church.[25]

If we are to take seriously the Great Commission, then we must recognize the need for a renewed missionary effort to reach rural America. If we are more concerned about numbers and recognition than we are about lost individuals, then we have forgotten the nature of the gospel. Longenecker continues, "In America's small towns and rural areas, there is still need for those who are prepared to take the gospel at whatever personal cost, by whatever possible means, and thus to form a local fellowship of believers that will stand as a permanent witness to God and His grace."[26] Perhaps the greatest indictment against the American church is that we have failed to carry out the Great Commission by abandoning those in the forgotten places. The Great Commission is not about success, accomplishments, and recognition, but about taking the gospel to each individual, wherever that individual might be.

The Importance of Applied Theology

It's one thing to affirm and clarify our theology, and it's quite another thing to live by our theology so that it shapes and guides our ministry. To understand the theology of the rural church begins by putting it in the context of rural people. For Andrew (not his real name), the value and importance of the rural ministry is not a hypothetical question. It's a life-changing reality.

Like many children in rural areas, Andrew's home life was marked by drugs and alcohol. But one Sunday, he walked to attend the small youth group in a rural church of one hundred people. There, he found more than just a youth group. He found a place where people cared about him, and the congregation "adopted" him as one of their own. Every Sunday, from the time he was just a freshman in high school, he would get up early to walk across the small town to attend Sunday school and church. For Andrew, the church was more than just a place to attend and be entertained with a dynamic service geared for youth. It was a family that gave him support and care. It was a place where he found acceptance. People in the church would invite him home for dinner and share their life with him. For Andrew, the little church located across the road from open corn fields became a home, and in the process, he came to faith in Christ. The church provided him the emotional support he lacked in his dysfunctional home. The other members of the youth group not only befriended him but also helped with his school work and showed him acceptance when they attended the small Midwestern high school together. The church gave him counsel and advice after he graduated from high school.

What would have happened to Andrew if the church had not been there, if the pastor, who has served in the church for the past fifteen years, had opted to pursue a more prestigious post? If there was no rural church located in a forgotten and dying rural community, Andrew would have gone the way of many other poor children with little hope. His only acceptance would have been from the kids involved in the drug culture, who desired nothing more than to use him for their own gain. He would have become another statistic on the welfare lists. But today, he has earned his degree and has a family of his own. And most importantly, he embraced Christ as his Savior.

The rural church today is crucial not only on a theological and biblical basis, but also because people like Andrew who face the struggles of poverty, broken families, and a lack of opportunities. Andrew would not have been able to walk sixty miles to the nearest Wal-Mart church. Even if he could have obtained a ride, they may have shown little interest in Andrew, for he could have become lost in the crowds, a nameless face from a nameless town who would have visited maybe once or twice but then drifted away. The rural church is important for no other reason than people like Andrew. While we may overlook them, all the angels in heaven rejoice because of them.

The rural church has more to offer than just a place, for the rural church has a significant part to play in the larger evangelical church. If we are to value the rural church, then we need to value the work it does in rural communities and the contribution it makes—and can make—even to the urban church.

The Contribution of Rural Ministry

IN THE AGE OF TEXT messaging and Facebook, we have lost the importance and value of interpersonal relationships. Reflecting upon my childhood in a small rural church, I realize that most of the lifelong lessons I learned did not come from the programs and educational material. The lessons that shaped me then and continue to shape me today came from the lives of the people within the congregation who provided simple godly examples. It was the simple faith of country people who lived by their faith in everyday life. It was the faith of Francis Dorhman, who gave out homemade treats and a tract each Halloween to all the kids who came knocking on her door. She taught me that evangelism is not an event, program, or marketing strategy, but is simply a way of life.

It was the example of Lola Flolo, who was willing to step in and play the piano when my mother was not present, even though she could hit only about every third or fourth note—just enough to keep us all on track. She modeled what true servanthood is about: stepping outside your comfort zone and serving even when you are not skilled but are needed.

George Dorhman and Vern Mitchell showed the importance of utilizing all our skills to serve the church when they made the pulpit and foyer furniture, still in the church today. They were master woodworkers who saw their skills as an opportunity to serve the church. We do not just serve the church in our areas of spiritual giftedness. No, we serve in all capacities.

It was the simple faith of Marie Barreth who never learned to drive a car but could quote Bible verse after Bible verse because she loved the Word.

I still reflect on the example of Bernice Tanner and her willingness to host a "King's Kids" children's ministry in her home every Wednesday afternoon. She was never rich by any stretch of the imagination, and her house was small and simple, but it was a place where kids learned to love Jesus.

The champions of faith were men like my father, who was not educated—from society's standpoint—but a man who exemplified and lived the wisdom of Proverbs.

The names and lessons could go on. But each of these individuals, who would never get an opportunity to serve in a large church because they were not educated or skilled or polished enough, modeled for me a simple faith that shaped not only my life, but also my ministry, more than the seminary training I received.

When we think of the contribution of larger urban churches, we often think of their programs, the recognition they receive, and the books their pastors have written. But to understand the contribution of the rural church, we find ourselves thinking of simple people who have lived their faith. They could not pontificate on great theological truths, but they could tell you how the sovereignty of God gives hope when the cattle market crashes and it means a financially difficult year.

Someone once said that city people want hymns that reassure them that God is at work in the world, and that rural people take it for granted that God is at work in the world.[1] Rural people could quote Bible verses relating to the disappointments and struggles of life to remind us of the providential care of God and how He sustains us through the trials of life. They taught us that Jesus loves the little children, because they loved the little children. Their worship was not with glitz and glamour and polished performances; it was the simple worship of the greatness of God, who revealed Himself in the Bible and sustained them in daily life. If you were to ask me what writers were the most influential to my thinking, I would point no further than to these people. They did not write with a pen but with a life. They are the heroes of the church, and it is upon their shoulders the church stands.

The Rural Church and the Future of America

Every indicator points to the fact that the moral and cultural war has largely won the day in the urban areas, but the rural communities have remained more steadfast. However, if rural America follows suit, then the moral heart of America will be lost. I believe that if we lose the rural church, we lose the nation. In the cultural conflict, rural America stands as the Bastogne of the church. If we are going to win average people back, it will be done through the heartland. If the American church turns its back on rural communities, then it will be inflicting its own mortal wound.

The rural church has long been ignored and overlooked. But as a church community, we recognize the value and importance of the rural church, not only as an important ministry to reach the rural population, but also as a contributor to the overall well-being of the American church. It is time we listen to the message of the rural church, for the lessons it teaches are critically needed in the church today. We should recognize how the small church remains an important member of the Christian community and why more value is to be given to this ministry.

In an age of programs, entertainment, glitz, and marketing, we need to be reminded of the simplicity of the church's ministry.[2]

The Contribution of the Rural Church

As the nation became more industrialized and urbanized, ministry focus shifted to the urban and megachurch. The church at large rightly recognized the value and contribution that these churches brought to American Christianity. With a renewed sense of evangelism and strategic ministries, the urban church reminded the rural church of the importance of being missional. It served to bring to the forefront the importance of the Great Commission and the great commandment in the lifeblood of the church.

But we have failed to see that the body of Christ always involves mutual interdependency. Just as the rural church can learn much from its urban counterpart, so also the urban church can learn from the rural church. Rural congregations "present the opportunity for celebration, community, intimacy and a depth of shared spirituality. Much can be learned by the wider church from rural churches' creativity in responding to the challenging circumstances as well as in their thirst for community, the opportunities for partnership and the potential of spiritual development."[3]

The Rural Church Is the Model of Church Health

Attend any church leadership seminar, and the speakers will often come from large churches proclaiming the latest principles of effective ministry. Many megachurches offer training materials, seminars, and pastors conferences taught by their staff on how to be effective in ministry, and pastors—many of whom come from small churches—flock to them in hopes of discovering the latest principles and programs ensuring their success. Yet studies indicate that the healthiest and most effective churches are not the megachurches but the small and rural churches.

After conducting extensive research on the spiritual and organizational health of churches of all sizes across the globe, Christian Schwarz identified eight qualities distinguishing spiritually vital churches. He concluded that small churches consistently demonstrate greater health in almost every category.[4] He states further that the small church—those under one hundred in average attendance—is sixteen times more effective in reaching people for Christ than churches over a thousand.[5] These numbers are not only astounding, but heartbreaking, for in an age where the small church continues to excel, it is often overlooked and denigrated.

Recently, one prominent national church leader made national news when he stated that people who attend small churches are "stinking selfish" and care nothing about the next generation.[6] We often view success by numbers and programs, and in a culture enamored with bigness, the small church can be considered irrelevant. Yet it is the small church that provides the spiritual growth of the global church today.[7]

Cynthia Woolever and Deborah Bruce surveyed over two thousand congregations and more than three hundred thousand worshipers and identified ten strengths of healthy US congregations. According to their research, small churches were the most effective in six of the categories (growing spiritually, meaningful worship, participating in the congregation, having a sense of belonging, sharing faith, and empowering leadership), compared to the mid-size church, which excelled in three areas (caring for children and youth, focusing on the community, and looking to the future). The large church excelled in only one (welcoming new people).[8] Instead of turning only to large urban church leaders to teach other churches and instruct the next generation of leaders, we should also be turning to small church leaders who are effectively leading healthy congregations.

The Rural Church Is the Moral and Theological Backbone of the Country

As recent elections have revealed, there is a wide divide between the rural and urban landscape that goes beyond political ideology and strikes at the center of the nation's moral ideology. Brown and Swanson comment, "Rural people and communities merit special attention because Americans generally accord them a value that far exceeds their material contribution to the nation's growth and well-being. The American public tends to see its rural population as a repository of almost sacred values and a stable anchor during times of rapid change."[9] The moral and spiritual divide was evident in a recent report by Barna and Summit Ministries. They revealed the following contrast between "practicing Christians" in both urban and rural communities (in each of the questions, the percentage indicates the number of those claiming to be a "practicing Christian" who strongly agree with the statement).[10]

	URBAN	RURAL
New Age Spirituality: All people pray to the same god or spirit, no matter what name they use for that spiritual being.	39%	22%
Secularism: A belief has to be proven by science to know it is true.	22%	3%
Secularism: A person's life is valuable only if society sees it as valuable.	27%	6%
Postmodernism: No one can know for certain what meaning and purpose there is to life.	31%	12%
Postmodernism: What is morally right or wrong depends on what an individual believes.	31%	18%
Postmodernism: If your beliefs offend someone or hurt their feelings, it is wrong.	30%	5%

Morality does not change or move in a vacuum, but is intricately interwoven with our theology and our understanding of the nature of God and the authority and inspiration of Scripture. Many churches have adopted a minimalist theology, where they affirm little more than the Apostles' Creed. The problem is not with what the Apostles' and Nicene Creeds affirm (both are orthodox), but what they leave out. Many of the theological questions the early church wrestled with and refined were still unresolved and, as a result, key issues of orthodoxy were not clearly affirmed until after these Creeds were written. Important doctrines such as the inerrancy and authority of Scripture, the centrality of the atonement, the necessity of personal confession of Christ, and others were not addressed when these Creeds were formulated.

Consequently, churches today that seek to maintain a broad appeal usually end up undermining the theological underpinnings of the historical church. In contrast, the rural church is still likely to maintain a strong foundation of both theology and biblical morality.[11] The rural church reminds us that biblical morality and theology are not only important, but still central to how we live, both privately and publicly. In the name of evangelism and church growth, we can undermine the gospel if we soften on biblical truth. In the quest to be liked by the world, we run the risk of becoming like the world. Theological and moral compromise will never make the church stronger.

David Smith identifies the small church as "the guardian and instructor of sound doctrine, which has been discarded by the big-church movement."[12] He goes on to write,

The teaching of sound doctrine produces strong, healthy believers who are not tossed around by the latest fad. . . . In the small membership congregation, this work (it is work because it's not easy, and it takes time) is done by the pastor. . . . This process is found in small churches all across America. Maybe that's why they are small. This process is not found in many large churches. Maybe that's why they're large. There's no one there to tell them the truth. Corruption loves a dark corner that is not illuminated by the light of biblical doctrine.[13]

Some may label the warning of theological and moral compromise coming from rural pastors as "being old fashioned and legalistic," but to do so is perilous. We all would do well to listen to its cry.

The Rural Church Provides a Model of Community

In an individualistic age, we need to return to community. In many churches, people attend a depersonalized service where they don't know anyone around them. They worship with a group of strangers and then head home without any meaningful connection with others in the congregation. In contrast, the rural church is centered on community. There is a place for everyone, and everyone has a place. We can measure community not by the number of people who attend or enroll in a small group, but by how long people stay after the service to visit. It is not uncommon in our church to have people standing around and visiting for forty-five minutes after the service.

What Barna describes as authentic fellowship is an organic reality in the rural church: "It is being real with one another, loving and caring for one another genuinely and without hypocrisy. It is the knowledge that if someone is having difficulties, we know that person well enough to recognize the signs. It is learning to take off the masks that we all wear and allowing people to know us as we really are."[14] Thus, Woolever and Bruce conclude, "Simply put, this means that worshipers in small congregations have a greater sense of belonging than participants in large congregations. This finding should challenge large congregations to do what they can to help people feel they are in the right place."[15]

Today, young people are leaving what they perceive to be impersonal churches in search of a deeper sense of community. They're not looking for another worship service designed to entertain them with age-determined music. Rather, they are looking for a family, a place where they belong.[16] One contribution the rural church can make to the urban church is the understanding of what constitutes biblical community. It includes relating to one another throughout the week. It includes caring for each other and being present when people are enduring a crisis. It includes coming to church and sharing prayer requests during the service, and people praying for those requests through the week. As Kennon Callahan points out,

> The vision of a small, strong congregation—if it ever thinks in terms of vision—is that of the Good Samaritan and the Good Shepherd. Small, strong congregations are not interested in vision-driven statements, challenge-driven goals, or commitment-driven objectives that advance the organizational growth of the congregation or institutional welfare of the denomination. What stirs people in a small, strong congregation is their spirit of compassion.[17]

Biblical community happens when we recognize the value and importance of everyone. Ministry is not about programs, but one person ministering to another. People serve one another because they know one another. Discipleship is not a program but a relationship that enables the older person to come alongside and informally mentor a younger person. When I ask young families why they are leaving our church, the most common answer I get is, "The church doesn't have enough young people and youth-related programs." What they fail to grasp is that we have something even greater to offer than a program. We have people who have lived a life of faith through all the difficulties and struggles of life, who can mentor and come alongside the youth to teach them how to live their faith. This kind of relationship is worth far more than the latest program. It is what Paul had in mind when he instructed older believers to encourage younger ones to love their families and to live in godliness, "so that the word of God will not be dishonored" (Titus 2:3–5). Mentoring is not a program but a relationship. It may certainly include programs, but it is first and foremost about relationships.

In the search for community, we can learn much from the Hispanic and Native American church. The Navajo church gives us a model of the interconnectedness that should characterize the church. For them, the clan and extended family binds them together into a brotherhood. Instead of seeing the Navajos simply as Native Americans to evangelize, we can learn from their actions and listen to what their pastors say is genuine community. They can teach us the importance of respecting and learning from the elders who are honored for the wisdom they possess. The same is also true in the Hispanic congregations where the focus is upon family and relationships. In our success-driven Anglo culture, we can glean much from our Hispanic brothers and sisters about the importance of family and community connections.

The Rural Church Provides a Model of Involvement

Researchers of church health have pointed out that healthy churches have approximately fifty-five percent of the people volunteering in the various ministries. However, if you were to look at most rural churches, the number is near eighty percent.[18] Woolever and Bruce discovered that sixty-three percent of small church members are active participants—which they define as joining a study group, assuming leadership, and giving of time, talent, and money to the church—in the church compared to forty-eight percent of larger churches.[19]

Rural churches don't have the luxury of having paid professionals develop, organize, and provide leadership for the various programs and departments in the church. As a result, people not only become more involved, but also help lead the church. Authority is shared between the pastor and the people. People are involved at all levels of leadership and, in many cases, perform several different roles. A local teacher serves as the Sunday school director as well as the Awana leader. A contractor maintains the facilities and serves on the elder board. A farmer teaches the adult Sunday school and serves as the church treasurer. As Dennis Bickers points out, "Smaller churches can't afford to have people sitting on the sidelines. Limited people and resources require that every member of the small church must be engaged in ministry if the church is to have an effective witness in its community."[20] Small church leaders trust the laity, for they have recognized that the ministry of the church is not conducted by paid professionals, but by everyday people who get involved. The pastor provides the teaching, training, and modeling, but the laity carry on the ministry.

But service is not just an expression of one's spiritual gifts; it is also a part of the community. When people gather for meetings, often more time is spent discussing personal issues—sometimes even about how the local fish are biting—than the actual business of the church. As Jean Risley points out,

> If you see something that you think needs doing around the church, and it matters to you, you'll probably be the only one who ends up doing it. If you're thinking clearly, you'll probably get a couple of friends and a newcomer to help. If you bring some coffee or iced tea and a snack, what you'll have is a party with a purpose. You'll find that work gets done, friends get to enjoy each other's company, and you get to know the person behind the new face.[21]

This relational approach to ministry and involvement may frustrate many task-driven pastors, but it builds community within the congregation.

Yet this involvement not only trains people to be leaders, but also fosters a global outlook within the church. People get involved not simply because they are needed, but because they have a burden for the church. This translates into a global mission. Rural churches become strong financial supporters of missions, and, per person, they far out-give larger churches. It's not uncommon for rural churches to give well beyond ten percent of their budget to overseas missions. While large urban churches often focus on internal ministries and give little overseas,[22] the rural church sees overseas missions as part of their responsibility.[23] When missionaries visit a rural church, they are not assigned to a Sunday school class or given five minutes for a "missions moment" in the worship service. Rather, they are given the whole message time to share what God is doing on the field and how the church can better support them. As a result, the small church (both in urban and rural settings) not only supports missionaries financially but also raises up pastors and missionaries by providing approximately fifty percent of all pastors.[24] The rural church not only provides young people a model for involvement in ministry, but also trains them for ministry by getting them involved in church activities at an early age. Since more than half of all pastors sense a call to ministry between the ages of fourteen and twenty-one, this early involvement is critical in helping them identify their call as well as develop skills necessary for them to realize their call to ministry.[25]

The Rural Church Provides a Model of Intergenerational Ministry

When the church meets on Sunday, it is often the most generationally segregated day of the week. Young people attend newly planted churches, and older people attend established congregations. For some families, the only time spent together is in the parking lot as they arrive at and leave church. The rest of the time, each hustles off to their "age-appropriate" worship service—the youth to a service that resembles a rock concert, the young adults to their contemporary service, and the older people to their traditional service of hymns and organs. David Kinnaman writes, "The generation gap is bigger today than ever."[26] He goes on to state, "For too long, we have assumed that we do good youth or young-adult ministry when we separate kids from the rest of the church. . . . We have segregated (believe me, this is not a verb I use lightly) students and young adults from the rest of the church—and it's hurting their faith."[27]

Yet throughout Scripture, we find the focus is not upon generational separation, but multigenerational involvement and interaction. Older men are to set the example by being temperate, dignified, sensible, sound in faith, in love, in perseverance. Young women are to learn from older women how to be godly mothers and wives (Titus 2:4–5). Grandparents are to provide spiritual instruction for the grandchildren (2 Tim. 1:5). Likewise, young people are to serve as models for the older generation in faith and conduct (1 Tim. 4:12; 5:1–3).

Tragically, we have largely lost the importance of generational cross-pollination. Young people need the wisdom, guidance, and spiritual discernment of the older generation. In an age of moral compromise, young people easily become enamored with the latest trends and cultural pressures. To combat this, they need the theological and moral stability of older saints. Likewise, the older generation needs the fresh perspective, enthusiasm, and passion of the younger generation. At times, those of the older generation develop blinders that hinder them from seeing new needs and opportunities for ministry. Further, they can become discouraged, so they no longer have a passion for ministry. They need the idealism and zeal that the younger generation brings.

In rural communities, intergenerational worship and community remains. Because rural communities are small and have only a few churches, there is not the population base for multigenerational churches, much less multigenerational services within the church. Moreover, because the rural church functions as a family, the value and importance of intergenerational worship is maintained. Children not only remain in the worship service—except perhaps those below the age of ten who go to children's church just before the sermon—but they actively participate in the service as well. Children sing specials and help collect the offering. One of my great joys as a pastor is to have children raise their hands and share prayer requests during our prayer time in the worship service. They are learning not only the importance of prayer, but also what it means to be part of a community where we care and pray for one another. They get to know the older generation at church on Sunday and can see them throughout the community during the week as well. In the process, they have the privilege of seeing the reality of faith lived out in the context of daily life.

Further, because the rural church is small and family-oriented, the children get to know the pastor. They do not see him as some figurehead standing behind a pulpit, but as a real person living life. They get to see him at the store, at the school activities, and at the local fair. In an age when many children do not know the name of their pastor, much less actually know him on a personal level, the rural church draws us back to a church culture that functions as a family, one in which children see the pastor as *their* pastor.

The Rural Church Provides a Model of the Simplicity of Ministry

America has become addicted to the latest fad. Whether it be clothes, iPhones, or cars, we quickly discard what is outdated in pursuit of what is now in vogue. Our obsession with what is trendy even creeps into the church. Whether it be the seeker-sensitive church, the emergent church, the contemporary church, or any other fad-focused church, it seems that no one wants to be ignorant of the latest ecclesiastical fashion. Like teens obsessed with being in the "in-crowd," we purchase the latest books, attend the latest seminars, and implement the latest programs, all so we are on the "cutting edge" of ministry. Our greatest fear is that we would be labeled "old-fashioned" and "outdated." In the process, we've lost the simplicity of the gospel. Instead of seeing the power of the gospel in the gospel itself, the church has become market-driven, seeking to empower the gospel by following programs and methodology determined by the latest formula.

Amid this, the rural church "naturally rejects faddish and market-driven church formula programs because they are faddish and market-driven. Most small membership congregations have been there and done that. They've been set up by the hype and then let down when the promise of a pot-of-gold at the rainbow's end didn't materialize. The small community congregation has a single strategy that has worked and continues to work for its situation."[28] The rural church provides a corrective by showing that church health is connected to the gracious activity of God rather than to programs.[29] The power to transform lives comes from the message of the gospel itself (Rom. 1:16). Because of this, Paul eschewed the use of gimmicks and man-centered methodology (1 Cor. 2:1–5). In our age of pastoral celebrities, we have developed the notion that the power of the message is found in the ability of the messenger. Thus, a church is better served by an eloquent preacher on a screen than a live pastor behind the pulpit. Therefore, the voice of the rural church needs to be heard, for they remind us that the success and health of the church comes through the sovereign work of God rather than the wisdom of men, that God's presence, not the size of the congregation or the popularity of a program, determines the health of the church. Kent Philpott provides a timely warning:

> Nearly all of the movements I have ever seen . . . are diversions from the primary goal of the gospel ministry. Movements waste our money, steal our time, and embarrass us. My suggestion is to avoid movements. . . . It has been my observation that those who have experienced true conversion are satisfied with Jesus. Growing up into the stature of the fullness of Jesus and bringing Him glory and honor, these seem to be enough.[30]

The rural church brings us back to the simplicity of ministry. Worship doesn't require laser lights and special effects fronted by a worship team comprised of professional musicians where the focus is upon "our experience" in the service. Such worship becomes more entertainment and emotionalism rather than genuine worship. Worship today is often more narcissistic and self-centered than God-centered.[31] Genuine worship is not about what we experience. Rather, worship is about our response of obedience to the loving and redemptive God revealed in Christ. As Daniel Block points out, "True worship involves reverential human acts of submission and homage before the divine Sovereign in response to his gracious revelation of himself and in accord with his will."[32] True worship involves the recognition of and a loving response to who God is and what He has done for us. And we do this by submitting ourselves to Him and serving Him in all aspects of life. Genuine worship is not a worship team performing up front while a thousand people sit back, clap their hands, and watch. Worship is active participation of the whole congregation affirming the nature and activity of God. This is central to the rural church. It is authentic so long as the whole congregation participates.[33]

The simplicity of ministry is discovered when we realize that the church was never meant to be run by paid professionals who implement specific programs. Rather, the church was designed to be a community of people who faithfully serve one another and the community by using their spiritual gifts and talents for the advancement of the kingdom. As Shawn McMullen points out, "Regardless of the location or size of your church, you have the potential to engage in life-changing ministry that transforms your community. You don't need to relocate. You don't need an advanced degree in church growth. You don't need additional staff. With God's help, you can begin right where you are and make an eternal difference."[34] The most effective servants in the hands of a living God are not those who are the trained professionals, but those who faithfully serve God in complete dependence upon Him.

The Rural Church Is a Model of Community Involvement

Several years ago, a large urban church made national news when they donated eleven tons of food to a local food bank that had been the victim of theft. It truly was impressive. But this got me thinking about our own church. Every other month, we take a collection of food to contribute to the local food bank for distribution. Rather than run our own food closet, we have found that it is much more effective to come alongside the local food bank and donate to them. So, every other month, we donate between three hundred and five hundred pounds of food. Compared to the massive amount donated by this megachurch, our contribution seemed insignificant. However, when I calculated the amount of food per person who attended the church, the megachurch contributed less than two pounds of food per person while our church contributed approximately five pounds per person. While they did it only once, our church continues to do it six times a year while also donating gifts for children during Christmas. My point is not to belittle the contribution that the urban church made. It was significant and a positive testimony to the community. Nor do I intend to brag about my own congregation. There are other rural churches doing far more. The point is that rural churches often do more than large churches in terms of community involvement, but without the fanfare.

The rural church excels at caring for people, not only in the church, but also in the community as well. When a tragedy strikes a local community, the church usually reacts immediately with food and support for victims. In the rural communities, the church serves the whole community, and the pastor is often seen as the community's pastor. People who never attend the church will introduce the pastor as "our pastor." When the new pastor arrives, most of the people will know who the pastor is even before the pastor has met them.[35] They are often seen as community leaders along with the local doctor, lawyer, and teachers. Their influence often extends beyond the size of their church.[36]

People who attend the rural church are often actively involved in the community. They serve on the school board; they are active in the local museum; they are members of the local volunteer fire department. They serve on the town council and are the directors of the local Public

Utility Department. When disasters hit, the church provides emergency assistance, whether that means providing food for the firemen fighting a nearby forest fire or providing emergency housing during a crippling blizzard. When people cannot pay their rent or utility bill, they will often turn to the church for help. Whether or not they have "Community Church" in their church name—and many of them do—most rural churches see themselves and are seen by the rest of the community as a "community church" that gives strength and hope to people by their presence. As Dennis Bickers points out, "When life begins to crumble around these people, they're often attracted to that small church in their community to see if there are any answers to be found there that can help them. In a healthy small church they'll find those answers and will often find a personal relationship with Jesus Christ."[37] While many churches provide "token" community involvement such as going out into the community twice a year to do a service activity, rural churches are usually integrated into the community and serve the community on a daily and weekly basis.

The Student Has Become the Master

Some denominational leaders often regard the rural church as the poor stepchild of the denomination. Old-fashioned, small, and insignificant, they have little to offer the larger church community. Or so it seems. Once, when I suggested to a denominational leader that they should honor a pastor who had served faithfully for forty years in a small community church in a town of one-hundred and forty people, he responded, "But how much has the church grown?" For him, the little church of forty people and the faithfulness the pastor demonstrated in such a forgotten place had little merit. Yet the reality is that the small rural church is far healthier and a better example of a dynamic church than many of the larger urban churches. If we are going to discover the key to revitalizing the church of America, we can start by looking to the small and rural church. Instead of looking at the rural church as a blight upon the ecclesiastical landscape, we should listen to its voice, for in many rural churches we discover vibrant, healthy congregations that can teach much to the urban and large church. But for this to happen, we need to move beyond the paternalistic attitude that many have toward rural churches and begin to see them as equals, fellow coworkers in the kingdom. Only then can we develop more synergistic relationships that will benefit both urban and rural churches.

While the rural church has its strengths, it also has its weaknesses. It can easily become paralyzed by traditionalism. At times, it becomes indifferent to the social issues confronting people within the community. In the enjoyment of community, it can become ineffective and unmotivated in evangelism. Here is where the urban church can help. It can help in training rural communities to be more effective in outreach. It can help the rural church see that traditionalism and legalism are just as dangerous as liberalism. It can help them see that social action does not undermine the gospel, but becomes the soil in which the gospel can flourish. If the church in America is to maintain its spiritual health and be a powerful force of the gospel, then we need to develop strategic partnerships between the urban and rural church. It is to this that we now turn our attention.

11

Developing Strategic Partnerships

WORK ON THE FARM was never dull. For some, this seems unlikely, for what could be more boring than driving around in circles all day at five miles an hour. But spend a day with a farmer and you will find that in the apparent monotony of working the land day in and day out, there is continual fluctuation and challenges. As the seasons change, so do jobs and tasks. If one were to list all the jobs a person does on the farm by its parallel urban profession, a farmer would have a résumé that seems to encompass many different lives. One minute, they are a heavy equipment operator, the other a mechanic. They are a CEO, CFO, project manager, salesman, and veterinarian. They are a supervisor, strategic planner, commodity trader, and human resources person. All this, and it is not yet noon. Not to mention that everything they do involves some degree of danger. For many ranchers, "running with the bulls" is a daily experience. Farming may be difficult and dangerous, but it is never boring.

But the complexity of farming also points us to the importance of teamwork. Possessing many different pieces of equipment, each having a different task, the farmer goes throughout the day dependent upon every piece of equipment functioning properly. A combine cannot plant wheat, and a drill cannot bale hay. While most people look at the flashy tractor or combine, perhaps the most important is the "trap wagon." This is an old dilapidated pickup we used to haul fuel, grease, and tools to keep the tractors running. It's dirty and ugly, and no one wanted to drive it. But without it, the farm work stalled. Farmers depend not only upon the different pieces of equipment to work together to get from the planting to the harvesting, but also upon each other. A single farmer can never have all that he or she requires to cover all the needs and contingencies on a farm. As a result, neighbors depend upon each other. If one farmer gets stuck in a mud hole—which happens each spring—he needs the help of his neighbor to bring his tractor and pull him out. Everyone needs others, and every piece of machinery needs the contribution of the other pieces to get the job done. In many ways, farming becomes a microcosm of the church. Every person is dependent upon other people, every program succeeds or fails by what happens in other programs, and every church needs the assistance and help of other churches to build the kingdom.

When Christ first formed the church, the focus was not upon each individual church, but upon the community of believers who together formed the body of Christ. While the local church provides the visible organization and presence, it is connected to the broader body of believers. When Christ prayed for the unity of the church in John 17, He did so with the whole community of believers in mind. Thus, "the highlight is on relational unity and mutual support within that great community, with structural or organizational unity necessarily in the background. The fundamental idea still is that Jesus conceived of all His disciples as 'one people.'"[1] Yet in recent years, the focus has shifted to the local church, with little thought given to the unity we all have in Christ. While we give it theological lip service, churches compete for parishioners and recognition. The market-driven church has little place for promoting the well-being of other churches in the same area. Rex Koivisto's warning against the megachurch movement can serve as a warning to all churches, where there "is the tendency for a megachurch congregation to understand itself as a full-service church, capable of meeting the needs of Christians more effectively than smaller fellowships."[2]

Before we get on our theological soapbox and condemn the megachurch, often we in small or midsize churches fall prey to the same ecclesiastical arrogance. In 1915, Edwin Earp warned the small church of the dangers of forming church and denominational silos. He wrote,

> There is present today competition with those who should be our cooperators. This . . . has been manifest in our church life to a degree that is almost tragic in some rural communities. I saw a photograph . . . of seven churches on one street in a little town in Tennessee . . . and the only sign of the cooperating spirit in the town was the fact that they all used the one stove, it being carried from one building to another in turn as the absentee pastors may have had occasion to preach in their respective pulpits.[3]

When we cooperate with other churches only by sharing a wood stove, we have failed to understand the biblical theology of the church. We often look down at other denominations and churches in the area, believing that we are somehow better equipped to serve the community than they are. Instead of seeing them as a part of the worldwide church, our brothers and sisters in Christ, we see them as our competition. We divide the church into groups based upon size, denominational affiliation, theological perspective, location, and style. In the process, we view others with a degree of self-superiority, believing that our church and our approach to ministry are better. Instead of holding onto this mentality, we should realize that the health of every church should be the concern of all churches. While we may have our philosophical and theological differences, we are joined together by our common affirmation of Christ and His redemptive work.

The Importance of Partnerships

In the formation of the early church, a partnership existed. Rather than being concerned only with their own congregation's well-being, or even that of the congregations in one geographical area, the early Christians had a sense of mutual participation and partnership in the gospel encompassing all churches. The church at Colossae had a deep love and concern for all the saints (Col. 1:4). Epaphras was deeply concerned for the well-being not only of those in Colossae, but also of those in Laodicea and Hierapolis (Col. 4:13). The level of interchurch partnership was further evinced when the letters of Paul were circulated among congregations in the region (Col. 4:15–16). The church at Philippi supported both Paul and the churches in Thessalonica (Phil. 4:16). Paul exhorted the troubled church in Corinth to join with the churches in Galatia to help support the congregation in Jerusalem. Normally, when a sermon today is preached concerning the importance of tithing and giving, the focus is upon giving to the local church to support its own ministry. However, when Paul wrote about the importance of giving, the focus centered on giving to the needs of other churches. While instructing the church at Corinth concerning the importance of generosity in giving, Paul highlights the churches of Macedonia, who gave generously from their poverty to the support of Christians in other churches (2 Cor. 8:1–7). The tradition of having a weekly offering was not to support the local church but to take a collection to send to other churches (1 Cor. 16:1–2).

For the early Christians, giving expressed their understanding that every congregation and member was part of the church. The New Testament saints recognized the mutual responsibility that every congregation and member had for one another. To say that one church or one location is more important than the other, or to turn one's back upon the needs of other congregations, is not simply foreign to the New Testament but violates the intrinsic nature of the body of Christ. What Paul writes in 1 Corinthians 12 applies both to the attitude of each member toward others in the local congregation and to our attitude toward all people and all congregations. If I isolate myself from other churches and fail to be concerned about the well-being of every congregation, whether urban or rural, then I disregard the synergistic nature of the body of Christ. If we belittle a church because of its size and regard it as unimportant, if we deem one church to be insignificant, if we do not show concern when another church becomes spiritually unhealthy, then we violate biblical ecclesiology (1 Cor. 12:14–26) and fail to embody the love that is to exist within the church (1 Cor. 13).

A biblical theology of the church does not begin with structure and polity but with our attitude toward other congregations. Donnie Griggs rightly summarizes, "Real collaboration, however, starts where every godly initiative does; in the heart. We need our hearts to be convinced that we don't have everything we need. We need to learn from other workers in this 'field' who can help us do our job better."[4] If all we see is our own church and our own community, without seeing beyond the arena of our ministry, then we do not understand the church. Urban churches must see the presence, value, importance, strength, and contribution that the rural church demonstrates. Likewise, rural churches must recognize the importance and value of the urban church. When we drive through a rural area and see a closed church, it should cause us deep grief, for the witness of the gathered body of Christ is no longer present. If we evangelize the whole city but lose rural people, we have not advanced the kingdom.[5] The kingdom is not built by individuals, or even individual churches working in isolation from one another, no more than our physical body functions when the hand remains isolated from the foot (1 Cor. 12:14–22). Our willingness to partner and support other churches is a fragrant aroma, an acceptable sacrifice, well-pleasing to God, and becomes the basis for God's supplying all our needs (Phil. 4:15–19). If we are going to be effective in reaching a post-Christian, postmodern world, then the church needs to develop a spirit of cooperation and partnership that is reflected in the New Testament. If we fail to do so, we will soon find ourselves isolated and irrelevant.

This is not only true of the urban-rural church relationship; it is equally true of the ethnic church as well. We need to value and learn from the African American church, the Hispanic church, the Asian American church, and the Native American church. The church needs to be a model of unity to our racially-divided world.

Partnership Killers

While Scripture points to the importance of cooperation and mutual partnership within the Christian community, often this cooperation is thwarted by our approach to ministry. Instead of working in cooperation with one another, churches operate in isolation from others or in domineering ways.

Silo Churches

Patrick Lencioni identified the existence of silos within dysfunctional organizations. Silos "are nothing more than the barriers that exist between departments within an organization, causing people who are supposed to be on the same team to work against one another. And whether we call this phenomenon department politics, divisional rivalry, or turf warfare, it is one of the most frustrating aspects of life in any sizable organization."[6] In other words, silos exist when we become more concerned about our own interests rather than the interests of the group. Sometimes, it can happen because of jealousy or conflict. Other times, it occurs when groups (and churches) operate in isolation from one another.

Silos are formed not only within a specific congregation, but also within the larger Christian community. Because we tend to focus on our own specific ministry, we fail to recognize the value and contributions others have and how we mutually benefit one another. Karl Vaters points out, "Lack of cooperation between churches may be [the] #1 reason why small churches don't see their true value and aren't as effective as we should be. We're not working together. . . . Because of our limited resources, it's critical for small churches to tear down the silo walls between churches and work together to advance the kingdom of God."[7]

Imperialism

Imperialism exists when one nation seeks to extend their authority over another by gaining indirect control over the political or economic life of others. Ecclesiastical imperialism exists when a larger church becomes involved in a small church in order to adopt the smaller church as one of their satellite locations.[8] This often happens with the best of intentions, because of financial hardship or the lack of other resources, or at the request of the smaller church. Instead of forming a true partnership where the larger church seeks to encourage and assist the small church, the "relationship" results in the large church controlling and/ or assimilating the small one. Many churches falsely see no real value in forming partnerships with other churches if they do not directly benefit from them. Thus, they will form cooperative works only if there is something in it for them. This danger is especially true in forming urban and rural cooperative works. As Griggs points out, when large churches assimilate rural churches into their satellite system, it "reinforce[s] the negative stereotype that big city people have no real value for small towns if it doesn't directly benefit them. This is what people fear the most about large cities. 'If they are here, they are here to take over.'"[9]

Paternalism

Perhaps the greatest danger of the urban-rural cooperative work is paternalism. Instead of seeing the rural church as an equal, the urban church often views it as inferior. The relationship is not mutual or peer to peer, but one in which the superior condescends to the inferior. The relationship becomes paternalistic, where the urban church helps the small church but with strings attached. While they may come into the rural church with good intentions of trying to help them by providing money and resources, they often dictate how the support is to be used. Programs may be implemented without regard for the rural people and their culture. The relationship is not two-way, but one in which the urban church comes to, as the saying goes, help the "country bumpkins get in touch with the real world."

To build God's kingdom, churches need to value one another. This requires the formation of partnerships between rural churches and urban churches, denominations, and educational institutions.

Cooperative Works with Other Rural Churches

Developing a cooperative ministry within the church body begins by working closely with those nearest you. Rural congregations face limited resources—time, money, and volunteers—often restricting the amount of work they can accomplish. One of the dangers of a rural church is that they attempt to become the mini-megachurch by seeking to provide all the ministries a large church provides. In attempting to do everything, they do nothing well. For the rural church to be effective, it must focus upon what it is uniquely gifted and called to do. Rather than try to include all ministries, it can support and work cooperatively with the other churches in the area so that, through their cooperative work, the collective can achieve what each congregation cannot do on its own.

The first way churches in rural areas can cooperate is by supporting each other's ministries. For example, one church may provide quality children's ministries while another can focus upon the youth in the community. Rather than the church with the strong children's ministry attempting to duplicate what the other church is doing for the youth, it can support and encourage its own youth to be part of the other youth ministry. By working together, the two churches can accomplish more than each could do individually.

This involves not only supporting each other's ministry by attendance, but also providing financial support to other churches. Village Missions is built upon such cooperative efforts. Churches within the mission, that are able, give a portion of their tithes back to the mission. These tithes are then used to support missionaries in rural congregations that cannot afford to pay the full salary of a pastor. Consequently, thirty percent of the churches unable to hire a full-time pastor within the mission are able to have a full-time resident pastor. The long-term benefit of this is that these non-supporting churches eventually move to become self-sustaining congregations.[10]

A second level of cooperative ministry comes when the two churches combine resources to work together to implement a program. Several churches can band together to have a Valentine's banquet or an outdoor show in order to reach out evangelistically to the community. Or rather than each church having its own food bank, churches can form one large food bank in the local community that is accessible to everyone.

A third level of partnership is found by working with other churches and organizations to develop cooperative ministries to address the needs of rural communities. As we have seen, rural communities are facing critical issues and often lack the necessary resources to address them. Churches can join together to develop strategic plans to deal with these problems. It's easy in rural ministry to feel a sense of futility and inadequacy in dealing with the complex issues of poverty, drugs, and caring for the needs of the elderly. However, by forming cooperative ministries, together they can address specific problems within the community. For example, they can work together with the local school and sheriff's office to develop a comprehensive drug-prevention program for teens. This might include assisting with the local D.A.R.E. program, providing counseling on drug addiction, hosting drug- and alcohol-free parties for teens, and offering other activities that encourage youth to "say no to drugs." The church may form a cooperative ministry with the local Senior Center to provide counseling and assistance on Medicare. Another ministry might be to develop a "Helping Hand" program within the local community to provide home maintenance in areas of safety, warmth, and keeping dry.

Cooperative Partnerships with the Urban Church

Rural and urban churches not only can learn a great deal from one another, but by building synergistic relationships they can mutually encourage and benefit the spiritual growth of one another. As was pointed out in the last chapter, there are several lessons the rural church can teach the urban church. By forming positive cooperative ministries, urban and rural churches can mutually help each other think outside the box and see aspects of ministry and spiritual growth that we would otherwise overlook.

First, cooperative partnerships prevent us from being trapped by our natural tendency to become inward focused, in which we devote our efforts to building our own little kingdom rather than building and strengthening the whole body of Christ. It enables us to develop a universal view of the body of Christ rather than a microscopic view in which we only look inward to our own challenges and needs. If we fail to widen our focus, we can become narcissistic and self-centered, having an over-inflated sense of our own role in the kingdom.

Second, cooperative partnerships provide us the opportunity to be challenged in our understanding of the church and Scripture. It's easy to become clouded in our view of the church. Driven by the desire for growth and effectiveness, we can easily compromise the gospel and our theological integrity. The urban church can benefit from listening to the voice of the rural church, which reminds us of the simplicity of ministry. By interacting with the rural church, balance can be restored to many urban churches, and their understanding of success within the church can be refined. The rural church can likewise benefit from the input of the urban church, which helps the congregation break out of the traditional blinders hampering the ministry of the church in the community. We may not always agree, but interaction and honest, open dialogue from both perspectives can help us think more clearly and in ways that accord more with Scripture. By forming sister church relationships, we can provide a context for greater mutual learning within the community of God's people. This may involve pastors trading pulpits several times a year as well as holding joint elder board meetings where leaders discuss the challenges and opportunities within their respective churches. This would also provide opportunities for joint leadership training.

Third, cooperative partnerships enable us to help one another in ministry. While we have already examined some of the contributions the rural church makes to the broader church family, there are also ways that the urban church can encourage and strengthen the ministry of rural congregations. The urban church can partner with rural congregations to provide ministry opportunities in rural communities. In light of the epidemic of opiate addiction in rural areas, the inner city church can help the rural church develop effective drug and gang prevention programs. Many of the principles that the inner city learned in dealing with these issues are becoming more relevant to the rural church today. Conducting a VBS program can benefit the rural community by providing needed assistance while supplying urban teens with ministry training. Having joint youth events can connect Christian young people in rural communities with the broader youth community. Rural and urban churches can work together to provide internships and mentoring programs to train future pastors and leaders for both urban and rural ministry. By having the internships in both congregations, students will be able to learn lessons from both rural and urban ministries.

Such cross-pollination will further strengthen the church as the student learns lessons from both congregations and thus will be able not only to minister in either location but also be able to promote unity among rural and urban churches.

Fourth, cooperative efforts can maximize resources. Often large churches have access to materials and resources unavailable to rural ministries because of the cost. The larger churches can assist rural churches by providing these resources for nominal fees. They can further assist rural churches by providing beneficial training for the church to help them implement the programs. Along with program resources, the large church can provide access to services that are unavailable in rural communities. For example, a staff counselor at a large church can provide counseling services at a rural church once or twice a month.

Fifth, cooperative partnerships can encourage and assist the rural pastor in his ministry. When the urban church treats the rural church as an equal in ministry, the importance and contribution of the rural church is validated. Further, larger urban churches can also provide critical financial support for the pastor and his family so that their needs are met and they can minister more effectively.

The opportunities and benefits of mutual partnership between urban and rural churches are countless, and together, rural and urban churches can more effectively advance Christ's kingdom. This work begins with the urban church identifying one or two rural churches with whom they can become a sister congregation in order to foster a mutually-beneficial relationship. Having identified and contacted the rural church, the leadership of the urban church can meet to discuss the details of the relationship and how it can be mutually beneficial. Last, the churches can have an annual combined board retreat where they discuss issues confronting them to gain advice and wisdom from the larger board. By doing so, each benefits from the collective wisdom of both churches.

Cooperative Partnerships
with the Denomination and Association

Denominations and the rural church often have had an ambivalent attitude toward one another. Denominational leaders often view rural churches as old-fashioned, stuck in the past, and unsupportive of denominational programs. Rural churches and rural church pastors sometimes view denominational leaders as distant and unconcerned about the rural church. Having served both on the executive team of an association and as a rural church pastor, I have experienced both sides of the coin. My conclusion is that both can benefit from mutual involvement. The rural church and pastor benefit by participating in the denomination and association, which is a support network critical for pastors in isolated rural areas. Further, the church can obtain assistance from the denomination when addressing issues within the congregation, especially when conflicts arise between the pastor and the congregation. The rural church also can obtain support and help during times of pastoral transitions and when the congregation is looking for a new pastor. Moreover, the denomination can assist churches in pooling money and resources, enabling churches to accomplish more for the kingdom than they can individually in isolation from one another.

However, the denomination needs to see the value and importance of the rural church. If the rural church exemplifies church health, the denomination needs to turn to the rural church for guidance and training. Too often, when looking for leadership for the organization or recruiting speakers for conferences, denominations look only at pastors from large churches. This reveals not only an unhealthy bias towards the urban church but also a failure to see the contribution that the rural church can make to the health of the whole organization. Rural pastors may not be eloquent or polished. They may not be recognized outside the circle of their local congregation. But they often possess wisdom in leading healthy churches. If we are to have healthy churches across the denomination, then the denomination needs to realize the contribution that rural churches make. We need to get away from being enamored with "church stars" and begin to realize that real wisdom often resides in the forgotten church. Denominations and associations should actively recruit rural church pastors and leaders to serve on their staff and corporate boards. They need to invite rural speakers to share their lessons of ministry. Instead of ignoring them as insignificant, we can appreciate their contribution and highlight their ministries. Too often denominational leaders discourage pastors from considering rural ministry because it "could harm the pastor's opportunities for further advancement in ministry."[11] Consequently, Dennis Bickers warns,

> Denominations must not ignore these churches, either. Invest in planting new churches in the larger cities if you choose, but if denominations continue to ignore the possibilities many of their small churches offer, they will find that God will do an 'end-run' and raise up ministries in churches that many did not believe possible. When that happens, those denominations that ignored their smaller churches for decades should not be surprised when these churches ignore them in the future.[12]

Cooperative Partnerships
with Seminaries and Bible Colleges

In *Hollowing Out the Middle: The Rural Brain Drain and What It Means for America*, Patrick Carr and Maria Kefalas describe a common crisis confronting rural America:

> Our country is in the throes of a most painful and unpredictable transition. In what has become an all-too-familiar story, rural states such as North Dakota and West Virginia share an unsettling problem: too many young people in their twenties

and thirties are leaving. . . . This hemorrhaging of people, specifically the younger generation, is hollowing out many of the
nation's small towns and rural communities.[13]

Consequently, they warn, "as the new century's first decade ends,
the loss of such a huge share of them could spell the end of small-
town America."[14] This migration not only means that rural America is
becoming older, but it results in the human capital attained through
education and training critical to the future socio-economic health of
a community being drained from rural communities. Young people
are leaving rural communities to pursue education and are not coming
back.[15] Thurston Domina writes, "During the last few decades a whole
new form of residential segregation has emerged. I call it educational
segregation: College graduates have become increasingly clustered in
a handful of places, while large swaths of America experience a long,
drawn-out brain drain."[16] The greatest division line in the educational
segregation of America lies between urban and rural communities.
Each year, rural communities lose six percent of those who have a
college education.[17] Six percent might seem low, but when you add it
up over a ten-year period, that results in a significant loss. While it is
not dramatic, it is a steady brain drain that ultimately undermines any
opportunity for economic growth. Consequently, rural communities
are left with inadequate medical care and educational opportunities as
rural communities struggle to replace aging doctors and teachers. The
"deepening educational segregation closes off opportunities for people
born into brain drain communities, creating new social and economic
inequalities."[18]

Tragically, this brain drain and educational segregation is seen in
the church as well. Young people who leave the rural communities to
pursue educational preparation for ministry are not coming back. The
result is that rural churches are being confronted with a crisis of leadership. The greatest challenge for Village Missions—a mission that targets

rural communities with a vision of "Keeping the Country Church Alive"—is not in finding churches asking for assistance but in recruiting students from Bible colleges and seminaries who are willing to serve in rural areas. The problem is not whether the harvest is plentiful, but whether workers are willing to go into the harvest (Matt. 9:37). Developing cooperative partnerships with Bible colleges and seminaries is critical for the future health of the rural church. This begins by raising the visibility of the rural church in educational institutions. Seminaries and Bible colleges need to actively look for and recruit individuals in rural ministries, not just those who serve a rural church for a short time before advancing to an urban church. Raising the visibility of the rural church involves having guest speakers in both the classroom and chapel to share the struggles, joys, and challenges of the small rural church. Internships can be developed with rural churches to provide students with an understanding of the needs and issues confronting the church.

Developing these partnerships is critical if we are going to reach rural communities. But this can happen only if we elevate the awareness of rural ministry and rural communities in evangelical thinking. In American society rural people are ignored and the focus is upon urban affairs. In the government, there is a secretary-level member of the cabinet to inform the president on urban affairs, but rural development comes under the Department of Agriculture, where the focus is upon the sustainability of the American farm and little attention is given to the broader rural issues. National news agencies assign reporters to cover the suburban and urban issues but have no equivalent to cover rural issues.[19]

In the universities, the urban and community section of the American Sociological Association focuses upon the issues concerning urban settings. "Meanwhile, rural sociology survives as a relatively minor sub-discipline pursued by a small and committed band of scholars. Despite the iconic place the Heartland inhabits in the national psyche, rural policy remains the most obscure of concerns."[20] Tragically, the same could be said of the rural church and evangelicalism. While Christian colleges and seminaries have programs and departments for urban research and training, the issues and needs of rural America go unnoticed.

The issues and opportunities facing rural communities and the rural church are abundant. To meet those challenges, the rural church needs the support of one another, denominations, urban churches, and the educational institutions preparing a new generation of pastors for these communities.

12

The Rural Community as a Mission Field

OTHER THAN THE six years I lived in Portland, Oregon, attending seminary, I have always lived in rural communities. My childhood was spent in a farming and logging community where people's livelihood was intricately connected to the land. It was a place where people cared for one another. Farm vehicles and implements were often shared. If a truck went missing from the farm, no one was concerned. They just assumed a neighbor borrowed it and would return it when they no longer needed it. If a person required help, a neighbor was only a phone call away. People watched out for one another and were there for one another.

The first church I pastored was located in a ranching and farming community on the eastern edge of Montana. Branding cattle was not only a necessary part of spring work, but also a community event, as ranchers banded together to help one another rope the newly born calves and brand them before turning them onto the summer range.

For the last twenty-five years, I have been serving in a community that was once predominantly a logging community in the Northwest. But the economic downturn undercut the logging industry, and the closure of the national forest for logging undermined the local economy. Since then, the community continues to struggle as it has turned to tourism as a new economic base. Yet in the transition from a logging community to a tourist community, people have continued to take care of one another.

In each of these communities, the people have understood the importance of caring for one another. When a crisis strikes a family, the whole community bands together to help. If you forget or neglect to lock your door, there is little concern. People watch out for one another. If you were to walk the streets of town, visit the local "watering hole" (otherwise known as the local coffee shop), or eat at the favorite restaurant, what you would find are good people who have a strong sense of moral values. They have a firm belief in God, although they might say that God "helps those who help themselves." They often will identify with a local church, even though they rarely attend.

However, the moral (and political) conservatism, the firm belief in God, and the community concern often conceal a darker reality. As we have already discussed, rural America grapples with increasing social and economic struggles that threaten the vitality of the community. However, even though many of the people identify themselves as Christian, they lack a genuine redemptive relationship with the living God. They are *good* people, but they are not *redeemed* people. In many ways, they may be characterized by the words of Paul: they hold "to a form of godliness, although they have denied its power" (2 Tim. 3:5). They are often religious but lack a vital relationship with Christ grounded in obedience to Scripture.

Rural America as a Mission Field

In Matthew 9:36–37, Christ seeks to change the perspective of the disciples. It's not difficult to identify with the disciples' view of the people clamoring to hear Jesus' teaching and receive His healing touch. At times, the disciples saw them as a nuisance. At others, they saw them as a distraction. Perhaps they saw them as good people who were already part of God's kingdom. But in the event preceding Christ commissioning the disciples to go forth and proclaim the gospel of the kingdom, Christ seeks to give them a different perspective. He described the people in graphic terms—as "stressed and dispirited"—to remind the disciples that the need for the gospel to be preached was great. The problem is never with the harvest, but with the availability of workers who not only see the need for the harvest, but also understand the spiritual condition of people.

When the church turned its attention to the urban centers, instead of expanding its vision for the lost, it narrowed it as it prioritized reaching the city. This was based upon the faulty assumption that rural America was already evangelized and in some cases over-churched. Again, reality does not match perception. Nationally, thirty-four percent of American adults do not have any affiliation with a church.[1] Except for the region of the Bible Belt, rural communities not only correspond to the national average, but exceed it in some cases. In the rural areas of the Pacific Northwest and the Rocky Mountain region, those who claim no religious affiliation exceed forty percent, and only approximately twenty percent would claim to have made a personal commitment to Jesus Christ.[2] The county in which I currently live is one of the most unchurched counties in the United States.

Yet the problem goes deeper than those claiming no religious affiliation. Many in rural areas describe themselves as Christian and claim affiliation with a church but live without any spiritual growth or transformation. Donnie Griggs rightly summarizes the problem:

Small towns often have, if they have anything, an assumed gospel. Don Carson wisely says that, 'One generation believes the gospel, the next generation assumes the gospel, but the next generation denies the gospel.' But, with the data so clearly showing sin as reigning in small towns, we have to question if they haven't moved past an assumed gospel to a full-blown denial of the gospel.[3]

When we examine rural communities, we discover many of them face social collapse with increases in suicide, alcoholism, domestic violence, and gambling that rival and even exceed urban areas.[4] While a number of reasons contribute to the crisis confronting rural communities, part of the problem stems from the church abandoning rural communities. Thus, Griggs summarizes, "Small-town America has fallen apart. Maybe it's not directly because of our focus that has primarily been on urban centers. That's certainly debatable, but what is not debatable is that small towns are just as in need of great leaders and great churches as any big city is."[5] It's time that we rethink missions in the United States and recognize that rural communities are unchurched and in need of the gospel.

Ultimately, this brings us to the heart of the Great Commission. The Great Commission was not a call to preach the gospel to urban centers but a call to penetrate every corner of the globe with the message of Christ. In light of the millions of people living in rural communities who have not embraced the gospel, the church should be motivated for a renewed vision for rural communities. Tragically, in a time when we need a new call for missions in rural communities, some promote the abandonment of it. Some have gone so far as to say that the closure of thousands of rural churches is not "an entirely undesirable condition."[6] To turn our backs on rural communities is to become indifferent to the spiritual condition of people. Abandoning the rural church neglects the Great Commission and distorts the personal nature of the gospel.

Tragically, there are still many rural communities in both the United States and Canada that do not have a church present in them.

To reach those who have not heard or embraced the gospel of Christ, we need to mobilize a new generation of people who see the rural communities as the mission field. The fields are white unto harvest. The task requires dedicated pastors willing to go to rural communities; it also mandates the training, equipping, and mobilizing of rural people to become missionaries. As Morrow points out, "Small towns desperately need normal, everyday people like farmers, factory workers, teachers, secretaries, and small business owners who think and act like missionaries to reach their friends, neighbors, co-workers and extended families for Christ."[7] Those who serve the rural church must not only see themselves as missionaries, but also see the importance of training and equipping rural people to become missionaries as well.

Cross-Cultural Ministry in Rural America

While rural churches often support global ministries, they now need to recognize that cross-cultural ministry has come to their own communities. As rural America becomes more ethnically diverse, especially through the Hispanic population growth, the church can become more involved in cross-cultural ministry at the local level. This requires people to accept and value the strong contribution minorities make within their communities and within the church. As we pointed out earlier, this means that the church needs to become the leader in seeking to assist them in the struggles they encounter. Hispanics, and many other minorities, often do not have access to formal healthcare services because of financial limitations, lack of insurance, transportation costs, language barriers, and cultural differences.[8] The church can assist them in becoming productive members of the community by helping to remove existing structural barriers. This begins by helping rural leaders "view their Latino residents as assets rather than liabilities and to invest in the development of their human capital in order for Latinos to help sustain their communities."[9] This is equally true of the church. The global community is now knocking on our front door so that we can have a cross-cultural ministry with our next-door neighbors, as only twenty percent of the Hispanic community is evangelical.[10]

Along with the growth of the Hispanic population, the Asian population is growing in rural areas as well. The percentage of people of Asian descent (Asian and Pacific Islanders) is a relatively small percent of rural population (1.1 percent, except in Hawaii, where it is 35 percent). However, the population of Asians in rural areas grew 37.4 percent between 2000 and 2010.[11]

The rural church needs to recognize the value of cultural diversity. Many declining rural communities are experiencing a resurgence of growth with the influx of Hispanics and other minority groups. In the rural communities of Western Kansas, for example, every county but one has experienced a decline in the non-Hispanic white population, while at the same time many of them experienced double-digit growth in the Hispanic population. And even as the Anglo population has declined, the overall population has increased.[12] This brings new opportunities for rural churches not only to experience needed growth but also to be enriched by the diversity and perspective other cultures bring. Instead of seeing this influx as a threat, we can embrace it as an opportunity for growth in the social and human capital of a community. What Um and Buzzard argue concerning the strength of urban centers can equally be realized in many rural communities: when there is connective diversity, the result is the "amplification of human potential in every dimension of life and culture."[13]

Our faith and understanding of God's redemptive program expands when we learn from other cultures and people groups. In my ministry, I have had the privilege of teaching and interacting with pastors and church leaders in Russia, the Philippines, and Mexico. In each case, while I was there to teach, I felt that I learned more from them than they did from me. Seeing the depth of their faith and their perspective of community expanded my own understanding that is at times clouded by my own cultural background. We can learn a great deal from other cultures, from people whose focus on community contrasts the rural mindset of individualism and self-determination. By embracing cultural diversity, our own faith will be expanded. When this happens, not only will we see the Hispanic, African American, Asian, and Native American members of our communities as our brothers and sisters, but we will also begin to value and recognize the contribution they give to the church.

The Rural Church and Native Americans:
The Challenge to Reach an Unreached People

When we think of missions to an unreached people group, we focus our attention on some forgotten, uncivilized people in the jungles of South America or the 10/40 window. Yet in our own backyard, the Native North American Indians remain largely unreached with the gospel. Of the 6 million Native Americans, only eight percent have been reached with the gospel.[14] In many of the 566 tribes, less than 4 percent claim to be evangelical.[15] Many of the Eskimo tribes have less than 2 percent evangelicals, and in the Creole tribe, the figure is less than .05 percent.[16]

While there has been a long history of missionary work within the tribes, little headway has been made. The reasons are complex, but there are several factors. First, the isolation of Native Americans on reservations left them isolated not only from mainstream culture, but also from the mainstream church. As the evangelical church turned their attention to the cities, there was little to attract them to Native American ministries. Out of sight, out of mind. Second, the long history of mistreatment of Native Americans has created an attitude of distrust toward Christianity, as Natives have seen it as political and cultural rather than redemptive. Third, in recent years, there has been the attempt to revive

Native culture that has also led to the resurgence of Native religious traditionalism and the revival of the peyote movement. Native American racial identity is interwoven into the Native spirituality and identity.[17] To be Native is to be embrace Native spirituality. As a result, the challenge to reach Native Americans is met with a double challenge: one challenge is ethnic/cultural, and the other is spiritual. For them, to embrace their Christian faith places them in direct conflict with their Native cultural heritage. As a result, they face the challenge of seeking to discern what it means to be a Native American Christian. The question of adaptation and utilization of cultural forms in worship within the Native Church remains one of the most critical issues confronting Native Christians. Finding the right balance is difficult to achieve.

This brings us back to the challenge of the church today. Reaching Native Americans with the gospel does not happen with an urban church sending out a "missions team" to do a week of service on the reservation. In doing so, we are often more concerned about doing something to make us feel like we are seeking "social justice" than we are about truly transforming people's lives. Our service becomes religious penance to assuage our guilt about our indulgent lifestyles. Reaching Native Americans involves devoting time to live with them, understand them, and respect them. It involves going back to the very heart and foundation of the gospel: building relationships so that the gospel may be modeled even as we communicate it. This begins with the rural church, which is present on and near reservations. It involves in-depth discipleship of Native Americans who have accepted Christ, enabling and equipping them to become missionaries to their own tribes. But it also involves helping them deal with and overcome the effects of the social and moral breakdown they have experienced on the reservation, where many Native women experience sexual and physical abuse and suffer long-term emotional scars. It's not an easy task, but our calling is never to go to those who are well; it is to go to the broken who need to have their life restructured by the gospel of Christ.

This is what brings us to the heart of our perception of the rural church. The effective rural church is not one that sees itself as a spiritual sanctuary to be served by a pastor who is there to marry, bury, and keep the doors open. The rural church must be a missional church that understands it exists on the mission field with the task of advancing the kingdom of God through the proclamation of the gospel.

The Rural Church as a Missional Church

We struggle to understand rural communities as a mission field because we assume they are already Christian. And we assume they are Christian because the moral conservativism existing in many rural communities supports and is grounded in a Judeo-Christian ethic. This is especially true when we contrast this ethic with the moral relativism that characterizes the larger society. As a result, the rural church is viewed as a maintenance church (that is, a church that maintains a Christian influence in the community) rather than a missional church (that is, a church that exists to evangelize and disciple people with the gospel of Christ).

We also struggle to see the rural church as a missional church because we fail to distinguish between missions and church growth. In rural ministry, we become discouraged because we do not experience the substantial growth we all desire. It doesn't take long in rural ministry to recognize that pursuing church growth is to pursue a mirage that is ever on the horizon but never obtainable. In many cases, when the church orients itself to outreach, the driving force does not come from an awareness of the lostness of people, but a fear of the church dying. But the "fear of dying is not an adequate reason for a church to want to grow and will usually mean the church will not grow."[18] However, because we equate growth with being a mission-driven church, when we abandon the pursuit of growth, we also abandon the pursuit of evangelism. As Zunkel rightly points out, "It needs to be said that *some faithful churches will not grow.* Indeed, some churches, because of special ministries of a unique calling to a prophetic ministry, should not expect to make significant growth."[19] However, he rightly goes on to point out, *"But all congregations share in the mandate of the Great Commission."*[20] Even as we flounder in the pursuit of church growth, we should not allow it to discourage us from the pursuit of reaching people with the gospel. To be a missional church is to be driven by the desire to see all people come to Christ so that none may perish. Kevin Ruffcorn identifies this struggle for rural churches: "Congregations have burdened themselves unnecessarily by trying to measure the results of their evangelistic activities. Rural congregations have looked out upon fields that, although ripe for harvest, are not plentiful, and they have despaired."[21] When harvest time came on the farm, the focus was never upon the quantity of the harvest, but on the quality of the harvest. The urgency came because the wheat was ripe regardless of yield. So also in the small rural church. Our focus is never upon the quantity of the harvest, but rather on the fact that people desperately need to hear the gospel.

A missional church is one driven by Matthew 28:19–20. It has a passion not only for reaching the lost, but also for making disciples. Missional churches focus upon building the kingdom rather than maintaining the existence of the church. They integrate discipleship into all aspects of ministry. While large churches have multiple programs for carrying out different aspects of the Great Commission, the rural church, because of its size, needs a more holistic approach in which the church weaves evangelism and discipleship into all aspects of its ministry. David Ray rightly points out, "Small church mission is integral to the whole life of the church. Working as it should, small church mission is inspired through worship, informed through education, and carried over from the member's care for one another. It is not a separate activity done by a separate group of people."[22] Social events designed to build fellowship and a sense of community provide opportunities for outreach. For the last several years, our most effective outreach has come from a group of people in the church meeting every week at the local coffee shop. However, this moves beyond just the local church, for it involves the universal church as well. A genuinely missional church sees the importance of taking the gospel both to urban and rural people. It does not prioritize one group over another based upon demographics, population, or expected results.

A Missional Church Recognizes the Importance of Presence

The apostle Paul recognized the importance of presence when he wrote, "How then will they call on Him in whom they have not believed? How will they believe in Him whom they have not heard? And how will they hear without a preacher? How will they preach unless they are sent? Just as it is written, 'HOW BEAUTIFUL ARE THE FEET OF THOSE WHO BRING GOOD NEWS OF GOOD THINGS!'" (Rom. 10:14–15). The heart of the gospel is relational. The gospel provides the means by which humanity is restored into a dynamic, vibrant, and personal relationship with the living God. It should not surprise us when God sets the proclamation of the gospel within the context of relationships. From the beginning of the church, the focus of evangelism was grounded in relationships rather than conveying information through impersonal programs. Peter points this out when he challenges us to always be "ready to make a defense to everyone who asks you to give an account for the hope that is in you, yet with gentleness and reverence; and keep a good conscience so that in the thing in which you are slandered, those who revile your good behavior in Christ will be put to shame" (1 Peter 3:15–16). We silence our critics and give legitimacy to our message when people can observe our life up close and see the hope we possess. The redemptive plan of God is centered upon one person building a relationship with another for communicating the gospel.

Reaching the rural community begins with the church being present in the community. The church needs to be involved in the lives of people, not isolated from the community. A regional church may attract a large group of Christians, but it will not penetrate the local community with the gospel of Christ to build relationships within the community. Harold Longenecker points out, "We can never successfully centralize our churches. At least we cannot do so and remain true to our commission. To go in this direction is to violate the very idea and genius of the church. The church was not meant to be a repository but a dispensary. She is not to conserve but to diffuse."[23] He goes on to state, "Rather than aim at bringing the people to the church, the church must be taken to the people."[24] Likewise, at the turn of the twentieth century, Gifford Pinchot and Charles Gill warned,

> While the preaching of a good pastor is an indispensable factor in the individual development of his parishioners and in the progress of community life, that of the non-resident is by comparison of little value. It is shooting in the air without seeing the target, like the fire of artillery without the aid of air scouts. There is no greater force for righteousness in a country community than a church with a resident minister, well educated, well equipped, wisely selected, whose term of service is not too short.[25]

Christ did not bring salvation to us by remaining in heaven and shouting an invitation to come and join Him. No, He brought salvation by entering into our world, becoming a personal substitute for our sins, and connecting with people as individuals and sharing the message of the kingdom with them. For this to happen today, we not only need to connect with people in the community, but we need to be actively involved in the community, ministering to people and meeting their needs.

A Missional Church Is Intentional

In rural ministry, it's easy to be driven by tradition and the status quo. While tradition remains important, providing an anchor in a chaotic world, it can also hinder the church when the church is more driven by the maintenance of tradition than the advancement of the gospel. To be missional requires the rural church to become intentional in all its activities. While valuing the past and traditions, they base their decisions upon what effectively reaches the community. The massive cultural and moral upheaval sweeping across the nation has not only transformed urban society, but has influenced rural culture and society as well. This is especially true regarding the young people living in rural communities. In addressing the potential of the rural church to reach the next generation, Terry Dorsett summarizes the changes occurring in rural society,

> The same technology that made it possible for outsiders to move in has also brought the outside world to small towns and rural communities. Teenagers from small towns and rural areas can now be just as connected and up-to-date on music, clothing styles, and philosophical concepts as their urban counterparts. Adults from rural and small towns are now exposed to more progressive ideas and concepts than ever before, and some of them are buying into these new ideas.[26]

The intentional church adapts its ministry to more effectively communicate the unchanging gospel of Christ.

A Missional Church Revitalizes Churches

For some, the struggling small church is a dinosaur needing to be closed. Rather than revitalizing the floundering rural church, they opt to close the church and either consolidate it with another regional church or start a new church under new leadership. While there are times when this is beneficial—especially when the church has a poor reputation within the community because of long-standing internal conflicts—in many cases, it is more effective to revitalize the church because it has already formed strong connections within the community. Rural people are reluctant to accept outsiders, so a church plant can be viewed with suspicion by the community. In contrast, an already established church has relational ties to the community that can become the springboard for new opportunities in ministry.

Revitalization is not about moving the church to a new form, such as the seeker-sensitive model. Nor is it about developing new programs and ministries. Instead, it begins with the heart of the church. Hazelton describes revitalization this way: "The revival we speak of here is not a series of special services nor an appeal to sinners. Revival is the need of God's people, the Christian believers. Revival is a fresh outpouring of God upon His Church."[27] So also, Shawchuck states, "Bringing God's people to a place where they can serve Christ fully, where they can do all that He asks of them—that is revitalization."[28] *Revitalization is the process of the Spirit of God moving the church to spiritual and organizational health by renewing the congregation's understanding of their responsibility before God so that they become obedient to Him and follow His will individually and corporately.* Revitalizing the church is not about church growth—although that may happen. Rather, it is about renewing the sense of mission within the congregation. As such, there are two types of revitalization.

Spiritual revitalization is necessary when the church has become spiritually anemic or weak and is no longer walking in obedience to God and driven by the Great Commission. In this case, the task of spiritual revitalization is to renew the people's focus upon God and His word so that they are living in obedience to Him. *Organizational revitalization* is necessary when the church's programs and structures hinder the work of the church and when the people focus upon doing the business of the church rather than serving Christ. In this case, the church is spiritually healthy but is channeling its efforts in a wrong or ineffective way. In such cases, the church needs to examine the needs and opportunities within the community and focus on ministering to people rather than maintaining past programs.[29]

A Missional Church Recognizes the Value of Planting Churches

Tragically, many rural communities are lacking churches grounded in the gospel, yet there is a marked neglect of planting churches in rural communities. Attend a denominational conference, and you will hear report after report of planting new churches in cities, but a silence regarding those being planted in rural communities. In one denomination, only 15 percent of the churches planted were in small towns and rural areas, and half of those were in one district that targeted rural areas.[30] Yet there are new opportunities for church planting in many rural areas.[31]

In recent years, there has been a population rebound in many rural communities, especially in areas of natural amenities. With the increased ability to conduct business from any location through the internet, more people are moving to rural communities that offer the enjoyment of natural resources. During a recent ten-year period, small towns grew by 4.9 percent.[32] As "urbanites" migrate to rural areas, they bring different expectations for the church and a new need for new churches to reach them with the gospel.

The increase of ethnic diversity has also resulted in a need for planting churches with an empasis on reaching multiple ethnic groups in rural areas, especially in those areas experiencing an influx of Hispanics as well as areas on or near Native American reservations. Even communities with a church may be possible locations for a church plant. Rural churches tend to be culturally homogeneous while the community is becoming multicultural, requiring new churches to reach different cultural groups.

Jim Montgomery writes that a group of people has been evangelized when there exists "1) an active, witnessing cell of believers in every village, town, urban neighborhood and ethnic community in the country; 2) a church for every geographical group of 300 to 1,000 people; 3) a viable church within geographical and social-cultural reach of everyone."[33] Tragically there are countless communities and areas in rural America where this is not yet realized. However, if churches are to be planted in rural communities, then rural rather than urban methodologies will be required. Many books on church planting are grounded in an urban context. For example, one book on church planting suggests that you start with a minimum of 50 people with at least 10 to 12 families. This simply is unrealistic in many rural settings. The goal is to establish a witnessing community in an area lacking one rather than establishing a church with the potential to grow beyond 200. One of the best means of planting churches comes from the rural church itself. As a rural church identifies a community in its surrounding area as needing a church plant, it can start by holding a Bible study in the community with the goal of forming a separate congregation with the pastor serving as the interim preacher.

As we turn our attention to the future, we should recognize that the rural church can no longer survive merely as a refuge for Christians to gather together and focus on our proverbial navels. It must see its community as a mission field where the goal of the church is to connect with people to share the gospel. Otherwise, there will be no future.

The Future
of Rural Ministry

RECENTLY, I RETURNED from helping my brothers with the Timothy Hay harvest. After driving a tractor for two weeks, I reflected upon the first time I operated a baler. It was when I was in my early teens driving my father's 35-horsepower diesel Ford Major, which was built in the mid-1950s. Behind the Ford, we pulled a New Holland baler powered by a Wisconsin, two-cylinder gas motor, having the same horsepower as the riding lawn mower I now use to mow the grass around our house. During the peak of the haying season, with a crew of 8 to 10 teens, we would put 1,000 50-pound bales (approximately 20 tons) a day in the barn. The hay was then used to feed the cattle belonging to my dad for the coming winter. In a good year, when there was more hay than my father needed, he would sell hay to other farmers and ranchers in the community.

When I recently baled hay with my brothers, I did so with a 310-horsepower tractor pulling a Massey Ferguson baler that made

1,100-pound bales. Together, with the three other tractors my brothers owned, we would bale and stack 1,500 to 2,000 bales a day (approximately 750 to 1,000 tons). Instead of the hay being used to feed their personal cattle—my brothers quit raising cattle several years ago—these bales will be trucked to a processing plant to be recut, compressed, and placed in containers to be shipped to Asia and the Middle East. In the last 40 years, not only has the production per day increased tenfold, but the market for the hay has become global.

To label rural America resistant to change and stuck in the past grossly misunderstands and misrepresents rural people. The tsunami of change sweeping across America and bringing the national economy into a global market has swept across rural communities as well. With the changes occurring in society at large, the rural church faces new challenges and opportunities as it moves forward in the twenty-first century. How the rural church and the church of America in general respond to these changes and challenges will determine their survival. In looking to the future of the rural church, there are several important challenges and opportunities confronting congregations dotting the rural landscape.

The High Cost of Losing Rural America

The heartbeat of the best rural church is where faith in the gospel is lived out in a caring community, where worship is not entertainment, and where preaching is not reduced to a soundbite. As Callahan writes, "Regrettably, however, we have virtually forgotten that small can be *very* strong."[1] One of the values of the rural church is found in that rural and small town communities often provide the leaders for our nation. Nine of the last twelve presidents find their roots in rural and small town America. Many influential celebrities and leaders come from small communities. This leads Griggs to ask a thought-provoking question: "What if we had great churches in all of these towns? How much different could the lives of these leaders have been? And, for us, if we take small town ministry seriously now, can we help shape the future?"[2] To abandon rural communities as irrelevant is to abandon the relevancy of the church in the larger community as well.

Tucked away in isolated and overlooked communities, rural communities and rural churches draw little notice. As a result, their struggles and crises often go unnoticed. In *Hollowing Out the Middle*, Patrick Carr and Maria Kefalas observe,

> We're not implying that no one is advocating for rural America; people are. Our concern is that those people expend far too much energy just telling the rest of the nation that they should be worried about the countryside's fate. The greatest challenge is getting people outside of the region to see that the place where 'real Americans' dwell has any serious problems at all. The time is long overdue for an awakening to the social and economic crisis in the Heartland.[3]

This is true of the rural church as well. The evangelical community is largely ignorant of the spiritual crisis in the heartland. Carr and Kefalas go on to warn,

> If, as a nation, we decide not to intervene, then we must accept a future with a myriad of social problems throughout the countryside, the spread of rural wastelands, and the unraveling of civic institutions such as churches and local schools. The economic, political, and social cost of allowing huge swaths of the countryside to decline in this manner are simply too extreme to comprehend.[4]

If we, as a church, choose to ignore the future of rural America, we too will pay a price that may prove costlier than we realize.

If we lose our passion for rural America, then we will have abandoned a critical part of the gospel call. The church denounces the moral erosion in our country as society has abandoned the moral foundation of a Judeo-Christian ethic in the pursuit of a morality governed by the pursuit of personal pleasure and fulfillment. The pursuit of righteousness has been abandoned for the pursuit of personal happiness. Yet the church has often adapted the same ethos as we have replaced the pursuit of Christlike self-denial with the quest for personal success and recognition, where the absolute truth of Scripture has been dumped for a morality governed by whatever makes us feel good. To neglect rural ministry because it lacks the prestige and opportunities of the urban centers violates the heart of the gospel, which focuses upon the necessity of the individual to accept Christ. The gospel calls us to value each person, to leave the masses of the ninety-nine in the pursuit of the one lost sheep. It is to recognize that the Ethiopian eunuch in the desert is just as important to the heart of Christ as the masses in Jerusalem. The gospel is about Christ dying for the sin of each person and bringing redemption to whosoever will accept Him. If the gospel becomes merely a tool for our own success, then we have undermined the very nature of the gospel.

As our country teeters on the edge of moral chaos, rural America can provide a restraining voice. But that voice is about to be lost. Secularism is slowly infiltrating rural America as mass media and the internet have brought the message of moral relativism to the country. If the church is not present to call people to a biblical ethos, then the last restraint will vanish. The larger evangelical community may ignore and even abandon the call to rural ministry. But it does so at the risk of its own existence.

The Rural Church and Coming Change

The winds of change blowing across the religious and moral landscape of our country have not left rural America untouched. While there remains a moral and spiritual conservativism in rural communities, it does not mean that rural people and communities have not also been influenced by these changes in the wider culture. As we have pointed out, rural America faces challenges and struggles that parallel many of the issues confronting the rest of the nation.

Ministry is not static, but dynamic. It is not conducted in a sterile test tube isolated from the winds of culture. Instead, we find that the culture in which we live intertwines with the programs we conduct. As a result, the trends that blow across the cultural landscape infiltrate the cracks of the church and affect the life and ministry of the congregation. Some of these trends are positive, resulting in new opportunities to reach people for Christ. The renewed passion for social justice, for instance, reminds the church of the importance that God places upon the outcast and those at risk of abuse. Other trends undermine the foundation of the church and, if not confronted, assault the stability of the ministry. If the church continues to follow the moral accommodation plaguing society, it will find itself losing its moral foundation. Still others—such as the advancement of technology—are neutral, having in themselves no moral or spiritual implications, but radically affect the way the church conducts its ministry.

Rural churches face the same challenge of moral diversity existing within our country. As already noted, the secularization creeping into mainstream culture is also infiltrating rural communities. While many rural communities often still hold to traditional views of marriage and morality, those views are slowly eroding. Schools are being forced to comply with federally mandated regulations grounded in a secular worldview. But it extends beyond morality to all levels of culture, from the style of dress to views of the environment. As Anthony Papas points out, "The creation of 'exurbia' means that people who do things in a city way now live in the country. And they go to the little country church and in all spiritual zealousness disrupt the monolithic stability of centuries." He goes on to write, "For example, they make short-term commitments only (marriage or study groups, the same), are motivated more by personal benefit than by duty, guilt, or the good of the whole, and view all of reality in terms of pluralism and relativism. These folks might sit in the same pews as their parents but they are not in the same cultural universe!"[5] As people migrate back to the rural communities from urban centers, they bring into the area progressive and pluralistic worldviews that will continue to challenge and conflict with the traditional worldviews and, more importantly, conflict with a biblical worldview. Like urban churches, the rural church will face the growing challenge of how to uphold biblical morality while at the same time engaging secularists in a loving way in order to develop avenues to communicate the gospel.

As the rural church moves forward, it also faces the challenge of the mobility of people. Where farmers once tilled only the land in close proximity to their home, now it is common for them to travel thirty to forty miles to reach segments of their farm. Ranchers have summer and winter ranges in different states to benefit from various climates. People in small towns will drive to larger cities for their shopping, socializing, and church activities. People will bypass several churches of varying sizes and denominations to attend the church of their choice. The effect of this movement means that the church, even in the rural areas, cannot assume that people will attend just because their doors are open. The church needs to carefully examine who it desires to reach, what it is doing to attract people, and how it will keep them once they start coming.

This mobility of people also means that many no longer regularly attend church. People attend in the summer but are "snowbirds" in the winter. They are more apt to be gone multiple Sundays a month. Consequently, the pool of regular attenders is shrinking while the number of people who call the church home may be increasing. However, this means that people are less likely to volunteer for long-term commitments and are more likely to serve in specific ministries with a set length of service. It also means that the informal communications used in the past must be replaced with more formal structures of communication.

Because of the migration of the youth to urban centers, the rural church faces the challenge of an aging congregation. As Wuthnow rightly points out, "small-town churches usually face the challenge of having mostly older members and thus finding it difficult to attract young people. The problem is partly that young people move away to find better jobs, meaning that the few who remain may be in congregations with insufficient numbers of children and other young adults to be appealing."[6] They face both the problem of their young people moving out of the community as well as the challenge of attracting those who do move into the community. To appeal to the next generation, the church needs to be open to new programs and approaches to ministry that might be attractive to young families. Something that's not easy to do.

The rural church faces the influence of the church growth movement. Whether we realize it or not, this movement has drastically influenced—both positively and negatively—the landscape of the small church. Positively, it has raised the awareness and importance of outreach and evangelism. It has shown the church the value and necessity of understanding our community and the worldview of the unsaved. It has assisted the congregation by providing helpful ideas for reaching people with the gospel.

Yet the church growth movement also negatively affected the rural church by redefining success in ministry. Success, and even spirituality, are now often measured by external results rather than the heart and character of people. Pragmatism rather than theology can become the driving force. As a result, many small churches and pastors become discouraged by the lack of apparent results. As the focus shifted to size and growth, both people's and the pastor's expectations changed so that if numerical growth does not occur, people blame the pastor and the pastor blames the people. For example, one denominational leader writes,

In North America most small congregations are small and remain that way because they are spiritually and organization-ally dysfunctional. Many large congregations have become large as a result of pursuing organizational health and in many cases spiritual health as well. If small congregations are truly healthy they will not remain small, but will grow and repro-duce in one way or another.[7]

While we should recognize the positive contribution the church growth movement has made, we should also guard against trying to take matters into our own hands. We need to be more evangelistic, but we must also recognize that salvation is ultimately the product of divine initiative rather than personal efforts, stemming from the convicting work of the Holy Spirit rather than excellent programs (1 Cor. 3:3–9). Thus, the focus shifts from the results of evangelism, which belong to God, to the process of faithful proclamation, which is the responsibil-ity of people. The critical question is not whether the church is adding to its numbers, but whether people are sharing their faith with their neighbors, friends, and coworkers.

As the church moves forward in the twenty-first century, the ques-tion is not, "Will the rural church be confronted with change?" but, "How will it manage the change it faces?" The church needs to distin-guish carefully between the changes that are merely cultural and those that undermine the authority and teaching of Scripture.

The Rural Church and Denominational Identity

As society becomes more secular, there is the increased need for churches to mutually support one another, for each to recognize the value and importance of the other and how they can benefit each other. Yet this will not happen without intentional action. Too often, the rural church is unrepresented in denomination gatherings—partly because of economics, for rural pastors often cannot afford to attend them. For example, in one denominational conference, four out of every five delegates came from churches with more than two hundred members, and half the delegates attended megachurches. As Kemp concludes, "These delegates were entrusted with decisions affecting the broad range of congregations and yet many had never experienced worship in the average-sized church of the denomination. They were oblivious to how some legislation, like a slotted spoon passing through vegetable soup, misses the needs of small churches while capturing the hopes of those of a more noticeable size."[8] Denominational and associational leaders need to not only recognize the existence of the rural church, but also start ensuring that it is represented in the leadership structures. As Peter Bush and Christine O'Reilly point out, "Since the small church is here to stay, it is incumbent upon church leaders at the congregational, middle judiciary, and national levels to move from simply reacting to the challenges facing small-membership congregations. It is important that these leaders take the initiative to support small congregations in their worship and witness."[9] Rural churches cannot be treated as the poor stepsister who has nothing to contribute and is therefore ignored. Instead, they need to be valued. They need to be recognized for the wisdom and contribution they can bring to the whole association.

Denominations also need to recognize the value and importance the rural church has as part of the mission strategy of the denomination in reaching all people with the gospel. Kemp summarizes, "The successful denomination of the future will provide appropriate clergy and in other ways support a diversity of church sizes. The small church has an important missional niche in our culture, and even the micro-sized congregation of a few dozen souls holds a vital part of the line against the advance of irreligious secularism."[10] A healthy national organization seeking to promote the health of the church will recognize the value and importance of every church, whether that church be rural or urban, small, medium, or large. As Carl Clark states, "Denominational leaders and local church leaders must band together to stop the leaks in the rural church situation. Too many churches have died. Too many churches are declining. Too many churches, though they have not died, are apparently in their last struggle. Working together, these two forces can turn the tide from a declining situation to a growing situation."[11]

The Rural Church and
the Future of Pastoral Leadership

The greatest challenge for rural churches in the future will be the recruitment and retention of pastors to serve their local congregation. While many associations experience a surplus of pastors, the rural church still confronts a shortage. Patricia Chang, in her research published in *Assessing the Clergy Supply in the 21st Century*, concludes that the church, as a whole, does not face a shortage of pastors, but a shortage of pastors willing to serve small congregations, especially isolated rural congregations. Thus, she summarizes, "Small congregations in rural areas appear to have an even greater problem retaining pastors because the distance between congregations is greater, making the possibility of pastor sharing or yoked congregations more difficult. Rural congregations are also more isolated and have fewer job opportunities for spouses who might otherwise be able to supplement the pastor's salary and benefits."[12] For example, she cites the Presbyterian Church (USA) where in 2000, 76 percent of congregations with an average attendance less than fifty people and 47 percent of churches between fifty and one hundred do not have a pastor. This was an increase of 70 percent and 41 percent, respectively, from 1990.[13] The issue was not so much the availability of pastors but the willingness of pastors to serve small and rural churches.

Finding a solution, however, is not easy. The reasons that pastors overlook rural ministry are complex. The financial package the rural church offers, the lack of prestige, the lack of young pastors willing to go to rural areas, and the focus of seminaries and Bible colleges on urban ministries all contribute to the problem. Further, the loss of pastors due to burnout, stress, and migration to urban centers further influence the shortage experienced by rural churches.

It's always easier to identify the problem than it is to suggest a solution. Nevertheless, there are steps that denominational and association leaders can take to address the problem. First, they must elevate the status of rural ministry so it is not seen as simply a place to either start in ministry to gain experience and then move on to a more prestigious ministry, or a place to end one's career after the urban church has moved on to find a younger pastor. Instead, rural ministry needs to be seen as both vital and important within God's redemptive program. The rural church must not be seen as a dependent child requiring the assistance of the denomination, but an important member of the family contributing to the health and stability of the universal church. What Andrew Nurse and Raymond Blake point out regarding rural communities in general could equally be said regarding our attitude towards the rural church:

> Political discourse propagates a distorted and self-serving view of reality in many rural areas by continuing to deal with the rural development issue as a relief operation, or as humanitarian aid to threatened regions. Many public policies work that way: tell us you are in bad shape, and we will help. If you show some vital signs, off they go to the next area that can show it is in greater trouble than its neighbour. Such an approach clearly maintains rural regions in a state of unhealthy dependency. ... In the meantime, public opinion quite naturally comes to question the benefit of supporting these regions which, ultimately, cost too much in tax dollars for too little return.[14]

Tragically, this is often the attitude that denominations and associations have toward the rural church. They judge churches solely upon economic terms. As a result, they see the rural church as the welfare child. While the rural church may have little to contribute financially—or may even need financial support—what it contributes in other aspects of ministry and insight to the denomination can far outweigh the economics.

Second, denominations and associations need to develop creative ways to provide financial support for those in rural ministry. Various options include shared pastors, satellite campuses, "tent-making" pastors, the use of lay pastors, and other creative solutions. As Bush and O'Reilly remark, "Given the realities of the North American church and the North American economy, lay leaders in small-membership churches will need to take on roles in worship planning and leading and in preaching. There is no way around the fact that in purely economic terms, small-membership churches need to explore models of ministry that have longer-term economic viability than present approaches."[15] However, developing lay pastors who lead the church requires seminaries and denominations to think differently not only by developing programs for equipping the pastors, but also by training lay leaders to serve the local church as pastors as well. The future of the small church may well be built upon the shoulders of the laity who are trained to assist the pastor and provide pastoral care when no pastor is available. One place where the sun is shining brightly is over many of those small churches in which the traditional pastoral responsibilities are now carried by committed and equipped laypersons."[16]

Moving Towards the Future by Remembering the Past

As the rural church moves forward, it cannot do so in isolation from the past. Nor can it be governed by the past. It must move forward as an outgrowth of the past. In rural churches, heritage plays an important role. It provides not only an emotional and cultural anchor in a chaotic world, but a theological anchor as well. It serves to connect people with the previous generation as a reminder of the spiritual heritage that was passed on to them. This provides a steady reminder that faith and truth are not something we can treat willy-nilly, changing and adapting them as we please.

Within the small rural church, traditions are more than ruts; they are the stories and bonds that tie the present congregation to previous generations. Because the small rural church values not only the present membership but also the past members, traditions play an important role within the life and expression of the church. They are not interested in the latest fad and they are slow to change, for change constitutes a break not only from the past, but from the previous generations who built the church. Each church has a story, and each story has a person who is the hero within the story. To be a part of the church, new people need to learn the stories and value the heroes behind them. Tradition and the past are not hindrances to effective ministry in the future but are the foundation upon which the church can embrace and adjust to the changes occurring within the society and within the church. While the church must not be governed by tradition that leads to paralyzed ministry, it cannot be unwilling to adapt to the changes confronting the church. Indeed, it can celebrate the past traditions and learn from them. The past provides wisdom, enabling a congregation and leader to identify areas critical for the future. A healthy rural church does not live in the past. Nor does it try to replicate the past. Rather, it celebrates and learns from the past.

New Hope for the Forgotten Church

So often, we get caught up with the latest fad or program and we forget that what ultimately changes people is not programs or facilities or techniques. What changes people is the gospel of Christ, for "it is the power of God for salvation" (Rom. 1:16). The crisis of the rural church is not a crisis of resources or a shortage of opportunities or the failure to adapt to the latest strategies. The crisis of the rural church is *the shortage of leaders* who exemplify the words of John Wesley: "Give me one hundred preachers who fear nothing but sin and desire nothing but God, and I care not whether they be clergymen or laymen, they alone will shake the gates of Hell and set up the kingdom of Heaven upon Earth."[17] This shortage threatens not just rural churches, but the very existence of the church in America. The rural church needs men and women who are not enamored by numbers and prestige, but have a desire to take the gospel to all who have not heard it, whether they be in urban or rural communities. We need people who understand that the call to ministry is a call of self-denial, a call to the building of God's kingdom rather than the pursuit of our own success. In Bible colleges and seminaries, we need to continue preparing people for urban ministries, to be sure. But we also need to prepare people for rural ministry, to help them understand rural culture and to see the rural church not as the stepping stone to greater ministry, but as the essence of ministry itself.

The crisis confronting the rural church is *a crisis of the church*. How we view the forgotten church reveals our understanding of the church itself. The church is not a franchise where effectiveness is determined by marketing techniques and strategic planning, and where success is measured by the size of the church and the number of satellite campuses. The church is a community of believers, no matter how many gather together for mutual encouragement, support, and ministry. It is where "two or three have gathered together in My name" (Matt. 18:20). But this community goes beyond just the mutual care found within the local congregation. To be truly the church of Christ, we must recognize the value and importance of every congregation. It is to recognize that we are part of the broader community of faith where "the members may have the same care for one another. And if one members suffers, all the members suffer with it; if *one* member is honored, all the members rejoice with it" (1 Cor. 12:25–26). To truly be the church, we need to recognize and listen to the voice of rural congregations so we may see them as a vital member of the whole body of Christ.

The crisis confronting the rural communities is *a crisis of the Great Commission.* The church is missional, and its task is to take the gospel to every single person in the world. And only when the "gospel of the kingdom shall be preached in the whole world as a testimony to all the nations" (Matt. 24:14) is the mission accomplished. For this reason alone, the broader church of America should be deeply concerned about rural communities. The urban church should be deeply troubled that there are rural people who are "separate from Christ . . . having no hope and without God in the world" (Eph. 2:12). Likewise, the rural church should grieve when there are people living in the cities who are "distressed and dispirited like sheep without a shepherd" (Matt. 9:36). To be a truly missional church is to recognize that it will take the whole church (urban and rural) reaching the whole world (city and country) with the whole gospel.

But all is not lost to despair. Even in the darkest days of Israel's spiritual decline, God reminded Elijah that He had His people scattered throughout the nation, standing firm against the onslaught of pagan idolatry. While some have distorted their call for prestige, recognition, and personal gain, countless others go willingly to any church needing a pastor. While some are directed by God to go to urban areas, others are sent by Him to the forgotten churches and overlooked places. They recognize the value and importance of the rural church, not only because there are millions of people living in rural communities who still need the gospel of Christ, but because the rural church is an important member of the broader American church. The rural church is not dying. It is growing, vital, and healthy. The rural church will continue to have an impact not only in the rural communities but throughout the world. The broader church of America will be strengthened by listening to the wisdom and lessons learned by the rural pastor and church, and by partnering with them. But that can happen only if they are not forgotten.

Appendix

What Church History Books Don't Tell

WHILE TRADITIONAL church history details the major movements impacting the broader church growth in America, it often overlooks the small events and activities of people and ministries that have made a difference in rural America. What follows is a brief history of some of these ministries.

American Sunday School Union

The *American Sunday School Union*—later named *American Missionary Fellowship* and subsequently *InFaith*—was initially established to address the needs of the poor children in Philadelphia who were unable to read. In 1817, the Union was formed by a group of businessmen and lay people from several different denominations and would eventually establish 43 schools in the region. Recognizing that the need was far greater than just the Philadelphia area, the mission hired its first itinerate missionary, Rev. William C. Blair, in 1822 to establish Sunday schools in the surrounding states. In the first year alone, Blair traveled approximately 2,500 miles on horseback, visiting six states and establishing 61 Sunday schools. He visited 35 more, helped revitalize another 20, and established 6 tract societies. As the country continued to expand westward, the American Sunday School Union recognized both the ministry needs and possibilities. In response, it recruited 80 to 100 missionaries to "establish a Sunday-school in every destitute place where it is practicable, throughout the Valley of the Mississippi." Covering an area of "about 1.3 million square miles, with a population of four million. It started Sunday schools in 5,000 communities." Even as the country expanded to the Pacific Ocean, they sought "to establish and maintain a Sunday-school in every needy community in the vast territory from the eastern base of the Rocky Mountains to the Pacific."[1]

The Union also developed Sunday Schools with Native Americans. Beginning in 1822, they established thirteen schools for instructing Native American children among the Cherokee nation, the Choctaws, and Chickasaws. In 1956, Emma Isaac, a Native American graduate of Prairie Bible Institute, began ministering to her own people at the Fort Berthold Reservation in North Dakota, working with the Mandan, Hidatsa, and Arikara tribes.

Now renamed InFaith, the mission continues to target unreached people by providing leadership and support for local churches. While it has refocused on church planting and urban ministries, it continues to have a presence in rural areas with its camps and church networks.[2]

Rural Home Missionary Association (RHMA)

In 1942, Rev. C. J. Rediger realized that rural communities were being overlooked. As he looked about the communities in Central Illinois, he became concerned that most of the ministries serving rural communities were focused on short-term ministries such as VBS, camp, and revival ministries. But few were providing long-term resident ministries. Later he would reflect, "I saw the great spiritual needs in the small towns of this land. And there developed a weakness of mine—an inability to forget the faces of the children. These dear ones didn't need another revival meeting. They need a rock-solid church, with a full program. They needed something for the long haul—to plan a church in every community in need of a solid church."[3]

This burden originated from his rural background and God's leading in his early life. When Rediger was eleven, he experienced a family tragedy: their car was hit by a train. While he and his father and brother survived, his mother and sister were tragically killed. Several years after this, his father left the farm and moved to Meadows, Illinois, where he opened a general store. While there, the family started attending the Salem Mennonite Church near Gridley, which proved to be instrumental for Rediger. He accepted Christ at age thirteen.

After college, Rediger sensed God's calling on his life, and started serving in urban churches. However, a turning point came when he started a work in Canton, Illinois. It was there that he had the opportunity to hear Rev. J. Lloyd Hunter, the founder of the Rural Bible Crusade (now the Rural Bible Crusade of Wisconsin), speak of his burden for and work in the rural schools. Over the next several weeks, he and Hunter traveled together, and he saw firsthand the needs of rural America. Soon he resigned from his church and, without any support or income, began the ministry of RHMA.

In the early years of his ministry, his "pay" often consisted of potatoes, apples, or a simple jar of rhubarb. Nevertheless, he remained convinced of God's calling and the needs of rural people. He began by traveling to Western Illinois where he found few in the community attending any church. Consequently, he visited several local farmers during the evening hours, following them as they did their chores and talking to them about the need for a Sunday School. Because of these conversations, in May 1942, they held their first public ministry, a Vacation Bible School in which two girls were saved. Thus, began the ministry of RHMA with a three-fold vision:

1. Because the spiritual need in rural areas was a national issue, the work would be nationwide.

2. Because reaching rural communities for the long haul is not likely to happen simply through ministries that come and go, and simply through children's work, RHMA would focus on establishing local churches that are for the long haul, through a total church program.

3. These churches which RHMA establishes will not be like stagnating ponds with no outlets; they will be 'feeders' for missions, home and abroad—providing personnel and support for the global missionary effort.[4]

The ministry of RHMA has continued to expand under the present leadership of Ron Klassen. Not only has RHMA provided leadership for rural churches, but they have been instrumental in expanding rural church ministry by conducting training and conferences for pastors of rural churches. Yet for all the work the Association has accomplished, at the end of his ministry, Rediger stated, "What then of the future? I am convinced that the needs of our particular ministry are so vast that all engaged in this work are hardly scratching the surface. . . . Rural missions must expand."[5]

Village Missions

In 1890, a young man named Walter Duff Sr. launched a full-time evangelistic and training ministry that would become known as the Irish Christian Worker's Union. After ministering in Ireland, he felt God calling him to move to America where he would continue conducting evangelistic services. As was the custom of the day, Walter Duff Sr. traveled first, with the plan of sending for his family once he arrived in the United States, and he made arrangements for their housing. Initially, his family purchased tickets to travel across the Atlantic on the ill-fated

Titanic. However, anxious to join Walter, they obtained passage on an earlier ship scheduled to arrive a few days before the Titanic. It was not until they reached Boston that they learned of the sinking of the Titanic and the loss of 1,200 lives.

Initially making their home in International Falls, Minnesota, they would eventually move to Portland, Oregon, which served as the base for his preaching and pastoral ministry. While his ministry was primarily in urban areas, he reported to his family of the many closed churches in rural America because of the lack of pastors. At the end of his life, his last request to his son Walter Jr. was, "Walter, having a pastorate is fine. But why don't you give your life to recruiting and sending out other ministers and missionaries to country churches without leadership. You should be able to send out at least one hundred men in your lifetime."

Rev. Duff's three daughters, Evangeline, Olive, and Helen, formed the Duff Sisters Gospel Trio with the purpose of conducting evangelistic services, first in rural communities and later in cities. However, it was this introduction to rural people that formulated a passion for rural people in their hearts. Because of this concern, Helen (who married Elwood Baugh) would establish Stonecroft Ministries (a national outreach ministry for women) and the Youth Home Missionaries. The purpose of the Youth Home Missionaries would be to send young women into rural communities to conduct Bible studies, Sunday schools, and Vacation Bible Schools.

As single women were being sent, three couples became missionaries to pastor several of the Sunday schools that were established in these rural communities. Helen approached her brother, Walter Jr., about forming an organization to send out and support these couples. As a result, on September 9, 1948, Village Missions was launched with Rev. Walter Duff Jr. appointed as the national director, and the final request given by a father was now being realized in his son. The goal and purpose of Village Missions was to send out couples as missionaries to plant and revitalize churches in rural communities. Over the course of his lifetime, Rev. Duff Jr. would send out over 600 rural missionaries.

In 1968, Village Missions expanded its ministry into Canada. With the theme "Preach the Word and Love the People," Village Missions now serves over 230 churches across North America, providing not only pastors for rural churches, but also financial support for pastors serving churches unable to support a full-time pastor. Under the leadership of Brian Wechsler, the mission has expanded to provide training to raise up future leaders through the Contenders Bible Initiative.

Rocky Mountain Bible Mission

In the spring of 1957, Darrel and Betty Burch, new missionaries with the American Sunday School Union, began to serve in the Bitterroot Valley of Montana. Their territory included the rural areas west of Helena, from the Canadian border south to Idaho. With 62,000 square miles to cover, they soon realized they would need assistance. Consequently, they recruited the help of Don and Ferris Rust, and Gale and Elsie Fister, who were working in a lumber camp at Port McNeil on Vancouver Island, British Columbia.

The Rusts moved to Stevensville, Montana, in July of 1957. Gale and Elsie followed a month later. All three families started driving the highways of Western Montana, knocking on doors and holding youth groups, Bible studies, Sunday schools, and small church services. While both Gale and Don held secular jobs, they ministered on evenings and weekends in the towns of Haugan and DeBorgia, Saltese, St. Regis, Frenchtown, Lolo, and Camas Prairie. Often traveling to communities a hundred miles away, Gale and Don each held services in eight different communities on a two-week cycle. In the spring of 1962, Sam and Marjorie Gupton replaced the Burches as the area's American Sunday School Union missionaries. With the help of newly recruited Frank and Betty Jackson, they reached out to the communities of Garrison, Gold Creek, Helmville, Lincoln, and others.

However, in 1968, the lack of income prompted the American Sunday School Union to reassign the Guptons. In response, the decision was made to form a new ministry to reach the rural communities of Montana. On February 21, 1969, the Articles of Incorporation of the Rocky Mountain Bible Mission became official. Gale Fister was president, Wallace Tucker was vice-president, Robert Lukey was secretary, and Frank Jackson was treasurer, with the Guptons serving as the only full-time missionaries.

In 1986, the leadership recognized the growing need for Native American ministries, and so they began an outreach program on the Flathead Reservation through the Ravalli and Hot Springs churches, and from these efforts a Native American children's ministry was developed. The venture, called "Pathwalkers," had been used in six western states by the summer of 1999.

Over the years, Rocky Mountain Bible Mission continued to provide leadership for rural churches in Montana and Northern Idaho, not only by providing pastors and leaders, but also through leadership training for adults and camp ministries for children. Along with a comprehensive pastoral internship program, the Mission expanded its ministry by developing a training program to raise up new leaders for rural ministry and by conducting an annual Shepherds' Conference to encourage and equip those in the area that serve rural ministries.[6]

United Indian Mission (UIM, International)

In August 1954, Donald and Donna Fredrick's life took a dramatic turn. After Donald resigned from the pastorate of Hunt Baptist Church in Hunt, New York, they moved west to disciple new believers and begin a new church, Navajo Bible Church, in Fort Defiance, Arizona. However, as they began their ministry, they soon encountered several obstacles. First, many of the mission agencies serving on the reservation were focused on providing food and clothing, with few seeking to establish indigenous churches. The result was that the people were not only not being evangelized, but they were becoming dependent economically upon the mission organizations.

Second, those mission agencies working to establish churches were working only with the Navajo, so that there was little being done with the neighboring Haulapai and Havasupai tribes. While the Navajo ministry was going well, there was an increasing realization that a ministry was desperately needed for the other tribes as well.

Third, the Fredricks recognized that they faced a significant hurdle in that the Native Americans viewed the missionaries and the church as "white man's church." If the tribes were to have healthy churches, they needed Native Americans to provide the leadership, something that had not yet occurred.

At the same time, Lemuel Paya, chairman of the Havasupai tribe, invited the Fredricks to come and establish a ministry with the Havasupai tribe. As a result, the Fredericks, along with David and Muriel Chambers, and David and Regina Clark, formed the United Indian Mission, Inc. They would later expand their ministries to indigenous people in Mexico and Canada, and change their name to UIM International. Eventually, they would serve tribes in Washington, Oklahoma, and Wisconsin, as well as the Navajo, Havasupai, Hualapai, and Pueblo tribes. In Mexico, they would develop ministries in Sonora, Chihuahua, Sinaloa, and Oaxaca. In Canada, they reached out to the tribes of Gitxsan and Wet'suwet'ens. Today, UIM International reaches nearly thirty-five tribal groups in Canada, the US, and Mexico as well as Mexican nationals and Spanish-speaking groups within various parts of the US. Their objective is to establish gospel-centered and Bible-based churches that are self-governing, self-propagating bodies of Christ.[7]

Notes

Seeing as Christ Sees

1. David J. Hesselgrave, *Planting Churches Cross-Culturally* (Grand Rapids: Baker Books, 2001), 64.

Chapter 1: The Forgotten Ministry

1. Harry Rimmer, *The Last of the Giants* (repr.: St. John, IN: Larry Harrison, no date), 39.
2. Thomas D. Whittles, *Frank Higgins, Trail Blazer* (New York: Interchurch Press, 1920), 33.
3. "Higgins, Francis 'Frank' E. (1865–1915)," *MNOPEDIA* website, http://www.mnopedia .org/person/higgins-francis-frank-e-1865-1915.
4. Whittles, *Frank Higgins, Trail Blazer*, 41.
5. "The Sky Pilot to the Lumberjacks," *The San Francisco Call*, January 8, 1911, http:// chroniclingamerica.loc.gov/lccn/sn85066387/1911-01-08/ed-1/seq-14/.
6. "The Sky Pilot to the Lumberjacks."
7. "Rev. Higgins Doing Much Good Work," *The Bemidji Daily Pioneer*, vol. 4, no. 264, March 2, 1907, http://chroniclingamerica.loc.gov/lccn/sn86063381/1907-03-02/ed-1/seq-1/#.
8. Rimmer, *Last of the Giants*, 56.
9. Harold T. Hagg, "The Lumberjacks' Sky Pilot," *Minnesota History*, vol. 31, no. 2 (June 1950): 67.
10. "Preaching in the Camps," *Bemidji Pioneer*, April 10, 1902, http://chroniclingamerica.loc .gov/lccn/sn90059048/1902-04-10/ed-1/seq-3/.
11. Ibid.
12. Hagg, "The Lumberjacks' Sky Pilot," 69.
13. Whittles, *Frank Higgins, Trail Blazer*, 5.
14. "James Washington Hall Family Home Page, IL, MO, IN?: Information about Richard Townsend Ferrell," Geneology.com, http://www.genealogy.com/ftm/k/u/r/Carolyn-H-Kurtz/WEBSITE-0001/UHP-0085.html.
15. "Timberland Parish," *Presbyterian Life*, September 17, 1949, https://digital history.pcusa .org/islandora/object/islandora%3A8459.
16. "Timberland Parrish."
17. "Parish in the Pines," *Presbyterian Historical Society*, http://www.history.pcusa.org/history-online/exhibits/parish-pines-page-4.
18. Greg Jaffe and Juliet Eilperin, "Tom Vilsack's lonely fight for a 'forgotten' rural America," *Washington Post*, September 26, 2016, https://www.washingtonpost.com/politics/ tom-vilsacks-lonely-fight-for-a-forgotten-rural-america/2016/09/26/62d7ee64-7830-11e6-ac8e-cf8e0dd91dc7_story.html?utm_term=.c097326fc941.
19. Thomas A. Lyson and William W. Falk, eds., *Forgotten Places: Uneven Development in Rural America* (Lawrence, KS: University Press of Kansas, 1993), 1–4.
20. Ralph Adcock, *What Am I Doing Here?* (Mustang, OK: Tate Publishing, 2004), 141.
21. Adcock, *What Am I Doing Here?*, 160–61.
22. Richard Wood, *Survival of Rural America* (Lawrence, KS: University Press of Kansas, 2010), xi.

Chapter 2: The Misunderstood Ministry

1. Richard Wood, *Survival of Rural America* (Lawrence, KS: University Press of Kansas, 2010), xi.
2. David L. Brown and Kai A. Schafft, *Rural People and Communities in the 21st Century* (Malden, MA: Polity Press, 2011), 8.
3. Within the government and sociological definitions, there is not a distinction between urban and suburban. What is normally referred to as *suburban* is included within the *urban* category.
4. Michael Ratcliffe, Charlynn Burd, Kelly Holder, and Alison Fields, "Defining Rural at the U.S. Census Bureau," December, 2016, https://www2.census.gov/geo/pdfs/reference/ua/Defining_Rural.pdf.
5. Calvin Lunsford Beale, *A Taste of the Country* (University Park, PA: The Pennsylvania State University Press, 1990), 78.
6. Richard Rathge, "Rural Demography," in *Encyclopedia of Rural America*, 2 vols., ed. Gary A. Goreham (Santa Barbara, CA: ABC-CLIO, Inc., 1997), 2:627.
7. Cornelia Butler Flora, Jan L. Flora, and Stephen P. Gasteyer, eds., *Rural Communities*, 5th ed. (Boulder, CO: Westview Press, 2016), 11.
8. United States Department of Agriculture, Economic Research Service, "Rural-Urban Continuum Codes Documentation," *United States Department of Agriculture* website, https://www.ers.usda.gov/data-products/rural-urban-continuum-codes/documentation/.
9. Robert Wuthnow, *Small Town America*, (Princeton, NJ: Princeton University Press, 2013), 8.
10. Karen Owen Facebook profile, https://www.facebook.com/karen.owen.7127.
11. David B. Danbom, *Born in the Country* (Baltimore: The Johns Hopkins University Press, 1995), 2.
12. Mayhill Fowler, "Obama: No Surprise that Hard-Pressed Pennsylvanians Turn Bitter, *Huffington Post*, November 17, 2008, https://www.huffingtonpost.com/mayhill-fowler/obama-no-surprise-that-ha_b_96188.html.
13. Frank L. Farmer, "Rural, Definition of," in *Encyclopedia of Rural America*, 2:624.
14. See England, J. Lynn, W. Eugene Gibbons, and Barry L. Johnson. "The Impact of a Rural Environment on Values." *Rural Sociology* 44 (1979): 119–136, Farmer, "Rural, Definition of," 2:624.
15. Jeanne Hoeft, L. Shannon Jung, Joretta Marshall, *Practicing Care in Rural Congregations and Communities* (Minneapolis: Fortress Press, 2013), 9.
16. Farmer, "Rural, Definition of," 2:833.
17. This definition thus distinguishes between rural and micropolitan communities (those between 10,000 and 50,000). However, this distinction is fluid at best, so that some areas classified as micropolitan may still be rural in culture. See also George W. Garner, ed. *Rural Church Planting* (Alpharetta, GA: North American Mission Board, SBC, 2011), 14–16.
18. Jed Kolko, "How Suburban Are Big American Cities?" *FiveThirtyEight* website, May 21, 2015, https://fivethirtyeight.com/features/how-suburban-are-big-american-cities/.
19. Josh Kron, "Red State, Blue City: How the Urban-Rural Divide is Splitting America," *The Atlantic*, November 30, 2012, http://www.theatlantic.com/politics/archive/2012/11/red-state-blue-city-how-the-urban-rural-divide-is-splitting-america/265686/.
20. Laura Meckler and Dante Chinni, "City vs. Country: How Where We Live Deepens the Nation's Political Divide," *The Wall Street Journal*, March 21, 2014, https://www.wsj.com/articles/city-vs-country-how-where-we-live-deepens-the-nations-political-divide-1395369321.
21. Ibid.
22. Linda Lyons, "Age, Religiosity, and Rural America," *Gallup*, March 11, 2003, http://www.gallup.com/poll/7960/age-religiosity-rural-america.aspx.
23. Victor Davis Hanson, "The Oldest Divide," *City Journal*, Autumn 2015, http://www.city-journal.org/html/oldest-divide-14042.html.

24. David L. Brown and Louis E. Swanson, *Challenges for Rural America in the Twenty-First Century* (University Park, PA: The Pennsylvania State University Press, 2003), 2.

25. Ned Ehrbar, "Taran Killam blasted for calling rural Americans 'stupid.'" *CBS News* website, November 9, 2016, https://www.cbsnews.com/news/taran-killam-blasted-for-calling-rural-americans-stupid/.

26. L. Shannon Jung and Mary A. Agria, *Rural Congregational Studies: A Guide for Good Shepherds* (Nashville: Abingdon Press, 1997), 30.

27. "Perceptions of Rural America," *W. K. Kellogg Foundation*, December 9, 2002, http://www.wkkf.org/resource-directory/resource/2002/12/perceptions-of-rural-america, 4.

28. Ibid., 1.

29. Fern K. Willits and A. E. Luloff, "Urban Residents' Views of Rurality and Contacts with Rural Places," *Rural Sociology*, vol. 60, no. 3 (1995): 463.

30. Ibid., 464.

31. Brown and Schafft, *Rural People and Communities in the 21st Century*, 10.

32. Lydia DePillis, "Farms are gigantic now. Even the 'family-owned' ones." *The Washington Post*, August 11, 2013, https://www.washingtonpost.com/news/wonk/wp/2013/08/11/farms-are-gigantic-now-even-the-family-owned-ones/?utm_term=.0b261eb8cd68.

33. "The Disappearing Family Farm," *The Real Truth*, https://realtruth.org/articles/100607-006-family.html.

34. Emery N. Castle, *The Changing American Countryside* (Lawrence, KS: University Press of Kansas, 1995), 4.

35. "Perceptions of Rural America," 4.

36. Calvin Lunsford Beale, *A Taste of the Country* (University Park, PA: The Pennsylvania State University Press, 1990), 79.

37. Ibid., 122.

38. Ibid., 113.

39. Castle, *The Changing American Countryside*, 420.

40. Brown and Schafft, *Rural People and Communities in the 21st Century*, 63.

41. Castle, *The Changing American Countryside*, 428.

42. For a more detailed examination of the characteristics of the rural church, see Glenn Daman, *Shepherding the Small Church* (Grand Rapids: Kregel Publications, 2008).

43. Wuthnow, *Small Town America*, 223–24.

Chapter 3: Rural Life: A Historical Perspective

1. Pamela Riney-Kehrberg, *The Routledge History of Rural America* (New York: Routledge Taylor & Francis Group, 2016), 365.

2. Ibid.

3. Orville Vernon Burton, "Reaping What We Sow: Community and Rural History," *Agricultural History*, vol. 76, no. 4 (Autumn 2002): 638.

4. Burton, "Reaping What We Sow," 641–42.

5. Riney-Kehrberg, *Routledge History of Rural America*, 7.

6. Nancy Isenberg, *White Trash: The 400-year Untold History of Class in America* (New York: Viking, 2016), 30.

7. R. Douglas Hurt, *American Agriculture: A Brief History* (West Lafayette, IN: Purdue University Press, 2002), 35.

8. Hurt, *American Agriculture*, 35 (emphasis his).

9. David B. Danbom, *Born in the Country* (Baltimore: The Johns Hopkins University Press, 1995), 70.

10. Edwin C. Hagenstein, Sara M. Gregg, and Brian Donahue, *American Georgics: Writings on Farming, Culture, and the Land* (New Haven, CT: Yale University Press, 2012), 10.

11. Isenberg, *White Trash: The 400-year Untold History of Class in America*, 18–19.

12. Riney-Kehrberg, *Routledge History of Rural America*, 42.

13. Hagenstein, Gregg, Donahue, *American Georgics*, 9.

14. Ibid., 13.

15. Danbom, *Born in the Country*, 67.
16. Hurt, *American Agriculture*, 77.
17. Danbom, *Born in the Country*, 134.
18. Thomas Isern, "History, Rural," *Encyclopedia of Rural America: The Land and People*, 2 vols., 1st ed., Gary Goreham, gen. ed., (Denver: ABC-CLIO, 1997), 1:339.
19. Danbom, *Born in the Country*, 134.
20. Ibid., 199.
21. David Louis Brown and Louis E. Schafft, *Rural People and Communities in the 21st Century: Resilience and Transformation* (Cambridge: Polity Press, 2011), 23.
22. Jerome M. Stan and Ron L. Durst, "Foreclosure and Bankruptcy," *Encyclopedia of Rural America*, 1:279.
23. Riney-Kehrberg, *Routledge History of Rural America*, 263.
24. Richard Wood, *Survival of Rural America* (Lawrence, KS: University Press of Kansas, 2010), 3.
25. Leo E. Oliva, "How low are wheat prices? Take a look back at the 1800s, 1900s, and you'll see it's an all-time low," *The Hutchinson News*, July 28, 2016, http://www.kansasagland .com/agblogs/how-low-are-wheat-prices-take-a-look-back-at/article_c3a60410-0fbb-581e-a4c5-cbf9d5d0a171.html.
26. Paul K. Conkin, *A Revolution Down on the Farm: The Transformation of American Agriculture Since 1929* (Lexington, KY: University Press of Kentucky, 2009), 132.
27. John Dinse and William P. Browne, "Emergence of American Agriculture Movement, 1977–1979," *Great Plains Quarterly* (1985), http://digitalcommons.unl.edu/greatplains quarterly/1832.
28. Harry P. Diaz, *Farm Communities at the Crossroads: Challenge and Resistance* (Regina: Canadian Plains Research Center, 2012), 108.
29. Eric Ramirez-Ferrero, *Troubled Fields: Men, Emotions, and the Crisis in American Farming* (New York: Columbia University Press, 2005), 1.
30. Calvin L. Beale and Peter A. Morrison, *A Taste of the Country: A Collection of Calvin Beale's Writings* (University Park, PA: Pennsylvania State University Press, 1990), 166.
31. For a further discussion, see Patrick J. Carr and Maria Kefalas, *Hollowing Out the Middle: the Rural Brain Drain and What It Means for America* (Boston: Beacon Press, 2011).
32. http://www.oregonlive.com/mapes/index.ssf/2012/01/charting_the_decline_of_oregon.html.
33. https://www.fs.fed.us/forestmanagement/documents/sold-harvest/documents/1905-2012_Natl_Summary_Graph.pdf.
34. Brown and Schafft, *Rural People and Communities in the 21st Century*, 26.
35. David L. Brown and Louis E. Swanson, *Challenges for Rural America in the Twenty-First Century* (University Park, PA: The Pennsylvania State University Press, 2003), 31.

Chapter 4: The Rural Church: A Historical Perspective

1. See Thomas A. Lyson and William W. Falk, eds., *Forgotten Places: Uneven Development in Rural America* (Lawrence, KS: University Press of Kansas, 1993).
2. Roger Finke and Rodney Stark, *The Churching of America: 1776–2005; Winners and Losers in Our Religious Economy* (New Brunswick, NJ: Rutgers University, 1997), 25.
3. Nancy Isenberg, *White Trash: The 400-year Untold History of Class in America* (New York: Viking, 2016), 13.
4. Finke and Stark, *The Churching of America*, 36.
5. Ibid., 27.
6. Ibid., 36.
7. Helen Olive Belknap, *The Church on the Changing Frontier: A Study of the Homesteader and His Church* (New York: G. H. Doran, 1922), 58.
8. Edwin S. Gaustad and Leigh Eric Schmidt, *The Religious History of America* (San Francisco: HarperOne, 2009), 162.

9. Robert William Monday, *Pioneers and Preachers: Stories of the Old Frontier* (Chicago: Nelson-Hall, 1980), 5.
10. Ibid., 7.
11. Finke and Stark, *The Churching of America*, 39.
12. Ibid., 81.
13. Gaustad and Schmidt, *The Religious History of America*, 61.
14. Pamela Riney-Kehrberg, *The Routledge History of Rural America* (New York: Routledge Taylor & Francis Group, 2016), 167.
15. Belknap, *The Church on the Changing Frontier*, 67.
16. Lyman Beecher, "A Plea for the West" (1835), *TeachingAmericanHistory.org*, http://teachingamericanhistory.org/library/document/a-plea-for-the-west/.
17. Finke and Stark, *The Churching of America*, 63.
18. Monday, *Pioneers and Preachers*, 187.
19. Lois E. Myers, Rebecca Sharpless, and Clark G. Baker, *Rock Beneath the Sand: Country Churches in Texas* (College Station, TX: Texas A&M University Press, 2004), 18–19.
20. See Riney-Kehrberg, *Routledge History of Rural America*, 260–71.
21. Dwight Sanderson, *Rural Sociology and Rural Social Organization* (New York: John Wiley and Sons, 1942), 322.
22. H. N. Morse, *The Social Survey in Town and Country Areas* (New York: George H. Doran Company, 1924), 41.
23. Sanderson, *Rural Sociology and Rural Social Organization*, 331–32.
24. Finke and Stark, *The Churching of America*, 9.
25. Edwin Lee Earp, *The Rural Church Movement* (New York: Hardpress, Ltd., 2013), 34.
26. Sanderson, *Rural Sociology and Rural Social Organization*, 712.
27. Earp, *The Rural Church Movement*, 62.
28. Sanderson, *Rural Sociology and Rural Social Organization*, 717.
29. Ibid., 332.
30. D. Keith Naylor, "Pinchot, Gifford (1865–1946)," *Encyclopedia of Religion and Nature*, ed. Bron Taylor (London & New York: Continuum, 2005), 1280, http://www.religionandnature.com/ern/sample/Naylor--Pinchot.pdf.
31. For the history of each of these organizations, see Appendix.
32. "Record of Tensed Community Church," Tensed Community Church, Tensed, Idaho (no date or author given), from handwritten church archival documents.
33. Ibid.
34. Ibid.
35. Ibid.
36. *The Christian Mission in Relation to Rural Problems*, vol. 6, Report of the Jerusalem Meeting of the International Missionary Council, March 24th–April 8th, 1928 (London: Oxford University Press, 1928), 9–10.

Chapter 5: Understanding Rural Culture

1. L. Shannon Jung and Mary A. Agria, *Rural Congregational Studies: A Guide for Good Shepherds* (Nashville: Abingdon Press, 1997), 30.
2. Cornelia Butler Flora, Jan L. Flora, and Stephen P. Gasteyer, eds., *Rural Communities: Legacy and Change*, 5th ed. (Boulder, CO: Westview Press, 2016), 61.
3. Ian Convery, Gerard Corsane, and Peter Davis, *Making Sense of Place: Multidisciplinary Perspectives* (Woodbridge: The Boydell Press, 2014), 57.
4. Jung and Agria, *Rural Congregational Studies*, 31.
5. Soshanah Inwood, Jill K. Clark, and Molly Bean, "The Differing Values of Multigeneration and First-Generation Farmers: Their Influence on the Structure of Agriculture at the Rural-Urban Interface," *Rural Sociology*, vol. 78, no. 3 (June 19, 2013): 365.
6. Ibid., 352.
7. Glenn H. Elder, Rand Conger, and Valarie King, *Children of the Land: Adversity and Success in Rural America* (Chicago: University of Chicago Press, 2014), 11.

8. Harry P. Diaz, *Farm Communities at the Crossroads: Challenge and Resistance* (Regina: Canadian Plains Research Center, 2012), 108. See also Eric Ramirez-Ferrero, *Troubled Fields: Men, Emotions, and the Crisis in American Farming* (New York: Columbia University Press, 2005).

9. Miriam Brown, ed., *Sustaining Heart in the Heartland: Exploring Rural Spirituality* (New York: Paulist Press, 2005), 35–36.

10. Elder, Conger, King, *Children of the Land*, 45.

11. Ibid., 52.

12. Brown and Swanson, *Challenges for Rural America in the Twenty-First Century* (University Park, PA: Pennsylvania State University Press, 2003), 87.

13. Ralph Brown, "Community, Sense of," in *Encyclopedia of Rural America: The Land and People*, 1st ed., Gary Gorham, gen. ed. (Denver: ABC-CLIO, 1997), 118.

14. Ibid.

15. Brown, *Sustaining Heart in the Heartland*, 92.

16. Flora, Flora, and Gasteyer, *Rural Communities*, 14.

17. Ibid., 15.

18. Emery N. Castle, *The Changing American Countryside: Rural People and Places* (Lawrence, KS: University Press of Kansas, 1995), 357.

19. Jung and Agria, *Rural Congregational Studies*, 31.

20. Castle, *The Changing American Countryside*, 362.

21. For further discussion on the challenges of working with local church power structures, see Glenn Daman, *Developing Leaders for the Small Church* (Grand Rapids: Kregel Publications, 2009).

22. Aaron Morrow, *Small Town Mission: A Guide for Mission-Driven Communities* (GCD Books, 2016), 96.

23. David L. Brown and Louis E. Swanson, *Challenges for Rural America in the Twenty-First Century* (University Park, PA: The Pennsylvania State University Press, 2003), 265–66.

24. Sarah Pulliam Bailey, "Some Evangelicals Question Whether They have Overlooked the Rural Church," *The Washington Post*, December 15, 2016, https://www.washingtonpost.com/news/acts-of-faith/wp/2016/12/15/some-evangelicals-question-whether-they-have-overlooked-the-rural-church/?utm_term=.471e50e1cb3e&wpisrc=_nlfaith&wpmm=1

25. Jung and Agria, *Rural Congregational Studies*, 32.

26. Bernard Quinn, *The Small Rural Parish* (New York: Parish Project, National Conference of Catholic Bishops, 1980), 19.

27. Morrow, *Small Town Mission*, 94.

28. Elder, Conger, and King, *Children of the Land*, 45, 163.

Chapter 6: The Rural Ghetto: Poverty in Rural America

1. Tish Harrison Warren, "I Overlooked the Rural Poor—Then Trump Came Along . . . ," *Christianity Today* website, August 22, 2016, http://www.christianitytoday.com/ct/2016/september/i-overlooked-rural-poor-then-trump-came-along.html.

2. Osha Gray Davidson, *Broken Heartland: The Rise of America's Rural Ghetto* (Iowa City: University of Iowa Press, 1996), 1.

3. Ibid., 158.

4. David Louis Brown and Louis E. Schafft, *Rural People and Communities in the 21st Century: Resilience and Transformation* (Cambridge: Polity Press, 2011), 194.

5. Emery N. Castle, *The Changing American Countryside: Rural People and Places* (Lawrence, KS: University Press of Kansas, 1995), 230.

6. Brown and Schafft, *Rural People and Communities in the 21st Century*, 195.

7. Davidson, *Broken Heartland*, 9. For a state-by-state comparison of rural and urban poverty, see *City and Rural Kids Count Data Book* (Baltimore: Annie E. Casey Foundation, 2004) and Amy Glasmeier, *An Atlas of Poverty in America: One Nation, Pulling Apart, 1960–2003* (New York: Routledge, 2006).

8. Jeanne Hoeft, L. Shannon Jung, and Joretta L. Marshall, *Practicing Care in Rural Congregations and Communities* (Minneapolis: Fortress Press, 2013), 115.

9. David L. Brown and Louis E. Swanson, *Challenges for Rural America in the Twenty-First Century* (University Park, PA: The Pennsylvania State University Press, 2003), 99.

10. Richard E. Wood, *Survival of Rural America: Small Victories and Bitter Harvests* (Lawrence, KS: University Press of Kansas, 2010), 17.

11. Thomas A. Lyson and William W. Falk, *Forgotten Places: Uneven Development in Rural America* (Lawrence: University Press of Kansas, 1993), 4.

12. Castle, *The Changing American Countryside*, 235.

13. Kristen E. Smith and Ann R. Tickamyer, *Economic Restructuring and Family Well-Being in Rural America* (University Park, PA: University of Pennsylvania Press, 2011), 27.

14. Cynthia M. Duncan, *Worlds Apart: Poverty and Politics in Rural America* (New Haven, CT: Yale University Press, 2014), 9.

15. Joyce E. Allen-Smith, Ronald C. Wimberley, and Libby V. Morris, "America's Forgotten People and Places: Finding the Legacy of Poverty in the Rural South," *Journal of Agriculture and Applied Economics*, vol. 32, no. 2 (August 2000): 323.

16. Brown and Schafft, *Rural People and Communities in the 21st Century*, 150.

17. Leif Jensen and Eric B. Jensen, "Poverty," *Encyclopedia of Rural America: the Land and People*, 2nd ed., Gary Goreham, gen. ed. (Millerton, NY: Grey House Pub., 2008), 777.

18. Nathan Bomey, "Coal's Demise Threatens Appalachian Miners, Firms as Production Moves West," *USA Today* website, April 19, 2016, https://www.usatoday.com/story/money/2016/04/19/coal-industry-energy-fallout/82972958/.

19. Jeff Mapes, "Charting the Decline of Oregon's Timber Industry," *The Oregonian* website, January 23, 2012, http://www.oregonlive.com/mapes/index.ssf/2012/01/charting_the_decline_of_oregon.html.

20. Skott Bailey, "Skamania County Profile," *Employment Security Department, Washington State* website, September 2016, https://fortress.wa.gov/esd/employmentdata/reports-publications/regional-reports/county-profiles/skamania-county-profile.

21. Brown and Swanson, *Challenges for Rural America in the Twenty-First Century*, 113.

22. Eric Ramirez-Ferrero, *Troubled Fields: Men, Emotions, and the Crisis in American Farming* (New York: Columbia University Press, 2005), 7.

23. Wood, *Survival of Rural America*, 5.

24. Brown and Swanson, *Challenges for Rural America in the Twenty-First Century*, 125.

25. Smith and Tickamyer, *Economic Restructuring and Family Well-Being in Rural America*, 110.

26. Ibid., 35.

27. Jensen and Jensen, "Poverty," 777.

28. Smith and Tickamyer, *Economic Restructuring and Family Well-Being in Rural America*, 30.

29. Ibid.

30. Hoeft, Jung, and Marshall, *Practicing Care in Rural Congregations and Communities*, 117.

31. Daniel T. Lichter and David J. Eggebeen, "Child Poverty and the Changing Rural Family," *Rural Sociology*, vol. 57, no. 2 (1992): 154.

32. Castle, *The Changing American Countryside*, 216.

33. Smith and Tickamyer, *Economic Restructuring and Family Well-Being in Rural America*, 128.

34. Brown and Swanson, *Challenges for Rural America in the Twenty-First Century*, 48.

35. Ramirez-Ferrer, *Troubled Fields*, 12.

36. Brown and Swanson, *Challenges for Rural America in the Twenty-First Century*, 124.

37. See Charles A. Wanamaker, *The Epistles to the Thessalonians: A Commentary on the Greek Text* (Grand Rapids: William B. Eerdmans Publishing Company, 2015), 286.

38. See Steve Corbett and Brian Fikkert, *When Helping Hurts: How to Alleviate Poverty Without Hurting the Poor . . . and Yourself* (Chicago: Moody Publishers, 2012); Steve Corbett, *Helping without Hurting in Church Benevolence* (Chicago: Moody Publishers, 2015).

Chapter 7: Racial Tension in Rural America

1. David Louis Brown and Louis E. Schafft, *Rural People and Communities in the 21st Century: Resilience and Transformation* (Cambridge: Polity Press, 2011), 125.
2. Ibid.
3. Daniel T. Lichter, "Immigration and the New Racial Diversity in Rural America," *Rural Sociology*, vol. 77, no. 1 (2012): 7.
4. Housing Assistance Council Rural Research Brief, "Race and Ethnicity in Rural America," *Housing Assistance Council* website, April, 2012, http://www.ruralhome.org/storage/research_notes/rrn-race-and-ethnicity-web.pdf.
5. Lichter, "Immigration and the New Racial Diversity in Rural America," 4.
6. Brown and Schafft, *Rural People and Communities in the 21st Century*, 129.
7. Emery N. Castle, *The Changing American Countryside: Rural People and Places* (Lawrence, KS: University Press of Kansas, 1995), 341.
8. Madeleine Thomas, "What happened to America's black farmers," *Grist* website, April 24, 2015, http://grist.org/food/what-happened-to-americas-black-farmers/.
9. David L. Brown and Louis E. Swanson, *Challenges for Rural America in the Twenty-First Century* (University Park, PA: The Pennsylvania State University Press, 2003), 35.
10. Ibid., 58.
11. Brown and Schafft, *Rural People and Communities in the 21st Century*, 138.
12. Brown and Swanson, *Challenges for Rural America in the Twenty-First Century*, 63.
13. Housing Assistance Council Rural Research Brief, "Housing in the Border Colonias," *Housing Assistance Council* website, September, 2013, http://www.ruralhome.org/sct-information/mn-hac-research/mn-rrr/81-housing-in-the-colonias, 2.
14. Ibid.
15. Ibid., 3.
16. C. Matthew Snipp, "Understanding Race and Ethnicity in Rural America," *Rural Sociology*, vol. 61, no.1 (1996): 130.
17. Paul Chaat Smith, *Everything You Know about Indians Is Wrong* (Minneapolis: University of Minnesota Press, 2009), 10.
18. Ibid., 4.
19. Alan Taylor, *American Colonies* (New York: Penguin Books, 2001), 40.
20. C. Matthew Snipp, "American Indian," *Encyclopedia of Rural America: The Land and People*, 2nd ed., Gary Goreham, gen. ed., (Millerton, NY: Grey House Pub., 2008), 55. See also Circe Sturm, *Becoming Indian: The Struggle Over Cherokee Identity in the Twenty-First Century* (Santa Fe: School for Advanced Research Press, 2011).
21. Cornelia Butler Flora, Jan L. Flora, and Stephen P. Gasteyer, eds., *Rural Communities: Legacy and Change*, 5th ed. (Boulder, CO: Westview Press, 2016), 80–81.
22. Housing Assistance Council, "Taking Stock, Rural People, Poverty, and Housing in the 21st Century," *Housing Assistance Council* website, December 2012, http://www.ruralhome.org/storage/documents/ts2010/ts_full_report.pdf, 95.
23. Brown and Swanson, *Challenges for Rural America in the Twenty-First Century*, 43.
24. Art Swift, "Americans' Worries About Race Relations at Record High," *Gallup* website, March 15, 2017, http://www.gallup.com/poll/206057/americans-worry-race-relations-record-high.aspx.
25. Michael O. Emerson and Christian Smith, *Divided by Faith: Evangelical Religion and the Problem of Race in America* (Oxford: Oxford University Press, 2001), 7.
26. Ibid.
27. Edward C. Stewart and Bennett J. Milton, *American Cultural Patterns: A Cross-Cultural Perspective* (Yarmouth, ME: Intercultural Press, 2006), 3.
28. Sherwood G. Lingenfelter and Marvin Keene Mayers, *Ministering Cross-Culturally: A Model for Effective Personal Relationships* (Grand Rapids: Baker Academic, 2016), 2.
29. J. Daniel Hays, *From Every People and Nation: A Biblical Theology of Race* (Leicester: Apollos, 2006), 48.

30. Ibid., 50.
31. John Piper, *Bloodlines: Race, Cross, and the Christian* (Wheaton, IL: Crossway, 2011), 18.
32. Jarvis J. Williams, *One New Man: The Cross and Racial Reconciliation in Pauline Theology* (Nashville: B&H Academic, 2010), 135.

Chapter 8: The Church and the Rural Community

1. See Glenn Daman, *Shepherding the Small Church* (Grand Rapids: Kregel Academic & Professional, 2008).
2. John Piper, *Bloodlines: Race, Cross, and the Christian* (Wheaton, IL: Crossway, 2011), 154–55.
3. Rockwell Smith, *Rural Ministry and the Changing Community* (Nashville: Abingdon Press, 1971), 60.
4. County Work Department, ed., *The Rural Church and Community Betterment* (Middletown: Leopold Classic Library, 2017), 83.
5. H. Andy Wiebe, *The Rural Pastor* (Lulu, 2015), 44.
6. For further discussion of the legal status of the foreigner, see James Hoffmeier, *The Immigration Crisis: Immigration, Immigrants and the Bible* (Wheaton, IL: Crossway Books, 2009).
7. Robert Wuthnow, "Mobilizing Civic Engagement," *Civic Engagement in American Democracy*, eds. Theda Skocpol and Morris P. Fiorina (Washington: Brooking Institution Press, 1999), 338.
8. Robert Putnam, *Bowling Alone: The Collapse and Revival of American Community* (New York: Simon & Schuster, 2007), 77.
9. Walter Curry Mavis, *Advancing the Smaller Local Church* (Grand Rapids: Baker Book House, 1957), 30.
10. Mark Rich, *Rural Prospect* (New York: Friendship Press, 1950), 53.
11. Donnie Griggs, *Small Town Jesus* (Damascus, MD: EverTruth, 2016), 143–56.
12. See Cornelia Butler Flora, Jan L. Flora, and Stephen P. Gasteyer, eds., *Rural Communities: Legacy and Change*, 5th ed. (Boulder, CO: Westview Press, 2016).
13. Putnam, *Bowling Alone*, 19.
14. Flora, Flora, and Gasteyer, *Rural Communities: Legacy and Change*, 160.
15. Ibid., 165.
16. Ibid., 166.
17. Putnam, *Bowling Alone*, 23.
18. Flora, Flora, and Gasteyer, *Rural Communities: Legacy and Change*, 168.
19. Putnam, *Bowling Alone*, 66.
20. Ibid., 66–67.
21. Stephanie Clintonia Boddie, "Social Services, Faith-based," *Rural Encyclopedia: The Land and People*, 2nd ed., Gary Gorham, gen. ed. (Millerton, NY: Grey House Publishing, Inc., 2008), 903.
22. Ibid., 904.
23. County Work Department, ed., *The Rural Church and Community Betterment*, 65.
24. Putnam, *Bowling Alone*, 409 (emphasis his).
25 Rich, *Rural Prospect*, 105.
26. For helpful book on working with children in rural communities, see Rona Orme, *Rural Children, Rural Church* (London: Church House Publishing, 2007).
27. Rich, *Rural Prospect*, 103–104.

Chapter 9: Developing a Theology of Rural Ministry

1. Edwin Lee Earp, *Rural Church Movement* (New York: Hardpress Ltd., 2013), 34.
2. Quoted in Harold Longenecker, *Building Town and Country Churches: A Practical Approach to the Revitalization of Churches* (Chicago: Moody Press, 1973), 27.
3. David J. Hesselgrave, *Planting Churches Cross Culturally: North America and Beyond* (Grand Rapids: Baker Book House, 2000), 66.

4. Ibid., 64.
5. Aubrey Malphurs, *Planting Growing Churches for the 21st Century* (Grand Rapids: Baker Books, 1998), 319.
6. Stephen T. Um and Justin Buzzard, *Why Cities Matter: To God, the Culture, and the Church* (Wheaton, IL: Crossway, 2013), 17.
7. Ibid.
8. Quoted in ibid., 57.
9. Ibid., 58.
10. Pete Nicholas, "Urban ministry – is it a biblical priority?" *Inspire London* website, September 9, 2014, http://www.inspirelondon.org/blog/urban-ministry-%E2%80%93-is-it-a-biblical-priority.
11. Um and Buzzard, *Why Cities Matter*, 68–69.
12. Eckhard J. Schnabel, *Paul the Missionary: Realities, Strategies and Methods* (Downers Grove, IL: IVP Academic, 2008), 285.
13. Ibid., 286.
14. Joachim Jeremias, *Jerusalem in the Time of Jesus* (Philadelphia, PA: Fortress Press, 1969), 305.
15. Donnie Griggs, *Small Town Jesus* (Damascus, MD: EverTruth, 2016), 37.
16. Johannes P. Louw and Eugene Albert Nida, *Greek-English Lexicon of the New Testament: Based on Semantic Domains*, 2 vols. (New York: United Bible Societies, 1996), 1:89.
17. Griggs, *Small Town Jesus*, 48.
18. William H. Willimon and Robert Leroy Wilson, *Preaching and Worship in the Small Church* (Eugene, OR: Wipf and Stock, 2001), 14.
19. Leith Anderson, *A Church for the 21st Century* (Minneapolis: Bethany Book House, 1992), 59–60.
20. Ruth Tucker, *Left Behind in a Megachurch World* (Grand Rapids: Baker Books, 2006), 42.
21. David Ray, *Small Churches Are the Right Size* (New York: The Pilgrim Press, 1982), 41.
22. Ibid., 90.
23. Kent and Barbara Hughes, *Liberating Ministry from the Success Syndrome* (Wheaton, IL: Crossway Books, 2008), 35.
24. Tucker, *Left Behind in a Megachurch World*, 64–69.
25. Longenecker, *Building Town and Country Churches*, 26.
26. Ibid., 30.

Chapter 10: The Contribution of Rural Ministry

1. Quoted in Kathleen Norris, *Dakota; A Spiritual Geography* (New York: Mariner Books, 2001), 166.
2. Glenn Daman, *Leading the Small Church* (Grand Rapids: Kregel Publications, 2006).
3. James Bell, Jill Hopkins, and Trevor Willmott, *Reshaping Rural Ministry* (Norwich: Canterbury Press, 2009), viii.
4. Interview with Christian A. Schwarz, "The Strong Little Church," CT Pastors, http://www.christianitytoday.com/pastors/2004/may-online-only/cln40525.html. See also Christian A. Schwarz, *Natural Church Development: A Guide to Eight Essential Qualities of Healthy Churches*, 4th ed. (St. Charles, IL: Churchsmart Resources, 1996).
5. NCD International, "Christian A. Schwarz on Small Churches," *YouTube*, August 12, 2012, https://www.youtube.com/watch?v=LdbOt7NozY8.
6. Karl Vaters, "Dear Andy Stanley, Please Be the Small Church's Ally, Not Our Enemy," *Christianity Today* website, March 3, 2016, http://www.christianitytoday.com/karl-vaters/2016/march/dear-andy-stanley-please-be-small-churchs-ally-not-our-enem.html.
7. Karl Vaters, "Your Small Church Is Big," *Christianity Today* website, http://www.christianitytoday.com/pastors/2015/spring/your-small-church-is-big.html.
8. Cynthia Woolever and Deborah Bruce, *Beyond the Ordinary: 10 Strengths of U.S. Congregations* (Louisville, KY: Westminster John Knox Press, 2004), 135.

9. David L. Brown and Louis E. Swanson, *Challenges for Rural America in the Twenty-First Century* (University Park, PA: The Pennsylvania State University Press, 2003), 1.
10. Robert Wuthnow, *Small-Town America: Finding Community, Shaping the Future,* (Princeton, NJ: Princeton University Press, 2013), 269.
11. For a further discussion of the importance of theology and doctrine for the church, see Daman, *Shepherding the Small Church.*
12. David B. Smith, *Small Does Not Mean Struggling* (Enumclaw, WA: Winepress Pub., 2011), 65.
13. Ibid., 66.
14. Tony Dale, Felicity Dale, and George Barna, *Small Is Big* (Carol Stream, IL: Barna Books/ Tyndale House Publishers, Inc., 2011), 72.
15. Woolever and Bruce, *Beyond the Ordinary,* 50.
16. Brandon J. O'Brien, *The Strategically Small Church: Intimate, Nimble, Authentic, Effective* (Minneapolis: Bethany House, 2010), 126.
17. Kennon L. Callahan, *Small, Strong Congregations* (San Francisco: Jossey-Bass, 2012), 70.
18. Ron Klassen and John Koessler, *No Little Places* (Eugene, OR: Wipf & Stock, 2002), 78.
19. Woolever and Bruce, *Beyond the Ordinary,* 41.
20. Dennis W. Bickers, *The Healthy Small Church: Diagnosis and Treatment for the Big Issues* (Kansas City: Baker Books, 2000), 129.
21. Jean F. Risley, *A Place Where Everybody Matters* (Eugene, OR: Wipf &Stock Publishers, 2010), 30.
22. ChurchLaw & Tax reports that the average church gives five percent to international missions. See "How Churches Spend Their Money," *ChurchLaw & Tax* website, August 28, 2014, http://www.churchlawandtax.com/blog/2014/august/how-churches-spend-their-money.html.
23. Smith, *Small Does Not Mean Struggling,* 67.
24. Barna, "Common Experiences of Pastoral Calling," *Barna* website, May 3, 2017, https://www.barna.com/research/called-to-pastoral-ministry/#.WQtowiwiJcA.mailto. See also Edward Wesley Hassinger, John S. Holik, and J. Kenneth Benson, *The Rural Church: Learning from Three Decades of Change* (Nashville: Abingdon Press, 1988), 11.
25. Ibid.
26. David Kinnaman, *You Lost Me* (Grand Rapids: Baker Books, 2011), 45.
27. Ibid., 227.
28. Smith, *Small Does Not Mean Struggling,* 65.
29. Ibid., 66.
30. Kent Philpott, *For Pastors of Small Churches* (Mill Valley, CA: Earthen Vessel Pub., 2000), 121–22.
31. Kirk E. Farnsworth and Rosie Farnsworth, *All Churches Great and Small* (Valley Forge, PA: Judson Press, 2005), 101.
32. Daniel Block, *For the Glory of God: Recovering a Biblical Theology of Worship* (Grand Rapids: Baker Book House, 2016), 23.
33. Klassen and Koessler, *No Little Places,* 83–88.
34. Shawn McMullen, *Unleashing the Potential of the Small Church* (Cincinnati, OH: Standard Publ., 2006), 20.
35. H. Andy Wiebe, *The Rural Pastor* (Lulu, 2015), 35.
36. Bill M. Sullivan and Paul M. Bassett, *The Smaller Church in a Super Church Era* (Kansas City: Beacon Hill Press of Kansas City, 1983), 34.
37. Dennis W. Bickers, *The Healthy Small Church* (Kansas City: Beacon Hill Press of Kansas City, 2005), 18.

Chapter 11: Developing Strategic Partnerships

1. Rex A. Koivisto, *One Lord, One Faith* (Eugene, OR: Wipf & Stock, 2003), 30.
2. Ibid., 116.

3. Edwin Earp, *The Rural Church: Serving the Community* (Classic Reprint) (S.I.: Forgotten Books, 2015), 37.
4. Donnie Griggs, *Small Town Jesus* (Damascus, MD: EverTruth, 2016), 161.
5. Ibid.
6. Patrick Lencioni, *Silos, Politics and Turf Wars* (San Francisco: Jossey-Bass, 2006), 175.
7. Karl Vaters, "Dismantling Ministry Silos in the Small Church," *Christianity Today* website, June 2, 2015, http://www.christianitytoday.com/karl-vaters/2015/june/dismantling-ministry-silos-in-small-church.html?paging=off.
8. Griggs, *Small Town Jesus*, 162.
9. Ibid, 163.
10. For a list of seven different types of cooperative efforts by local churches and the possible problems with each, see Lyle Schaller, *The Small Church Is Different* (Nashville: Abingdon Press, 1992), 168–176.
11. Dennis Bickers, "Why Your Denomination Shouldn't Ignore Rural Churches," *Ethics Daily* website, April 14, 2014, http://www.ethicsdaily.com/why-your-denomination-shouldnt-ignore-rural-churches-cms-21706.
12. Ibid.
13. Patrick J. Carr and Maria Kefalas, *Hollowing Out the Middle: the Rural Brain Drain and What It Means for America* (Boston: Beacon Press, 2011), 1.
14. Ibid., 2.
15. Ibid., 4.
16. Thurston Domina, "The Geography of Educational Segregation," *Inside Higher ED* website, January 19, 2007, https://www.insidehighered.com/views/2007/01/19/geography-educational-segregation.
17. Ibid.
18. Ibid.
19. Carr and Kefalas, *Hollowing Out the Middle*, 139–41.
20. Ibid., 140.

Chapter 12: The Rural Community as a Mission Field

1. Roger N. McNamara, *The YBH Handbook of Church Planting* (Longwood, FL: Xulon Press, 2005), 49.
2. Michele Dillon and Megan Henly, "Religion, Politics and the Environment in Rural America," *Carsey Institute Issue Brief*, no. 3 (Fall 2008): 1.
3. Donnie Griggs, *Small Town Jesus* (Damascus, MD: EverTruth, 2016), 65.
4. See David L. Brown and Louis E. Swanson, *Challenges for Rural America in the Twenty-First Century* (University Park, PA: The Pennsylvania State University Press, 2003).
5. Griggs, *Small Town Jesus*, 63.
6. Harold Longenecker, *Building Town and Country Churches: A Practical Approach to the Revitalization of Churches* (Chicago: Moody Press, 1973), 27.
7. Aaron Morrow, *Small Town Mission: A Guide for Mission-Driven Communities* (GCD Books, 2016), 13.
8. Brown and Swanson, *Challenges for Rural America*, 65.
9. Ibid., 70.
10. Joshua Project, "Americans, U.S., Spanish-Speaking in United States," *Joshua Project* website, https://joshuaproject.net/people_groups/10291/US.
11. Housing Assistance Council, "Rural Research Brief," *Housing Assistance Council* website, April 2012, http://www.ruralhome.org/storage/research_notes/rrn-race-and-ethnicity-web.pdf.
12. A. G. Sulzberger, "Hispanics Reviving Faded Towns on the Plains," *The New York Times*, November 13, 2011, http://www.nytimes.com/2011/11/14/us/as-small-towns-wither-on-plains-hispanics-come-to-the-rescue.html.
13. Stephen T. Um and Justin Buzzard, *Why Cities Matter: To God, the Culture, and the Church* (Wheaton, IL: Crossway, 2013), 48.

14. "Numbers on Native Americans: Will They Reach 9%," *Missiologically Thinking* website, November 2, 2011, http://www.jdpayne.org/2011/11/02/numbers-on-native-americans-will-they-reach-9/.
15. See Joshua Project, https://joshuaproject.net/filter.
16. See Joshua Project, https://joshuaproject.net/filter.
17. Circe Sturm, *Becoming Indian: The Struggle Over Cherokee Identity in the Twenty-First Century* (Santa Fe: School for Advanced Research Press, 2011), 68.
18. Dennis W. Bickers, *The Healthy Small Church* (Kansas City: Beacon Hill Press of Kansas City, 2005), 98.
19. Charles Wayne Zunkel, *Growing the Small Church: A Guide for Church Leaders* (Elgin, IL: David C. Cook Publishing Co., 1983), 83.
20. Ibid. (emphasis his).
21. Kevin Ruffcorn, *Rural Evangelism: Catching the Vision* (Minneapolis: Augsburg, 1994), 16.
22. David R. Ray, *The Big Small Church Book* (Cleveland, OH: Pilgrim Press, 1992), 125.
23. Longenecker, *Building Town and Country Churches*, 26–27.
24. Ibid., 27.
25. Gifford Pinchot, Charles Otis Gill, and The Macmillan Company, *Six Thousand Country Churches* (Charleston: BiblioBazaar, 2010), 50.
26. Terry W. Dorsett, *Mission Possible: Reaching the Next Generation through the Small Church* (Bloomington, IN: CrossBooks, 2012), 11.
27. Paul N. Hazelton, *7 Steps to Revitalizing the Small-Town Church* (Kansas City: Nazarene Pub. House, 1993), 18.
28. Norman Shawchuck and Lloyd Merle Perry, *Revitalizing the 20th Century Church* (Chicago: Moody Press, 1986), 9.
29. For more discussion on revitalization, see Ron Crandall, *Turn Around Strategies for the Small Church* (Nashville: Abingdon Press, 1995); Ron Crandall and L. Ray Sells, *There's New Life in the Small Congregation* (Nashville: Discipleship Resources, 1983); and Aubrey Malpurs, *Pouring New Wine into Old Wineskins* (Grand Rapids: Baker Book House, 1993).
30. Tom Nebel, *Big Dreams in Small Places: Church Planting in Smaller Communities* (St. Charles, IL: ChurchSmart Resources, 2002), 20.
31. See *Rural Matters: A Focus on Church Planting in Rural America* (Wheaton, IL: Rural Matters Institute, 2017); and George W. Garner, *Rural Church Planting: A Missional Footprint* (Alpharetta, GA: North American Mission Board, 2011).
32. Ron Klassen and John Koessler, *No Little Places* (Eugene, OR: Wipf & Stock, 2002), 57–58.
33. Quoted in Nebel, *Big Dreams in Small Places*, 19.

Chapter 13: The Future of Rural Ministry

1. Kennon L. Callahan, *Small Strong Congregations: Creating Strengths and Health for Your Congregation* (San Francisco: Jossey-Bass, 2000), 14.
2. Donnie Griggs, *Small Town Jesus* (Damascus, MD: EverTruth, 2016), 168.
3. Patrick J. Carr and Maria Kefalas, *Hollowing Out the Middle: the Rural Brain Drain and What It Means for America* (Boston: Beacon Press, 2011), 141.
4. Ibid., 142.
5. Anthony Papas, *Inside the Small Church* (Bethesda, MD: Alban Institute, 2002), 224.
6. Robert Wuthnow, *Small-Town America: Finding Community, Shaping the Future* (Princeton, NJ: Princeton University Press, 2013), 247.
7. Paul D. Borden, *Hit the Bullseye* (Nashville: Abingdon Press, 2003), 59.
8. Bill Kemp, *Holy Places, Small Spaces: A Hopeful Future for the Small Membership Church* (Nashville: Discipleship Resources, 2005), 5.
9. Peter Bush and Christine O'Reilly, *Where 20 or 30 Are Gathered: Leading Worship in the Small Church* (Herndon, VA: Alban Institute, 2006), 101.
10. Kemp, *Holy Places, Small Spaces*, 141.
11. Carl A. Clark, *Rural Churches in Transition* (Nashville: Broadman Press, 1959), 144.

12. Patricia Chang, *Assessing the Clergy Supply in the 21st Century* (Durham, NC: Pulpit and Pew Research Reports, Duke Divinity School, 2004), http://pulpitandpew.org/sites/all/themes/pulpitandpew/files/ClergySupply.pdf, 12.

13. Ibid., 13.

14. Andrew Nurse and Raymond Benjamin Blake, *The Trajectories of Rural Life: New Perspectives on Rural Canada* (Regina: Canadian Plains Research Center, 2003), 155–56.

15. Bush and O'Reilly, *Where 20 or 30 Are Gathered*, 111.

16. Lyle Schaller, *Small Congregations, Big Potential Ministry in the Small Membership Church* (Nashville: Abingdon Press, 2003), 200.

17. Beliefnet, "Beliefnet's Inspirational Quotes," *Beliefnet* website, http://www.beliefnet.com/quotes/evangelical/j/john-wesley/give-me-one-hundred-preachers-who-fear-nothing-but.aspx#VYWISxk4KTJuzwKx.99.

Appendix: What Church History Books Don't Tell

1. InFaith, "InFaith heritage," *InFaith* website, https://infaith.org/heritage.

2. The summary was gleaned from InFaith's history provided on their website.

3. Ron Klassen, Rural Home Missions Association, Morton, Illinois, email to author, April 4, 2017.

4. Ibid.

5. Ibid.

6. Rocky Mountain Bible Mission, "Why We Exist," *Rocky Mountain Bible Mission* website, http://rmbible.org/about/our-story.

7. Adapted from Donald G. Fredricks, email to author, February 10, 2017.

Acknowledgments

I WOULD LIKE TO express my appreciation for the staff at Moody Publishers for the hard work they have done in making this project possible. I especially would like to thank Duane Sherman and Kevin Emmert for the work they have done in editing and preparing the manuscript. Their work is an invaluable contribution and greatly appreciated.

I would also like to thank Emily Daman for her willingness to read through the manuscript to identify and correct any errors. It was truly an act of love. I would like to express my deep appreciation for the people of River Christian Church. They have given us the privilege of serving them for the past 25 years. They have been gracious in my mistakes, forgiving in my weaknesses, and supportive in my ministry. Last, I would like to especially thank my wife, Becky. She is a constant support and partner in our ministry. Her dedication to ministry, her compassion and love for people, and her faithfulness in service have been the foundation for our ministry. Without her support and encouragement, I would never have been effective in serving the body of Christ.

Small ≠ Broken

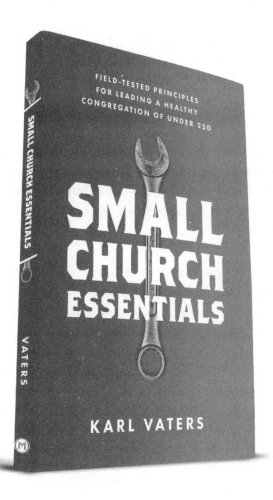

Small Church Essentials is for leaders of smaller congregations. It encourages them to steward their role well, debunking myths about small churches while offering principles for leading a dynamic, healthy small church. It will help small-church leaders identify what they do well, and how to do it even better.

978-0-8024-1806-7 | **ALSO AVAILABLE AS AN EBOOK**